PRESENCE OF MIND
Writing and the Domain Beyond the Cognitive

Edited by

Alice Glarden Brand
State University of New York-Brockport

and

Richard L. Graves
Auburn University

Boynton/Cook Publishers
HEINEMANN
Portsmouth, NH

Boynton/Cook Publishers, Inc.

A subsidiary of Reed Elsevier Inc.
361 Hanover Street, Portsmouth, NH 03801-3912
Offices and agents throughout the world

Acquiring Editor: Robert W. Boynton
Production: Melissa L. Inglis
Cover design: Julie Hahn

Every effort has been made to contact copyright holders for permission to reprint borrowed material. We regret any oversights that may have occurred and would be happy to rectify them in future printings of this work.

The editors and publisher wish to thank those who have generously given permission to reprint copyrighted material:

Letters of Emily Dickinson reprinted by permission of the publishers from *The Letters of Emily Dickinson* edited by Thomas H. Johnson, Cambridge, Mass.: The Belknap Press of Harvard University Press, Copyright © 1958, 1986 by the President and Fellows of Harvard College.

Poems of Emily Dickinson reprinted by permission of the publishers and the Trustees of Amherst College from *The Poems of Emily Dickinson,* Thomas H. Johnson, ed., Cambridge, Mass.: The Belknap Press of Harvard University Press, Copyright © 1951, 1955, 1979, 1983 by the President and Fellows of Harvard College.

"When I Am Asked" by Lisel Mueller from *Waving from Shore*. Published 1989 by Louisiana State University Press. Reprinted with permission.

"Some Rivers" by Richard L. Graves from *Teaching English in the Two-Year College* (December 1992: 279). Copyright 1992 by the National Council of Teachers of English. Reprinted with permission.

"Symposium" by Richard J. Murphy, Jr., is reprinted by permission from *The Calculus of Intimacy: A Teaching Life* by Richard J. Murphy, Jr., copyright 1993 by the Ohio State University Press.

Library of Congress Cataloging-in-Publication Data
Presence of mind : writing and the domain beyond the cognitive /
    edited by Alice Glarden Brand, Richard L. Graves.
        p.   cm.
    Includes bibliographical references.
    ISBN 0-86709-336-6
    1. English language--Rhetoric--Study and teaching--Psychological aspects.
I. Brand, Alice Glarden. II. Graves, Richard L. (Richard Layton), 1931- .
PE1404.P65   1994
808'.042--dc20   93-42727
                                                                                 CIP

Printed in the United States of America on acid-free paper
98 97 96 95 94   CM   1 2 3 4 5 6 7 8 9

PRESENCE OF MIND

To Ira Brand and Lois Graves

Contents

Foreword
James Moffett   ix

Acknowledgments   *xiii*

Introduction:
Defining the Territory Beyond   *1*

Silence

1   Silence: A Collage
Peter Elbow   9

2   Wait, and the Writing Will Come:
Meditation and the Composing Process
Donald R. Gallehr   21

3   The Pedagogy of Silence in Public Education:
Expanding the Tradition
Charles Suhor   31

Wisdom of the Unconscious

4   Traces in Texts: Reading the Waters
Anne E. Mullin   41

5   Let the River Run:
Exploring Personal Archetypes Through Writing
Richard L. Graves and Susan M. Becker   53

6   Behind the Screen of Consciousness:
Intuition, Insight, and Inspiration in the Writing Process
Elizabeth Holman   65

Wisdom of the Body

7   A Writer's Way of Knowing: Guidelines for Composing
Sondra Perl   77

8   The Write Moves: Cultivating Kinesthetic
and Spatial Intelligences in the Writing Process
Karen Klein and Linda Hecker   89

9   Generous Listening: A Deeper Way of Knowing
Trudelle H. Thomas   99

Images

10   Sites of Inspiration:
Where Writing Is Embodied in Image and Emotion
Hildy Miller   113

11   Mental Imagery, Text Engagement,
and Underprepared Writers
Kristie S. Fleckenstein   125

12   Visual Imagery Training and College Writing Students
Demetrice A. Worley   133

Emotions

13   Teaching Empathy Through Cooperative Learning
Nathaniel Teich   143

14   Defining Our Emotional Life: The Valuative System—
A Continuum Theory
Alice Glarden Brand   155

15   Defining Our Emotional Life: The Cool End (Plus Motivation)
Alice Glarden Brand   167

The Open Door

16   Where Do You Find Your Stories?
Donald M. Murray   181

17   The Butterfly Effect: Writing from Chaos to Composure
Sandra Price Burkett   189

18   The Heart of the Matter: Language, Feeling, Stories, Healing
Gabriele Lusser Rico   199

19   Symposium
Richard J. Murphy, Jr.   215

References   225

Contributors   243

Foreword

When I'm holding workshops with teachers I often ask them to take turns telling the group their first memories of writing. First we jot them down hastily as notes for ourselves to talk from, but usually neighbors are talking about them already as they recall. At a certain point we share them all around. The more we listen to one another, the more of our own memories come back to us—doing Prussian handwriting exercises in primary school or using cut-out letters to spell words and sentences on the floor. I go first.

My older brother hated school but liked playing teacher with me after school. We had acquired as part of our play gear a small easel chalkboard with tray and eraser, and he coached me to write words and phrases that came out of my schoolwork. I had already memorized the alphabet while jumping up and down on my parents' empty bed and flipping through somebody's alphabetized address book. During some of these preschool years we lived with my mother's parents, and I was often thrown together with my grandmother while the others were at work and before my brother came home from school. She made scrapbooks with me, pasting in pictures and writing captions underneath them. She harbored ideas of publishing and had even gone up to New York to take courses at Columbia. She wrote things that she squirreled away in the many drawers and cubbyholes in the den where she read to me and passed on some of her love for books and writing.

When we moved into our own home later and I was in school myself, I sometimes wrote a story just for fun, lying on the living room rug. "Twang sang an arrow," began one. I've never since got so promptly to the point. My fifth-grade teacher sponsored me. She encouraged me to write on my own and suggested I compete in an essay contest for my age at the town art museum, which invited us to write an appreciation or critique of one of the paintings currently exhibited. I wrote about a painting of a horse and won the prize, which was a stylized Southwestern Indian painting of two deer grazing in desert sparsity. Today it hangs on the wall in my office—my first remuneration for writing.

My sixth-grade teacher had the class write a thank-you letter to a local dowager who had subsidized our school library. She chose mine

ix

as the best but took me aside and quite tactfully suggested that I might tone it down some. We cut "undying gratitude," for example. My idea of writing was to pull out all the stops. Alas, I didn't heed her advice later in high school, because most teachers liked for me to pour it on, especially the ostentatious vocabulary. (I was to flunk my first theme in college.) But she also turned me off to writing for a while. My reward for writing the best thank-you letter was that I had to memorize it and deliver it personally to the dowager in a public auditorium along with a basket of fruit so heavy that by the time I had huffed and puffed my way on-stage with it I was so out of breath I could at first only stare stricken at her. If this was what happened to you when you wrote best, I was going to take an early retirement.

Some teachers in my workshops remember nothing about writing before adolescence but much after, others nothing in school but much out of school. The stories tumble out—about cruel nuns who bark and bite and Jewish mothers who go "Ai, ai!" when your performance disappoints them, about furtive note passing and messages on the fridge, the dreaded "long paper" that you ended up liking, dreamy wish lists, the ubiquitous ticketing of parts of speech and sentences, and that locked diary with secrets so dark that revelation was a fate worse than death. After we've feasted on this miscellany of memories about writing, I ask the teachers to get professional again and say what patterns they may have detected, what generalizations they infer from their collective youthful experience that may help us to teach writing.

No matter what region the workshop takes place in, the main generalizations run to type. Personal relating is important, some of it play with peers or some other form of socializing, some of it support from elders—spontaneous appreciation and response in either case. Schools go about writing far too mechanically and impersonally, we conclude, though often one teacher or so stands out for having tried to make writing assignments and circumstances authentic and interesting. Too much drill on form, too little choice on subject matter and occasion, too many "reports" and "papers," not enough personal expression or use of writing for pleasure and self-fulfillment. We discover, climactically, that most positive writing experiences occur out of school. A girl corresponds with her uncle overseas in war. A neighborhood mother organizes bored kids into a group that puts on skits for which they write scripts. Two or three friends habitually exchange stories they make up and write down for each other. Someone in trauma fills notebook after notebook with feelings and thoughts. A preschooler writes down what he learns and wants to fasten in mind, like a personal encyclopedia, or makes up ads and jingles and posters. Older kids write out for each other recipes or other directions for how to make or do something they want to share.

Why do the best writing experiences have to happen out of school? These memory sessions show me that the writing that people care about occurs under circumstances difficult to arrange in large institutions, which compartmentalizes learning. Primary school allows some mixing of activities—emotional, physical, social, and playful—as a ground for reading and writing, but schools progressively emphasize discursive learning and isolate it out from other experience. The Whole Language movement tries to offset this, but it has had most success in the lower grades, where classrooms still tend to be all-purpose and children still syncretic. Secondary school not only makes English a separate subject but writing a separate strand within that subject. Again, a special movement has arisen—Writing Across the Curriculum—to try to reassert integration against institutionalism. College consummates this fragmentation by separating writing out into a special "composition course" where not even all kinds of writing are treated but only those more abstract sorts called for in other courses—making (or paraphrasing) generalizations out of the content of the course.

Isolating writing to teach it intensively boomerangs. Specializing it as a service course in order to prep undergraduates to do term papers and essay exams for lit crit, econ, social relations, or government, makes it even harder, paradoxically, to learn to write even the so-called exposition and argumentation that the courses target. This is because, as the authors of this book indicate in their various ways, writing so isolated and so specialized loses its grounding in emotions and the senses, in private and social experience, in the body and the unconscious, in silence and intuition. This multifarious matrix can't be skipped or slighted, because it includes the sources and resources of writing, reasons to write, and the circumstances that prompt and reward writing. The futility of a course in which one is supposed to just *write,* in a vacuum, can be seen in several telltale symptoms, the most notable of which is the head-scratching, paper-staring search for something to write about. The instructor resorts to assigning "provocative" essays or other *texts* (not only supplying subject matter but the same subject matter for all). Other symptoms of stripping down to focus on the "cognitive" are notoriously poor motivation and chronically disappointing results.

Real cognizing occurs harmonically, at all octaves of our being—physical, emotional, intellectual, and spiritual—in such a holistic way that to single out one discursive activity and to feature even then only a certain range of the abstractive spectrum is bound to defeat itself. That is the essential reason that college composition courses frustrate students and faculty alike. The synergistic approach of this book may do for college what Whole Language attempts for the elementary grades and Writing Across the Curriculum attempts for middle and secondary school. The authors of the essays collected here aim to restore the integrity of human functioning that educational institutions unwittingly break up in breaking down learning into piecemeal, pragmatic goals. Outside, people write from desire and fear, imagery and impulse, recollection and reflection, expertise and authority, stillness and suspension. They write to work up and work through, to find out and break out, to show and let know, to prove to others and to improve themselves.

When my sixth-grade teacher supplied us with a subject, a motive, and an audience in order to teach writing, she made the same mistake that colleges do in setting up self-contained, self-referring courses. When my high school teachers applauded my five-dollar words and my pompous phrasing to develop vocabulary and style, they were sacrificing writing as a whole activity for whole people to some subsidiary objectives. The following essays root writing back into the richness of the total organismic life that academic courses mostly exclude and that future education must restore. Ironically, writing as a means of studying another subject and of evaluating results is best served when subordinated to writing for self-realization. Colleges need to honor writing in all its fullness as a central humanistic activity. If they heed these essays, they can ensure that the best writing experiences no longer have to occur off campus.

James Moffett

Acknowledgments

We would like to acknowledge first and foremost each other for the patience, grace, and loving support during the time we worked on this book. We look forward to a time beyond our work when we can meet, celebrate, talk about families, and share some of the simple joys of living.

We acknowledge the help of Rosemary Thorne who typed, mailed manuscripts, sent and received fax messages, decoded cryptic handwriting, and did countless other tasks to make our work successful. We appreciate SUNY Brockport's Drake Memorial Library and Bob Gillam for locating books and letting us check some out for as long as three years. Lorna Wiggins at Auburn's Ralph Brown Draughon Library was unsurpassed as a detective for locating obscure books and passages. The Yaddo artist retreat granted Alice winter weeks of quiet for her thinking to take written shape.

We are thankful for Bob Boynton's faith in this project from the outset, for his prodding as well as his patience. Bob passed the torch to Peter Stillman whose honest response and encouragement continued to be a source of motivation for us. We acknowledge too the keen eye of Melissa Inglis, our editor at Heinemann, and others who were helpful.

We appreciate the support of our colleagues in the Assembly on Expanded Perspectives on Learning. Their insights have been both informative and inspiring and continue to broaden our vision.

Finally we acknowledge the contributions of our students, both at SUNY-Brockport and Auburn University, who without knowing it sharpened our thinking about writing and living.

Introduction:
Defining the Territory Beyond

Up to now what has fallen within the cognitive domain seemed to be virtually anything that establishment theorists claimed. The first sessions of the "Beyond the Cognitive Domain" interest group at the 1991, 1992, and 1993 Conference on College Composition and Communication (CCCCs) certified that well over one hundred participants were in some way connected with everything else. Without defining the cognitive domain in any particular way, we asked participants what that everything else was. Terms were tossed around, spilling all over, colliding into each other, occasionally knocking each other out or eliminating the other. What emerged from one meeting was an ungainly list: affect, affect motivators, apprehension, attitudes, beliefs and their systems, consciousness, creativity, creative imagery, ideational fluency, emotion, emotional intelligence, empathy, feeling, felt sense, healing and writing, humanistic values, imagery, imagination, imagistics, insight, inspiration, intuition, kinesthetic knowledge, meaning beyond language, meditation, memory, motivation, mystical experience, self, subjectivity, writing as therapy, unconsciousness, values and their systems, and visualization.

It was clear that everyone had a different idea of what went on beyond the cognitive domain. In some instances individuals differed so markedly in their ideas that they threw everything in or almost nothing. Other areas seemed up for grabs. Many didn't know what or where the domain was. But they knew it was somehow different from cognition. And they knew important things happened there.

1

Of course, charting the territory beyond cognition depends on how cognition is defined and where boundaries are set. What is inside, outside, borderline? What does knowing mean for intellectual models of writing in order to understand what knowing means otherwise, or when knowing incorporates everything else as well?

Definitions of the cognitive domain vary widely. One of the more inclusive ones put forth by Ulric Neisser attributes to cognition "all the processes by which . . . sensory input is transformed, reduced, elaborated, stored, recovered, and used" (1967, 4). Another definition includes all mental processes that we exercise in order to learn, store, retrieve, and use information, the byword of the field for many years. The notion of humans as information processing systems has surely outlived its usefulness. For in actuality the pivotal term is *knowledge,* with which the word information seems interchangeable. The broadest definition of knowledge refers to that which may be acquired through reasoning, perception, and intuition. Very little is excluded here. However, the intellect, a frequent synonym for cognition and intimately related to knowledge (insofar as the intellect means the capacity for it), provides a more limited definition insofar as it means the ability to learn and reason through something, as distinguished from the ability to feel or will it.

To other specialists cognition has to do with intelligence that is driven by symbols (Simon 1981) which has to do with the faculties of thought and reason. Still to others, cognition means propositional thought, without necessarily meaning the use of logic formally but rather the use of logic inferentially or experientially — along with mental models of the world (Johnson-Laird in Norman 1981). This introduces cognition on the basis of symbolic structures, subdividing them into spatial, temporal, and motor types, after the work of Piaget (J. Mandler 1984). J.P. Guilford recognizes the way humans deal with different forms of information in its broadest sense with his Structure of the Intellect. Despite the apparent shifts in terms most psychologists agree that how we perceive, remember, and think is grounded in two attributes: 1) An internal symbol system from which springs structures, schemata, and/or representations that marks its static quality; and 2) Processes, their dynamic complement, which involve the "patterning" (Simon 1981, 14), "manipulation, combination, and transformation" (Norman 1981, 3) of these symbols. And one cannot be postulated without the other (Simon 1982).

At about the time that psychologists lamented the myopia of traditional cognitive science,[1] the cognitive group in composition studies

---

[1]Simon meant it should be cross-disciplinary and include artificial intelligence (1981, 14). Norman meant it should include the social and affective (1981). Neisser urged it to have ecological validity (in Gardner 1985, 134).

staked its claim to almost every form of mental functioning—with the possible exception of emotion. Although Flower and Hayes have asserted that most knowledge occurs as conscious, verbal processes, they enunciated their multiple representation theory which recognizes several "languages" of thought: auditory, imagistic, schematic, and other ineffable forms of representing knowledge, particularly at the planning stages of writing (1984). But an interesting thing happened. For writing specialists paying attention, the domain beyond the intellectual had shrunk substantially. Thus, what in 1980 was "everything else" slipped into "what is left over" by 1993.

Regardless of theoretical persuasion, most of us recognize knowledge as not limited to textual, logical, and fully conscious thought. Norman (1981) particularly complained that contemporary theories of the mind seemed to be "theories of pure reason" (275) and, as such, were "inadequate and misleading" (266). It is one thing to lament the conventionally narrow definitions of cognition. It is quite another to covet all internal experience, to colonize it with intellectual principles as if all knowledge and meaning could be forced into a cognitive shoe.

There is an obvious point to be made here: We are straight thinkers. We are symbol-processing organisms. The intellect is involved in almost all of what we do. But we are more. It is naive and inaccurate to believe that all ways of knowing may only be represented intellectually. It is not so much that the imperialism by cognitivists should be checked. Rather, we need to recognize the complex and unique qualities of the inner experience that do *not* fit readily into the prevailing structures. And this we try to do here.

Arguably this book has a thesis only if it endorses a limited definition of cognition. Our position is obvious and continuous with the way writing specialists generally view intellectual processes—in their more common and restricted sense as conscious, verbal, rational mental processes involved in acquiring and transforming knowledge.

Given that, we say there is an everything else, and a substantial one at that. What other ways of knowing seem to have in common is that in one way or another they don't fit the traditional paradigms. Let us briefly note *some* categories as we see them. In one class of internal events we come to know things without being able to explain exactly how we come to know them. Things pop into our heads. An implicit piece of knowledge is made explicit or clear, seemingly without mediation or discourse. Preceded no doubt by a complex selection process, these events happen instantly or slowly. Some of them may be termed intuition, insight, or inspiration. Another class of inner states is marked by biophysical changes. Our pulse quickens. We experience fluidity or tightness in our neck or shoulders, our stomachs or throat. We feel euphoric, in a peak experience, as Maslow (1968) called it, totally absorbed in an activity, in flow, as Csikszentmihalyi (1990) would say. We do not realize it because if we did, we probably would not be in flow. Kinesthetic/tactile and body sense—even emotion and motivation—might fall here.

Another group of mental functioning is characterized by images formed in our minds. The crucial pictorial/presentational mode that Langer and Paivio so brilliantly research stands sharply in a class of its own. We experience something without its original stimuli—commonly spatial or visual images. But some may be quasi-sensory like auditory, olfactory, even motor images. We can tell the difference between a musty and fresh room, a wet and dry hanky. Imagination, reverie, fantasy, and dreams fall here. Knowledge like meditative acts seems to bypass intellectual structures in part or almost entirely. Rather than registering inner speech, meditation works to suspend it.

The most common feature of noncognitive knowledge (shared perhaps by all the above mental functions) is in the way it first reveals itself. This knowledge may fall below our level of awareness or be verbally inept at the outset and remain that way or rise to the cognitive to express, justify, or verify itself. A seemingly not-conscious thing becomes conscious. The conscious thing becomes conceptualized, articulated, enacted. Even if it becomes part of thought, it still may resist rational explanation and, in some cases, conventional symbolizing.

An opposite phenomenon occurs in the therapeutic experience. Rather than internal experience serving written discourse, written discourse serves the inner experience. Here the salutary effects of language are central. And because therapy involves emotion, much of this essential experience, of necessity, falls outside the cognitive domain.

Clearly, most of these forms of knowledge may be placed in several categories. Most interact so profoundly with one another that the human mind has yet to fathom the intricacies of those relationships.

This whole notion of a meaning system beyond the cognitive is, of course, not new. Philosophers long before Kant and through Langer have reminded us that there is considerable learning that goes unaccounted for, that we are at a loss to explain. We undoubtedly experience all these internal events. And they influence our mental lives and our language.

But this line of inquiry remains underdeveloped in composition studies—for obvious reasons. It is impalpable, ephemeral, even potentially incriminating. As teachers many of us are unwilling to risk the approval of our students, the respect of our colleagues, and our professional stature for such an unexplored enterprise, no matter what it may hold, particularly given our recent history. The 1980s saw exponential growth in the cognitive psychology of writing. Social theories followed, with powerful ideas about culturally constituted thought. But some people still seem dissatisfied with what these models say, do, and lead to.

The greatest need for growth in composition studies lies now in the ways we create meaning beyond what is currently considered acceptable knowledge. A comprehensive view of composing conceptually and practically must include these other ways of knowing—call them unconscious, automatic, ineffable, inexplicable. There have been isolated advances in this uncharted area of composition studies. Topics at one time taboo are no longer excluded from conference presentations. People are talking about emotion in ways they never did before. People are using kinetics and imagery in ways they never dreamed of. People are hungry for transformation.

This book responds to that need. The intention of this collection is to explore ways of knowing that we experience and that influence written language but have yet to be legitimated in composition studies. This volume is an act of faith. But we do not mean to imply that it will send readers to the river Ganges. Nor do we believe that as we pick up the torch and use it for lighting our paths, we will not burn our fingers. We wish we could say that these essays would solve the mysteries of the discursive mind. But they will surely raise more questions than they answer. As well they should.

The fact is that we do not understand the psychological content of our mental life much beyond conscious and verbal reasoning. It is not well understood by those trained to understand it. Perhaps in our lifetime we will learn very little about our full psychological life because we do not have the tools to study it, test it, and verify it. But we can make a start, small inroads into this territory. We can acknowledge such meaning, legitimate it, get it on record. We needed to read this book so we needed to write it.

In planning this work we had two courses to follow: one that deals systematically with several aspects of internal experience— imagery, insight, emotion, felt sense—and relates them to theory, research, and practice. Or the other—more haphazard—that invites those already active in these areas to bring to this volume their knowledge, insights, and experience. We were not likely to get an even mix with either approach. First, work is not being done equally in all areas. Second, certain lines of inquiry are more amenable than others to professional or pedagogical activities. Progress, for example, is being made faster in imagery than in the unconscious, which, to no one's surprise, reflects their parent field, psychology. It was also premature to commission work, so to speak, to ask composition scholars to pursue a subject in which they might have only modest interest.

Because we are inexpert in many of the subjects, we have appealed to writing specialists who are exploring these new approaches. We have thus produced a collection of essays on several strands that are sequenced from silence or chaos to emotion and healing.

The work collected here is eclectic in another way. It reflects its authors' styles of inquiry, be they through personal experience, historical study, or empirical research. Because of this eclecticism, the use of specialized and unfamiliar terms is sometimes unavoidable. Nonetheless, the collection models not so much a paradigm for teaching as it does a paradigm for learning that we believe is desirable if not essential at this frontier. Clearly, the best teaching and learning embody both intellectual and nonintellectual strategies.

We in composition studies are just beginning to grasp the potential of the inner experience that helps writing develop and to legitimate the writing that helps our inner experience develop. And this means nothing less than the mind in its whole humanity.

A.G.B.
Rochester, New York

R.L.G.
Auburn, Alabama

Part One

Silence

The world is full of noise, full of loud and strident voices, each trying to drown out the other. Glibness is mistaken for wisdom. Volume poses as authority. Cacophony masquerades as progress. Into such a world, silence comes as welcome relief. The more we are bombarded with language, the stronger our wish for quiet.

Silence is a way of knowing—and a way of learning, a way of teaching, and ultimately a way of being. Out of the vast unknown of silence words are generated. Silence provides the universal backdrop for them. Without silence our words would not be heard. The very absence of words insures their privilege when they are uttered. We know the meaning of words, their lights and shades, but who is wise enough to understand the meaning of silence? Who comprehends the nuance of silence? In the night sky, stars and moon speak volumes—in splendid eloquent silence.

Writers value silence. Silence is the first teacher of writing, and it is everywhere throughout the process. So it is not surprising that this book begins with silence. Peter Elbow writes, "I have a hunger for silence." It is mysterious and inexpressible, he reminds us, like an open door inviting us into some deep mystical consciousness. Elbow's work calls us back again and again to mine the paradox and wonder in the world of silence. Most of all, he invites us to know directly the silence in our selves as a source of power for writing.

In a natural way meditation blends the principles of silence with the rhythm and routine of daily life. Don Gallehr shows us how meditation is valuable in the composing process. Extending beyond analysis and linear reasoning, beyond cause and effect thinking, meditative insights do not come through concentrated effort but through waiting, as for some undeserved gift from an unknown benefactor.

How does silence fit into the school curriculum? "A pedagogy of silence enriches the school environment," comments Charles Suhor. Suhor argues that silence squares with a variety of specific educational practices — scientific observation, note taking, composing, athletic events, and test taking. Like the perfect stillness of Meister Eckhardt, silence is neither sectarian nor dogmatic. To be sure, distrust of silence stems from a longstanding cultural tradition which favors activism over reflection. Nevertheless, those who have the courage to open their doors within may find not the dark side but a center of light and energy.

Silence reminds us to slow down, breathe, order priorities, discover essences. As we try to understand the vast domain beyond the cognitive world, nothing could be more appropriate than to begin with silence.

1

Silence
A Collage

Peter Elbow

Empty, empty, empty. That's the main impulse I feel now. Towards emptiness. I'm tired of words. The tyranny of words. I have a hunger for silence.

It makes me realize how committed to words I've been, how deeply stamped by certain formative experiences. Being inarticulate, unable to write, blocked, stuck—and therefore having to quit graduate school as a failure. And then some years later, being able to write. Losing my tongue, finding my tongue.

Having found I could write, I've kept writing, writing, writing. Afraid I'd lose it again if I stopped? Got to keep talking on paper for dear life? Perhaps a quality of desperation.

And not just the experience of writing but of actually succeeding in saying what I want to say! Despite the struggle. What a miracle! It's left me with an insistent feeling that we can write anything. I get mad at the deconstructive idea that language always fails. No, damn it, we can say anything. Language doesn't fail. A stubbornness. Shrillness? Fear?

But now I think I'm ready to move on. Tired. I think I want to wander now into the place that values silence, emptiness, inarticulateness. To celebrate nonlanguage—silence—not having to write or say all the time.

And in fact perhaps these two impulses—toward language and toward silence—actually go together in some paradoxical way. For I have a sense this morning of my whole life—even my writing life—as a stubborn if underground celebration of inarticulateness and brokenness. That's what I've been fighting for in my writing. I've always been angry at the articulate and fluent people.

* * *

9

I wrote those words (slightly more jumbled) at a workshop at Pendle Hill, a Quaker Retreat Center near Philadelphia, in June 1991. In the last few years, my interest in voice has gradually led me to feel some correlation between powerful or resonant voice and silence. In fact I've always been interested in people who don't write or talk—the silent ones. When they say something, their words often seem remarkably powerful: more umph, more conviction, more presence—their words more "gathered up." I think I see it even in small versions: if we sit in silence for a while, there is apt to be more gathered energy and focus in what we say. Is this really so?

I think of Billy Budd: he stutters, and at the most important moment is utterly silent. Wordsworth praises the speech of country folk. Of course this seems like dubious sentimentality, but isn't it true that something special does happen—or rather can happen—when people spend a lot of time locked inside their own heads, talking and listening inside in silence? The rural, solitary life is apt to enhance this inner life. Freewriting is an attempt to imprison people inside their head.

So with some of these intimations in my head, I was happy to accept the invitation from Pendle Hill to direct a weekend workshop on Voice and Silence.

We wrote and talked a lot. I talked more about voice than about silence, but what figured most in all our conversations and our written reflections at the end was silence: the various periods of silence we had—and particularly the unbroken silence we had both mornings stretching from wake-up through breakfast till the end of "silent meeting" at around ten o'clock.

Charlie Janeway:

> Breakfast. Eating slowly, carefully. A shy furtive glance at the person next to me, avoiding eyes.
> Strange sensual intimacy, sitting next to someone and not speaking, knowing that another time and place we might be speaking.
> [Silent] meeting. Through half closed eyes, peoples' legs and shoes on the shining waxed floor.
> Silence. Except for my breathing and the occasional stomach gurgle, only the chattering of the birds outside the Barn.
> My thoughts run in the silence. . . .
> Breathing in. Breathing out. One in. One out. Two, three, four. . . . Thoughts slow down, slip away. Calm. Peace.
> I feel as close to happiness as I can recall. Right now.

Torrey Reade:

> Strikes me that there are all kinds of silences. Yesterday's was dreamy, this morning's verged on the prim. The kind I thought I

had from laziness really comes from fear. Silence in meeting is a peaceful non-event or something that vibrates. Here in this group we are on the one hand dealing with the polite silence we've all been bred to, and on another with some deep nurturing thing that emits from its darkness things that turn into words.

Ardeth Deay:

WORDS WORDS WORDS pouring out and over me, drowning my core, distracting my integrity.

This is the first time I've been able to articulate how painful it is for me when we use words to separate, to disconnect, to ignore each other. To cover up who we are? that we don't know? fear? lack of trust? indifference? pain? power?

What would happen if we all only spoke when we had something to say? Would we go about our lives with the comfortable feeling of connection I felt at breakfast? Lovely silence—opportunity to notice we are here together. Space to feel our spirits overlapping. [See William Johnson 1979]

Diane Cameron:

The silence has helped me hear the voices better, to listen to myself. I feel more connected to myself, more grounded than I have in a long time.

Me:

I was so grateful at breakfast at the realization that we had permission to be with each other without having to figure out what to say— how to be with each other. . . .

In this silence, are we more together or apart? The question gets at the paradox of it. One feels the distance, awkwardness. And yet the communion is deeper too. . . .

[Silence is] a chance to attend to what's inner. Not that chatter in the brain. Actually, of course there is a chatter—for me, most of the time, anyway. It's louder in the silence, but I can sort of peep around the chatter just a bit and wonder what's behind it. Get a few glimpses of something quieter behind it. . . .

For a few moments in the Barn [silent meeting] I had a sense that I might really be able to open the door, still the noises, go into a dark place—scary but somehow desirable. But I got nervous and the door shut and I was back to the distractedness. Still, a lingering sense of feasibility.

The collage form is important here. The force of the collage is the force of embedded silence: asterisks, gaps. Parts don't "flow" in the "logical order" demanded by "good writing." The collage is jagged and broken rather than smooth. What a relief. Hypotaxis rather than parataxis: nonconnection, nonsubordination. And the collage doesn't say what it's saying. It's just a bundle of fragments. [See Weathers (1976) on "crots."]

This explains why I hate sentence combining exercises. They always want you to change, "He stepped on the gas. The car surged forward" into, "After stepping on the gas, the car surged forward" (or some such subordination). There's something wrong with their very model of good writing. They assume that everyone wants what I, for one, don't want. Readers may think they want smoothness, flow, connection, but I'll bet that's not what affects them most.

James Seitz (1991) points out that we tend to accept fragmentary texts and alternative syntactic structures only in freewriting which doesn't "count" as real writing: it's too "easy" and a "sign of failure" (819). He looks to Barthes who celebrates the fragmentary text as serious and valuable. Also to Woolf, Faulkner, Barthelme, and Paley who "reveal the rhetorical and aesthetic power generated by disruptive discontinuity and disorder . . . " (823).

By using unconnected fragments and putting them in the "wrong" order, the collage sucks the reader in. The reader has to make the connections. Whenever there is silence, the reader must enter in, read in, participate. "Finally, the reader of silence is implicated in the text in a new way in Woolf's novels, for she or he must join with the writer to understand and decipher the silences in the novel: a mode of subjectivity" (Laurence 1991, 217).

The principle of negativity; absence. What makes writing good is not what the writer puts in but what she or he leaves out. Silence is often what's most powerful in music; space in art and architecture. We hear the pulsing energy in certain rests in music—especially in Beethoven's quartets (Brown 1992). We see the force in the spaces in certain line drawings, say, by Picasso, especially as an old man. I think of Frank Lloyd Wright. This is the gift of old timers and seasoned professionals. They do the most with the least. The old tennis pro who never moves and makes his young opponent move.

It seems as though smooth logical prose is "regular" and the collage is odd or deviant. But actually the collage—because it is just a bundle of fragments that don't say what they are saying—gives us a better picture of how language really works. The collage is the universal paradigm (like the relativity model), while smooth logical prose (the Newtonian model) disguises how things actually work.

I read my collage out loud to a friend. He ended up thinking I had the opposite opinion from the opinion I really have. Is it because

I wrote so badly? No, it's not badly written. It's because, as a collage, it doesn't try to say anything: it just presents material. Yes. And I like that about collages. They can settle for throwing lots of material at readers and asking them to experience it and make up their own mind.

But his "misreading" leads to a subversive thought. Perhaps he's right. Perhaps—now that I look at my collage again—I don't think what I thought I thought. Perhaps my collage allowed me to find words for what I didn't know. My collage—and my reading it out loud to my friend—are making me start to disagree with my old self.

Ron Padget (1992) writes about Picard's *The World of Silence* (1952):

> Max Picard, the author, was a Swiss philosopher whose work is known in this country only by professors of philosophy and aesthetics and by a handful of poets. . . . For years I have recommended this book to friends and colleagues, but because it was out of print for so long . . . and the messianic look in my face as I spoke about it, no one ever seemed to take my advice. Every once in a while, though, the response would be explosive: "You know about *The World of Silence?* Isn't it the most amazing book you've ever read?" It is an amazing book, hypnotic and almost crazy, partly because the word silence appears in 95% of the sentences. After a while you realize you don't quite know what the author is saying, but by then you have been floated into the mysterious dreamy mental space he has created, and it's wonderful to be there. How can you use this book in the classroom? I don't know. All I can do is urge you to get this strange and beautiful book before it goes out of print again. (16)[1]

Silence and felt sense. The source and foundation of verbal meaning often lies in the silence of what is felt nonverbally and bodily. When writing goes well, it is often because we periodically pause and say, "Is this what I mean to be saying?" It's amazing that we can answer that question: that we can tell whether a given set of words corresponds to an intention. The source of the answer is the feelings and the body—consulted in silence. When writing goes badly, it is often because we don't make these pauses for quiet consultations with our felt sense.

Here is a passage from Anne Dalke's, essay, "'On behalf of the standard of silence': The American Female Modernists":

[1]Readers may also be interested in *The Problem of Pure Consciousness: Mysticism and Philosophy* (1990), particularly the introductory essay on Meister Eckhart by the editor, Robert K.C. Forman. See also the interesting book-length treatment of the rhetoric of silence by George Kalamaras (1993).

Surprisingly, what we found encapsulated in the majority of these works [by Stein, Glasgow, Cather, Wharton, Hurston, Welty, and O'Conner], and expanded considerably in some of them, was a paean to the values of silence: to a full, rich and sustained well-being that needs no sharing, no expression, that finds the striving to talk largely gratuitous. These texts offered a testimony to silence as a fertile resource for understanding. Each of them fell silent at one or more critical points; each acknowledged the limitations of language. Some actually celebrated its absence.

This stance surprised us, because we were guided to these writers by contemporary feminists convinced both of the power of language and of the urgent need for women to find an authentic means of expression. [She goes on to quote critics like Gilbert and Gubar and artists like Olsen and Rich.]

The texts of the early female writers of this century chronicle the acquisition, but also the inadequacy, of language, which often fails to express the centrality of human experience. In acknowledging the limitations of language, these authors assert their affinity with a foundational premise and practice of modernism, what Jeanne Kammer, in *Shakespeare's Sisters,* defines as the "aesthetic of silence" (1979, 163). These women writers acknowledge "the difficulty of articulating . . . experience," the belief "that there is more to it than language can convey" (154). For them, "silences are deeper than the words" (156); "Silence takes the place of linguistic connections" (158).

These writers are fundamentally modernist both in their denial that language constitutes reality, and in their assumption of a reality of experience, mysterious and inexpressible, which precedes articulation. Accordingly, language becomes in their works not only inadequate to expression; it can be a hindrance to, even a falsification of, genuine understanding. The acquisition of language, they say, is not an unadulterated virtue; it may mean a loss of great value. Several of them celebrate silence as a great gift: they suggest that, when we do not speak, we may listen, hear, understand, even communicate in other ways. Silence may function as an altogether alternative means of communication, not dependent on speech for fulfillment.

. . . The extent to which, and the ways in which, American women authors value language seem to me to have changed. The contemporary feminist equation of language with power, of selfexpression with self-empowerment, strikes me as a relatively new— and relatively naive—development in American women's writing. The earlier twentieth-century writers . . . see further than our contemporaries, in their refusal to accept as definitive a binary opposition between silence and discourse. . . .

Foucault (1978): ". . . There is no binary division to be made between what one says and what one does not say . . . . There is not one but many silences, and they are an integral part of the strategies that underlie and permeate discourses (27)." . . . Sontag (1969):

". . . Still another use for silence: Furnishing or aiding speech to
attain its maximum integrity of seriousness . . . [W]hen punctuated
by long silences, words weigh more. . . . Silence undermines 'bad
speech'" (19–20). [These passages come from Dalke's first six
pages. She then explores specific works by the seven women writers.
What follows comes from her concluding pages, 22–23.]

   . . . In evoking a mysterious reality inexpressible in language,
Cather represents an aspect of modernism which has been overshad-
owed in the postmodern striving for speaking voices.

   This essay will act as a reminder, I hope, of Lyotard's definition
of the modern as the evocation of the "unpresentable," of what I
would term "the unsayable":

   [M]odern art devotes its "little technical expertise" . . . to present the fact that the unpresentable exists. To make visible that there
is something which can be conceived and which can neither be seen
nor made visible . . .

   [M]odernity takes place . . . according to the sublime relation
between the presentable and the conceivable . . . (78–79).

   . . . . Silence for these writers is not the product of weakness or
fear, but the result rather of acknowledging a realm, both psychological and spiritual, which language alone can not encompass.

Analogies between silence and freewriting:

- Both are quiet. (It's such a relief just to have quiet in the classroom or meeting room.)

- Both get you to live inside your head.

- Both involve relinquishing control, letting go; thus sometimes
  fear.

- Both tend to start with jabber, jabber, jabber, noise, static, baloney.
  Yet both often lead to or at least clear space for—voice, non-
  baloney, language and thinking that are grounded in actual experience rather than in convention or external authority. If there is a
  class or meeting or conversation that has gone wrong in some
  way—even if only very subtly "off"—a period of either silence or
  freewriting tends to help people both notice the problem and begin
  to deal with it. ("How come everyone is avoiding the main issue
  we came here to talk about?" Or "Why are no women speaking?")

- Experienced silence-sitters say they can somehow feel it in the air
  when the silence in a group is deep, when a meeting is "gathered." I think I can feel the same thing in the silence of a group of
  people freewriting—when it is deeper rather than resistant or
  sullen (as sometimes happens in an exam or when people don't
  want to write).

- In silent sitting and freewriting, there is often a feeling of fellow-ship or companionship—in a gathered separateness.

- Both silence and freewriting are hard to classify in terms of "input" vs. "output." Both are times of "producing" but also "waiting for things to arrive."

- Both give relief from logic and linearity.

- Both consist of one part of the self ministering to another part of the self.

Here is a mini-collage of passages from Erika Scheurer's disser-tation on Emily Dickinson and Voice:

> Two passages from a letter (L271) by Emily Dickinson to Colonel Higginson: "Then there's a noiseless noise in the Orchard—that I let person's hear. . . ." She explains that she shuns society because "they talk of Hallowed things, aloud—and embarrass my Dog. . . ." Dickinson is saying a lot about silence. First, there are certain things, "Hallowed things," that should not be spoken of aloud, and when people do so it bothers her so much that she secludes herself; sec-ond, she wants it clear that her silence is not a sign of ignorance or lack of words—she chooses silence as a response to certain situa-tions; and third, silence is central to her poetic project—her work is to enable us to hear, not ordinary sound, but a "noiseless noise": the fullness of silence? it's meaningfulness?
>
> L[etter] 572: "Why the full heart is speechless, is one of the great wherefores."
>
> > The words the happy say
> > Are paltry melody
> > But those the silent feel—
> > Are beautiful—
> > 1750
>
> I want to discuss silence, not as an opposite of, or negation of, voice, but in relationship to voice. We have enough from Dickinson on both silence and voice to infer that she did not see them as mutu-ally exclusive either. First, on the qualities of silence and how they relate to voice: the usual opposition we see is of writing/ silence/absence and speech/voice/presence. Post-structuralists like to emphasize the division here . . . but I want to say that silence can be as present as voice, that silence is a part of voice, or even maybe has voice. The resonance of silence.
>
> The first observation I'd offer to break up the tidy dualism of writing/silence/absence and speech/voice/presence is that silence requires presence to give it meaning. If I am silent and nobody is aware of it as silence—say I'm sitting home all day working on a piece of writing, receiving no calls and making none—that silence

doesn't mean much. However, if someone repeatedly tries to reach
me, knowing I'm home, and I don't pick up the phone, then that
silence has meaning (it could mean any number of things). In this
sense, the power of silence is just as wedded to presence and connection as the power of speech.

> We talked with each other about each other
> Though neither of us spoke—
>   1473

> Speech is one symptom of Affection
> And Silence one—
> The perfectest communication
> Is heard of none
>   1681

Communication specialists are now looking at silence in the
context of speech as well. In *Perspectives on Silence* (Tannen and
Saville-Troike 1985), a collection of articles by linguists and anthro-
pologists, Muriel Saville-Troike points to the increasing attention
that silence is getting—that it is no longer considered simply as what
surrounds the important thing, speech. She writes, "The significance
of silence can usually be interpreted only in relation to sound, but
the reverse is also the case, with the significance of sound depending
on the interpretation of silence" (3). In other words, silence is an
equal part of conversation, not just the space around it. I'm reminded of my discourse-analysis research with collaborative writing
groups. One of the groups had turned on the tape recorder's speech
activation mechanism for recording their group meetings, so no
pauses in the conversation are recorded, only speech. Listening to
this sort of recorded conversation is like listening to one where the
speech of one group member has been erased—the conversation is
ultimately misrepresented. So the silences within speech are speech
acts themselves.

> My will endeavors for its word
> And fails, but entertains
> A rapture as of Legacies—
> Of introspective Mines—
>   1700

Dickinson doesn't just express a philosophy about the inexpressible; her writing, with its elided syntax, pervasive dashes, and
ambiguous meanings is replete with the inexpressible itself. What
are these qualities of her work if not silences—places in which she
refuses to (or cannot) speak? What happens when we read her work?
We speak in the silences. We try—even if we ultimately fail—to
fill in the meaning, to figure it out. Often we leave the poem with the
meaning just as unclear as when we began, but the silences have a
different character after we try to create meaning in them: they

become resonant silences. I'm wanting to say, odd as it sounds, that this sort of silence has voice—it engages us in the act of filling it. We're engaged in dialogue with silence and the words surrounding it. Dickinson's voice comes not only through her words, but through the silences that pervades them.

L614: "Vocal is but one form of remembrance, dear friend. The cherishing that is speechless, is equally warm."

> If what we could—were what we would—
> Criterion—be small—
> It is the Ultimate of Talk—
> The Impotence to Tell—
>   407

How often do we truly feel comfortable with long periods of silence? When we're with strangers, or even casual friends, when the conversation falters, we panic and do anything to fill up the air. At first this seems strange; when we're talking we're revealing ourselves, which you'd think would be more frightening than anything else. Could it be that silence reveals even more than speech does, and that's what we fear? Again, I'm thinking of silence replete with meaning, resonance. And to be willing to share that meaning—not fear it—requires a relationship of some trust.

And this is exactly the same context required for voice, isn't it? To write or speak in a voice that is not put-on from outside, but comes from the person's reality, a reality of perpetually shifting borders, requires the context of trusting relationship.

> My best Acquaintances are those
> With whom I spoke no word—
>   932

> When Bells stop ringing—Church—begins—
> The Positive—of Bells—
> When Cogs—stop—that's Circumference—
> The Ultimate—of Wheels.
>   633

From Eva Hoffman's *Lost in Translation: A Life in a New Language* (1989):

I am writing a story in my journal . . . . I make my way through layers of acquired voices, silly voices, sentennous voices, voices that are too cool and too overheated. Then they all quiet down, and I reach what I'm searching for: silence. I hold still to steady myself in it. This is the white bland center, the level ground that was there before Babel was built, that is always there before the Babel of our multiple selves is constructed. From this white plenitude, a voice begins to emerge: it's an even voice, and it's capable of saying things straight, without exaggeration or triviality. As the story progresses, the voice grows and diverges into different tonalities and timbres; sometimes, spontaneously, the force of feeling or of thought compresses language into metaphor, or an image, in which words and consciousness are magically fused. But the voice always returns to its point of departure, to ground zero (275–6).

Here is the last piece I wrote during the Pendle Hill workshop: I want to bring more silence into my teaching. Here are some things I want to do more:

- Writing itself brings in silence. It's such a relief to end the yammering in classrooms and sit quietly writing.

- Stress freewriting as listening to the voices within—as waiting and receptivity and input—silence—not agency and output and pushing.

- Work on listening. Especially by more emphasis on sharing: just having the writer read and listeners listen in silence. Remember the non-necessity of response—whether to speech or to writing.

- Stress how the writer can be a silent listener to her own writing. "Please read your piece out loud. No feedback from listeners or from yourself. Just listen to your own words. Don't try to judge or diagnose or fix your writing, just ask yourself, 'What do I hear? What is this telling me?'"[2]

- Just as I often ask for five and ten minutes of writing in class, I think I can ask for five and ten minutes of silence now and then. They can't think I'm crazier than they already do.

- Stress silence—and writing—as a way to reach for the unspoken, the meanings that are hard to find or don't want to go into words. Try to explain and exploit felt sense more. As a way to tap the tacit knowledge we all have; a way (as Dena Muhlenberg wrote) "to get in touch with the parts of the self we often push away."

- In this connection: the silence and nonverbal of the bodily as opposed always to the mental.

- I am always saying, "Write, write, write." I need to have the courage to say (as Don Murray does), "Wait, wait, wait." (See Don Gallehr in this volume.)

[2]Thanks to Anne Mullin and her UMass dissertation for this idea.

Peter Elbow

From John Cage's "Lecture on Nothing" (1974, 369–70):

                                    What we re-quire   is
silence   ;   but what silence requires
        is   that I go on talking   .
                                            Give any one
thought
                a push   :   it falls down easily   .
        but the pusher   and the pushed   pro-duce   that enter-

tainment   called   a dis-cussion   .

                    Shall we have one later ?

                                    •

Or   we could simply de-cide   not to have a discussion.   .
                                        I have nothing to say
            and I am saying it   and that is
poetry   as I need it   .

                This space of time   is organized
.   We do not fear these   silences, —
we may love them   .
                                        This is a composed
talk   ,   for I am making it
        just as I make   a piece of music.   It is like a glass
            of milk   .   We need the   glass
and we need the   milk   .

2

Wait, and the Writing Will Come
Meditation and the Composing Process

Donald R. Gallehr

Do you have the patience to wait
till your mud settles and the water is clear?
Can you remain unmoving
till the right action arises by itself?
      Tao Te Ching, Stephen Mitchell, trans.

I am standing in my backyard, bow drawn, staring at an archery target seventy-five feet away. I am about to release my ninth arrow. The previous eight have hit the bull's eye. My mind is fluttering: I don't want to blow it. It want to hit all ten. My breathing is erratic, my left hand tired and shaking. I lower the bow and breathe abdominally, letting go of my fears and hopes. When calm returns, I again raise the bow. This time I think of snow sliding off a leaf at just the right moment. I draw the bow, wait for the moment, then release the arrow. Bull's eye.

My neighbor has been watching and calls over, "Good shot." To him, I am playing. He smiles and waves. He does not know that I am practicing meditation, the focusing of my whole body and mind on one point. If I were to sit cross-legged on a cushion, he would think

An earlier version of this article was published in *Life-Studies,* 4 (Winter 1988), 24–29.

me odd. He also does not know that I use this and other forms of meditation as an integral part of my writing. I do not know what he would think of my joining writing and meditation, but I know what my students think. For them it makes considerable sense.

Over the years I've been fascinated by the complementary nature of writing and meditation. Writing empowers meditation; meditation empowers writing. Insights derived from meditation are the material for writing, and vice versa. And some of the results seem identical—a sense of rejuvenation and control, a centering accompanied by courage, a clearer mind. Even the recent Western histories of writing and meditation seem to complement one another.

Until the 1950s, for instance, knowledge about the inner lives of writers writing was limited largely to conversations and correspondence between them. With the publication of the *Paris Review* interviews starting in the 1950s some of the secrets were finally out. In writing education this was followed by the pioneering studies of Janet Emig and Donald Graves, as well as the perceptive texts by journalist Donald Murray and teacher Ken Macrorie. Unlike their predecessors, these scholars, writers, and teachers described what they saw—the actual writing practices of writers.

At about the same time Eastern methods of meditation found their way West. This movement was led by the Japanese scholar D.T. Suzuki whose works appeared in the late forties and fifties, and included practical, psychological, and philosophical aspects of Buddhism (1956, 1964). Suzuki influenced young Englishman Alan Watts (1955) as well as the Beat Generation of writers and poets, including Gary Snyder, Jack Kerouac, Philip Whalen, and Alan Ginsberg.

In the sixties and seventies, a number of individuals established highly influential meditation centers, including that of Soto Zen master Shunryu Suzuki, whose talks were published as *Zen Mind, Beginner's Mind* (1970); Chogyam Trungpa, the Tibetan Rimpoche who established Dharmadatu centers in several major cities and published such works as *Meditation in Action* (1969); Tarthang Tulku, who established a famous center in Berkeley and was the first to bring Tibetan practices to the West (see Anderson 1979); Dainin Katagiri, Japanese Zen Master in Minneapolis, author of *Returning to Silence* (1988), and teacher of Natalie Goldberg; and Vietnamese peace activist Thich Nhat Hanh who headed the Vietnamese Buddhist Peace Delegation to Paris and whose works such as *The Miracle of Mindfulness* (1987) introduced readers to meditation. And, of course, Hindu Marharishi Mahesh Yogi, who not only influenced hundreds of thousands through his Transcendental Meditation techniques, but also medical researchers such as Herbert Benson and Miriam Klipper (*The Relaxation Response*, 1975). The arrival of meditation in the West was also accomplished by Americans who journeyed to the East to study meditation and later returned to establish centers and training programs for laity and monks alike: in Massachusetts Joseph Goldstein wrote *The Experience of Insight* (1976), and with Jack Kornfield wrote *Seeking the Heart of Wisdom* (1987); Philip Kapleau in Rochester, New York, wrote *The Three Pillars of Zen* (1965), and *Zen: Dawn in the West* (1980); and Walter Norwick in Maine described by Janwillem van de Wetering in *The Empty Mirror* (1973) and *A Glimpse of Nothingness* (1975).

This parallel disclosure of the practices of writers and meditators resulted in a wealth of "how-to" books and instructors. Some were reputable; others were not. The American hunger for a quick fix led to outrageous claims for learning writing or meditation in incredibly short periods of time, and for those who followed such paths, the disappointment and failure were certain and swift. "I tried it and it didn't work," or "I tried it for a while and use it from time to time," became by-products of these fast food approaches.

Fortunately, some Americans took the long road and wrote or meditated on good days and bad, deepening their understanding and broadening their abilities. A few continued to practice both, including James Moffett, the best known meditator/educator whose "Writing, Inner Speech, and Meditation," (1981b) continues to serve as the theoretical foundation for practicing both writing and meditation.

Before connecting writing and meditation, let me briefly describe the activities involved in each. First, writing. Although composing is not linear, it has direction and form which hold true for most writers. Donald Murray was among the first to identify three stages: prewriting, writing, and rewriting, with the following subcategories:

Prewriting: collect, connect, rehearse
Writing: drafting
Rewriting: develop, clarify, edit

Later he revised the seven-step list to five: collect, focus, order, develop, and clarify. Betty Flowers (1981) took another approach by describing writing in metaphoric terms:

Madman
Architect
Carpenter
Judge

Regardless of the way individuals cut the pie, writing involves ideas, emotions, and language which change recursively over time, through reordering, adding, deleting, substituting, and reconceptualizing.

Like writing, meditation provides alternative approaches, but most contain the following: *Posture, Breathing, Awareness, Letting Go, Concentration.*

Posture

The posture for meditation is usually a sitting position, often on a cushion on the floor with legs crossed. When practiced in a classroom, students sit in chairs with their feet on the floor and their backs balanced, leaning neither forward nor back. Their hands are folded in their laps and their chins are tucked in slightly. Their eyes are either open or closed; if open, they rest on a point some six to nine feet in front of them.

Breathing

Several approaches to meditation begin by focusing attention on breathing, with meditators watching their inhalation and exhalation. Some proceed to breathing exercises which deepen the breath and concentrate the attention.

Awareness

As thoughts and feelings occur—as they invariably do even if meditators are trying to stay focused on breathing—meditators become aware of them, neither clinging to nor running away from them.

Letting Go

In some approaches meditators note or label their thoughts or feelings before letting them go, a mental decision which is often accompanied by physical relaxation.

Concentration

Letting go may be followed by a period of concentration in which thoughts cease. For most beginning meditators, it is a brief period lasting only seconds. Continued practice enlarges this period and allows it to recur several times during a twenty- to thirty-minute meditation.

When writing and meditation are joined, they produce four qualities of mind: *Awareness, Concentration, Detachment,* and *Balance.*

Awareness

Awareness of feelings and thoughts occupies a large portion of a beginner's meditation. Some call it witnessing, that is, watching thoughts and feelings as they arrive; watching as they stagger, strut, and bump into one another; and watching as they leave, some scurrying away, some shoved off the stage by more powerful thoughts and emotions. During meditation there is no jotting down but there is a noting — a rise of language to label and recognize, even, at times, to recall afterwards. Obstacles to this witnessing such as desire, aversion, sleepiness, restlessness, and skepticism, make it difficult to stay seated or to let go of thoughts and feelings.

Writers are involved in a similar process of awareness. For instance, Peter Elbow talks about nausea which may overcome writers during revision: "Revulsion. The feeling that all this stuff you have written is stupid, ugly, worthless — and cannot be fixed. Disgust"(Elbow 1981, 173). Successful writers, of course, know they can acknowledge and let go of disturbing thoughts and feelings until their mind once again clears. They also know that they will survive nausea, joy, doubt, or anything else their minds throw at them.

Janwillem van de Wetering travelled to Japan in the fifties to learn Zen meditation from a Zen master. Even though he was discouraged from reading about meditation on the premise that he would be tempted to compare his experiences to the "texts," he and others kept notes on their experiences. A similar technique employed by those using language to learn is called note-taking/note-making. It refers to *taking notes* on one side of the page about what happened, and making observations about those notes on the other or *note-making* side of the page. The activity is strikingly similar for both writers and meditators: awareness, reflection, and letting go.

In addition, successful writers and meditators know that hindrances, problems, and struggle are part of the territory. By treating them as old friends rather than enemies, they disarm them.

Based on my practice of meditation, I have added two awareness exercises to my advanced non-fiction writing classes. The first I call the worry sheet which uses mapping to discharge thoughts that bother students. In the center of a blank page we write thc word WORRIES, circle it, then map words and phrases that represent our worries. After approximately ten minutes, we do a progressive relaxation exercise, letting go of our worries as we relax each part of our bodies, much as I let go of my fears and hopes before releasing the arrow in archery. Students say that increased awareness enables them to write for longer periods of time without interruption.

The second awareness exercise is based on the Steppingstones technique developed by Ira Progoff. Students jot down twelve events in their lives as writers — such things as writing letters to family, receiving particularly good or bad grades on a school writing assignment, and learning how to write in a new form (research paper, report,

resume, proposal, etc.). They then choose one steppingstone and write
the story of that event.

We differentiate between active and inactive steppingstones—
between those that do or do not play a role in the students' current
composing practices. Inactive steppingstones are merely memories.
By "sitting with" active steppingstones, students de-activate them.
Awareness of these steppingstones enables students to develop their
identities as writers. Releasing these memories frees them to write.

Concentration

Among several forms of concentration, two relate to writing and meditation: focusing on one object; and focusing on objects as they occur.
In meditation the mind can pay attention to a candle, mandala, artistic
configuration, archery target, or any object of significance. Or the
mind can focus on thoughts and feelings as they arise. The same is
true of writing. The writers' mind can focus on an object or focus on a
succession of events, ideas, or things. In both activities concentration works when we relax and hold the mind steady. Tightening up, of
course, tires the mind.

Concentration allows us to see in detail. Betty Edwards, in
Drawing on the Right Side of the Brain and *Drawing on the Artist
Within*, sees this as a shift in hemispheric dominance that occurs when
artists draw. We notice the stripes of the tulip, the lines around the
eyes, the space that forms the backdrop of the portrait. Concentration
also allows us to move beyond preconceived thought and cliché. As
the veil of language drops, we see the object of our concentration
clearly.

In the middle of my advanced writing course we develop our abilities to concentrate by practicing drawing exercises developed by Betty
Edwards. We turn Picasso's line drawing of composer Igor Stravinsky
upside down, then we draw it as we see it. Relaxed and attentive, we
move our eyes and pencils slowly and carefully. I watch students,
guiding them to draw only what they see, not what they imagine.

We also concentrate on listening without thinking, letting go of
thoughts as they arise, working toward an uninterrupted attention to
sound. We also practice with our other senses. When we eat, we just
eat; when we touch, smell, and think, we notice the temptation of the
analytical mind to distinguish one sensation from another: to compare, contrast, compartmentalize, and categorize. We acknowledge
the presence of the discriminating mind, and make an appointment
with it for later. We train our minds to concentrate for longer and
longer periods, to observe in greater detail, and thus bring to our writing a rich collection of experiences.

We talk about the ability of the mind to observe itself (Sekida). For instance, we *observe* the computer screen with a story on it, we *reflect* on our observation, and we are *aware* of ourselves reflecting. We see that distractions from one-pointed concentration— that is, focusing on a single object—come not only from skipping from one object of observation to another, but also from shifting from observation to reflection to self awareness. We notice that the power to concentrate is only one side of the coin; the other is the power to let go. When we try hard to concentrate, the trying gets in the way. The observation, for instance, has a smudge on the lens, the smudge of trying. So we let go of the trying. We wait for the mind to settle until we are attentive without effort.

Detachment

Donald Murray says of writers, "They must detach themselves from their own pages so they can apply both their caring and their craft to their work" (1982, 68). He then cites Ray Bradbury's practice of putting a manuscript away for a year before revising it, acknowledging that not many writers have the discipline or time to do this.

Beginning writers not only have problems with deadlines, they must also struggle with topics they identify closely with. Most writers, beginning and experienced, in fact benefit from being able to detach themselves because it helps them move more quickly from writer-based to reader-based prose before their drafts are due. Detachment in meditation comes from adequate attention to thoughts and feelings arising in us. It also comes from an ability to practice letting go. For beginning meditators, letting go is rarely final. Strong thoughts or feelings in particular return repeatedly in the same meditation or in subsequent meditations. Over time, however, meditators develop the "big mind" as Shunryu Suzuki describes it, a form of detachment that sees from a distance and places things in perspective. In addition, continued meditation reveals a dynamic rather than a static world, a world in which previously perceived solids are seen as consisting of moving parts. This is true on the physical level (as in atoms in motion) as well as in the world of thought collections of interrelated ideas.

When writers perceive a writing problem as a solid entity, they are apt to deal with it as a total rather than as parts and connections. Writers' block, for instance, is not a monolith but a combination of actions and reactions to discrete writing problems. By becoming aware of and letting go of these different pieces, writers can move on.

Zen, one form of meditation, uses koans or word puzzles to trick the mind into detaching, much as the upside down picture does in drawing.

Koans cannot be answered logically. The question, "What is the sound of one hand clapping?" does not have a logical or rational answer. To practice detachment, I adapted the Zen koan to ask questions about writing which can be answered only intuitively. For instance, "What does this writing want to become?" forces us to move away from a rational identification with the writing to a detached intuition.

Answers to koans do not come immediately. We relax and wait, and waiting is one of the most difficult parts of both writing and meditation. Doubt begins as niggling and annoying, and as we wait the doubt grows and grows. I encourage my students to trust themselves, to relax and observe the question just as they observe the drawing.

Answers to koans have certain characteristics. They are *holistic*. Even if they are working on a segment of writing, they take it as whole unto itself. They are *surprising*. Because koan answers are not a product of the analytical mind, our intuitive mind is "surprised." Koan answers are *delayed*, that is, they take a period of time to arrive (Zen koans, which deal with issues as large as the meaning of life, may take months or even years to answer). Students who receive quick responses to koan questions say they have thought about the koan over a period of time, sometimes in response to a question previously posed by another student. Koan answers arrive *suddenly*, not in drips but in a gush. And koan answers appear *when least expected and often while writers are physically in motion.*

In the latter part of the course, we custom-make koans or questions about a particular work. For example, Irene spent her early childhood in Cyprus until her parents brought her to the United States. As a college student, she visited her relatives in Cyprus over the summer. When she returned to the United States she found herself writing about whether she should make Cyprus or the United States her permanent home. Analytical thinking to answer her question, "Where should I live?" was giving her usual, logical pros and cons. She couldn't decide. Nor could she complete her writing until she asked the koan question, "Where do I belong?" Then her answer was, "I'm an American." She had become not only a U. S. citizen but also an American. Where she lived at any given point in her life seemed less important than knowing her national identity. In addition she felt she was not ready to make a lifelong decision on where to live; for now, she would stay in the United States with her friends and, after graduation, look for a job.

Balance

I think of balance as scales. When the needle hits the middle, the scales are balanced. For instance, writing from too little or too much information is imbalance. Similarly, revising too early leads to nit-picking; revising too late restricts writers to sentence-level changes. Gauging the right moment is balance.

In meditation, sitting without leaning forward or back; watching thoughts and emotions without clinging to or rejecting them, develops balance. Meditators find that too busy a schedule distracts. Too much sleep leads to sluggishness. Too much excitement results in overload. Balance is in the middle.

Students who let go of praise and criticism, maintain balance. Students who let go of the wish to get an "A" keep their focus on writing. Students who wait until distracting thoughts leave, proceed with their minds clear.

Applying meditation to writing in its most secular sense serves several purposes. It preserves the connection between meditation and its Eastern heritage. It refuses to reduce this profound and complex practice to gimmicks. And it is an enlightened response to the question of how to bring *all* our abilities to bear on writing that instructors have long sought.

3

The Pedagogy of Silence in Public Education
Expanding the Tradition

Charles Suhor

Silence as a means of centering, of witnessing our feelings and thoughts, is something we seldom talk about in public schools or in teacher education. For a variety of legal, pedagogical, and ideological reasons, we avoid serious consideration of silence in public education. Advocates of pluralism in the schools staunchly (and rightly) oppose attempts at introducing silent prayer into the classroom, and court decisions support them. Fundamentalists who once directed their energies toward promoting "moments of silence" for sectarian prayer now seem more concerned with preventing students from engaging in any reflective activity that might be connected with "New Age religions" (Jenkinson 1988).

Religious schools typically have a tradition of silence that is available, if often neglected, as a pedagogy productive for personal growth. Private schools grounded in holistic theory (e.g., the Crossroad School in Santa Monica, California and Rudolph Steiner schools) have often taken the lead in exploring the educational uses of silence (Kessler 1990). But in recent years the dramatic movement in pedagogy has not been toward cultivating creative silence but toward collaborative learning and language-rich classroom environments. This movement is a healthy reaction to mind-numbing worksheets, desks riveted to the floor, dust-dry lectures and recitations, and—worst of all—the use of silence as punishment. The hum of language in the classroom is now viewed as evidence of learning, and student discussion is correctly seen as an integral part of meaning-making (Hynds and Rubin 1990). *Dimensions of Thinking*, the framework for teaching thinking from the Association for Supervision and Curriculum Development (ASCD), places oral discourse at the center of all thinking processes—not just the composing process but also problem solving, decision-making, comprehending, researching, and concept formation (Marzano 1988).

A sound, multidisciplinary research base supports this emphasis on oral language. Reciprocal teaching, inquiry methods, cooperative learning, and collaborative learning all call for thoughtful and lively student talk as core learning experiences (see, for example, Palincsar and Brown 1985; Collins 1986; David W. Johnson, et al 1984; Golub 1988). These techniques are consistent with Piaget's statement that "language is but one among . . . many aspects of the semiotic function, even though it is, in most instances, the most important" (1970, 45–46).

A Pedagogical Tradition

But the traditions of teaching and research in public education have not completely ignored the importance of silence. Instructors in all disciplines acknowledge several well-established practices calling for it. Such practices are found in schools and classrooms that also value oral language instruction: observing scientific experiments; composing—both written and graphic; reading, making notes on, and editing peer writing; seeking textual evidence for class discussion; pausing during "wait time" after class questions; test-taking; engaging in craft and shop activities; practicing and executing athletic activities; and participating in sustained silent reading.

Teachers at various grade levels report other activities in a pedagogy of silence. "Listen to the Silence" is a language arts exercise in which students sit quietly and attend to the background sounds in their environment. Then they write and talk about things they have heard and about their feelings as they listened. For example, one strategy for working on mathematical concepts and problems involves suspending analytical thought and simply looking and feeling "with the intention and expectation of understanding" (Noddings and Shore 1984, 83; see also Allender 1991). With this as a backdrop, we have a double-pronged rationale for exploring the uses of silence in public school classrooms. Besides being an important part of holistic, new paradigm teaching, the psychology of silence builds on existing pedagogical traditions.

Let me underscore one point. These traditions bear no resemblance to the enforced sepulchral silence of teacher-dominated classrooms of the past (and too often, of the present). Silence pursued for new insight is decidedly friendly, regenerative (when sustained), and conducive to creative response when part of a dynamic of reflecting, listening, and speaking. James Moffett, a leading theorist in language education, puts it this way: "People who can suspend discourse think and speak better when they turn it back on" (1981a, 171).

The Case for Suspending Discourse

Moffett has been a most ardent and articulate advocate of silence as a vital part of pedagogy. He effectively extends the traditional repertoire of activities that call for silence with visualizing, suspending inner speech, witnessing internal experience, and observing one's breathing. For Moffett, silence is not anti-language but an appropriate—and important—aspect of developing students' language skills.

As simple and as sane as this sounds, many find it frightening, even infuriating. To Christian Fundamentalists it smacks of New Age indoctrination. To civil libertarians it opens the door to prayer in the classroom. But these are knee-jerk responses—right knee and left knee, respectively. Radical religionists do not view meditation and other silent exercises as wholesome instructional practices. They have already attacked antiseptic materials like ASCD's *Tactics for Thinking* (Marzano and Arredono 1986) and Holt, Rinehart, and Winston's *Impressions* (see Davis 1991) series as wicked manifestations of the occult. Their mindset is expressed by Texe Marrs, a radical fundamentalist who claims that "Atheism and Secular Humanism . . . were only first crude attempts by the Devil. In the New Age movement and religion, Satan has latched on to something far more effective and direct" (1988, 230).

Civil libertarians have their own closet full of demons, but they generally work within the tradition of intellectual analysis. For example, the National Council on Religion and Public Education has long endorsed the study of religions in history, comparative religions, and the Bible (and other scriptures) as literature in public schools. Similar positions are held by the Interfaith Consortium for Pluralism and the First Liberty Institute. A logical extension of that pluralism would call for non-mainstream and non-Western modes of knowing—again, with proper insistence on a nonsectarian approach. Arthur Foshay, curriculum theorist and former president of the John Dewey Society, states that "our knowledge of how to take advantage in education of the transcendent experience . . . is impeded by our cultural reluctance to acknowledge that such experience deserves serious attention, since it is not obviously rational" (1991, 131).

Moffett frankly states that Eastern belief systems are an important source of techniques for cultivating useful silence. While he

cautions that meditative techniques can be trivialized, used manip-
ulatively, and misused by denominational zealots, he insists that
the techniques are essentially nonsectarian. An enriching public
school education must balance the empirical view of the world, in
which "knowledge derives from material experience ordered by
reason," with the meditative view, in which "people learn by resonance, by going into themselves in order to tune into things outside" (1990, 10).

New Research and New Dialogues

The problem of whether and how to teach silence in public schools is
indeed thorny, but that is no reason for closing the doors on it. Even
by empirical standards alone, the cultivation of inner awareness mer-
its our attention. A recent Stanford University meta-analysis of
research found meditation and other relaxation techniques useful in
reducing anxiety (Eppley 1989). "Mindfulness" meditation is clearly
connected to metacognitive understanding, as discussed in the educational literature. In a Canadian study researchers found that symptoms of stress were reduced for students practicing both meditative
and cognitive self-observation (Greene and Heibert 1988). Another
study found that "long-term meditators" were highly capable of dealing with conflicts as learning experiences rather than resorting to self-
blame or blaming others (Shapiro 1992).

The very language of Western scholarly discourse and Eastern
meditative traditions converge as they rise. Educational theorist and
researcher Gavriel Saloman (1987) discusses metacognitive mindfulness as a factor in the transfer of learning. Burmese teacher
S. N. Goenka (see Hart 1987) is among many using the concepts and
vocabulary of modern physics to describe meditation. Noddings and
Shore (1984) discuss intuition in education in terms of the similarities
between Zen Buddhism and the ideas of Pestalozzi, Martin Buber,
and Jerome Bruner.

Equally important, scholars from a wide range of disciplines have
recognized meditative techniques and religious beliefs as not inher-
ently linked. Psychologist Mihaly Csikszentmihalyi (1990) of the
University of Chicago, characterizes any transporting experience—
whether intense immersion in work, athletic activity, meditation, or
religious ritual—as "flow," a state that contributes to contentment
and mental health, regardless of the context of that belief. Stanislov
Grof (1985), a pioneer in contemporary theory and research of psychotherapy, describes transpersonal phenomena clinically as the feeling that one's consciousness has expanded ego boundaries and tran-
scended time and space limitations.

Shinzen Young, an internationally known teacher of Vipassana meditation, describes his pedagogy as "an approach that would cut across belief systems . . . so that people wouldn't think they had to become 'Buddhists' in learning techniques from the Buddhist tradition" (Tart 1990, 155). Catholic priest and psychologist Peter Lourdes agrees that methods such as Vipassana can be useful, even though "the theory (or theology, if you will) . . . does not generally fit" his Catholic belief system (1989, 2).

Secular and religious writers are growing increasingly comfortable with the idea that transcendent experiences are variously interpreted within different belief systems. Novelist Salman Rushdie, writing candidly as an atheist, defined transcendence as "that flight of the human spirit outside the confines of its material, physical existence which all of us, secular or religious, experience on at least a few occasions" (1990, 103). His view parallels that of theist Claudio Naranjo, who holds that meditation is restorative as a *"natural* mode of perception" accessible to believers and nonbelievers alike (1989, 150). The point is stated eloquently by noted psychotherapist Frances Vaughan:

> Spirituality is not the special property of any group or religion. It exists in the hearts of men and women of all races, creeds and cultures, both within and outside of religious institutions. Spirituality presupposes certain qualities of mind, including compassion, gratitude, awareness of a transcendent dimension, and an appreciation for life which brings meaning and purpose to existence. (1991, 105)

Elsewhere I have argued that transcendent experience, whether achieved through meditation, cognitive insight, athletic "highs," the arts, or everyday human empathy and love, is ultimately inexpressible. Thus, transcendence and silence are intimately linked (Suhor 1991). The highest of human aspirations and experiences are ineffable and asemiotic (Corrington 1989), and the rich symbol systems employed in education function best when they lead students to an uncoded and undifferentiated sense of—in Keats' phrase—truth and beauty.

A pedagogy of silence, besides being good mental hygiene (in Csikszentmihalyi's sense) enriches the classroom language environment (in Moffett's sense). Beyond that, a conscious pedagogy of silence results in greater receptivity to the worlds of silent transcendence toward which literature, the arts, and productive human living point us. As music educator Bennett Reimer (personal correspondence, September 10, 1991) puts it, "When we approach the transcendent quality of experience, the breadth we feel is more like silence than sound (even when musical), more like quietude than action."

Psychologist Charles Tart succinctly states: "See something *fully* and it is transparent, hear *fully* and it is silence" (1989, 257). For violinist and poet Stephen Nachmanovich, "direct and personal spiritual experience" is also inexpressible in words, but it leads to a "visionary attitude" that "expands . . . art, science, and daily life" (1990, 12). Psychiatrist and researcher Claudio Naranjo emphasizes the accessibility of such experiences, stating that "the experience of selfless identification with an object or being is known to all of us in some measure, for it underlies all genuine aesthetic experience, human empathy, and the religious attitude" (1989, 29). For novelist Iris Murdoch, peak experiences are derived from viewing paintings (Murdoch and Krishnamurti 1984); for playwright and poet Imamu Baraka (Jones 1963), from listening to jazz and blues (1963); for Trappist Monk Thomas Merton, from meditation (1958); for essayist and poet Annie Dillard, from communing with nature (1982). The most universally shared peak experiences probably come from human empathy in family relationships, with religious and aesthetic experiences varying more widely in form, intensity, and accessibility in different cultures.

Ultimately the current productive emphasis on rich and varied talk in the classroom merges with the productive use of silence. The movement from direct experience to a sense of transcendence applies to intensive class discussion. I have spoken to teachers around the country who have experienced, as I have, the absorbing spiritual involvement that class discussion can produce. The feeling of unity and transcendence that emerges from such discussion—another aspect of Naranjo's "selfless identification" and "human empathy"—is central to the joy of teaching.

In this sense, then, silence has always been a major educational *goal*. What is needed is a reconsideration of silence as *method* in public education. Clearly, our tradition includes a *continuum of instructional practices* that already make use of silence, ranging from unplanned, wondrous pauses during heady discussion to DEAR (Drop Everything And Read) time to intense self-searching while composing. There is no philosophical reason why that continuum should not include wider use of techniques such as visualizing, guided imagery, and meditation. Many of these methods already appear in our pedagogical literature, as in Moffett and Wagner's K–12 curriculum (1992), Thompson's imaging and writing work for college students (1991), and Hughes' writing and meditation materials for adult learners (1991).

We have come a long way from the time when the social debate over spiritual reality was limited to spitting contests between evangelistic atheists like Paul Kurtz and arch-rivals from the religious right, who spoke in black and white terms of backwoods Fundamentalism and godless humanism. The new rhetoric is dialogic and communal, seeking areas of overlap, if not consensus. The educational community needs to participate vigorously in this generous sharing of texts so that a pedagogy of silence is accessible to all students. Again, the wisdom of Arthur Foshay:

> I have become convinced that transcendence lurks in every part of the formal curriculum, and that it can be found in the other parts of the offering, too—the technical subjects, the school culture, . . . and in sports and other public performances that are usually a part of school life. It doesn't come free, however. If we wish to make the experience of transcendence in school learning more likely, we will have to learn to plan teaching in depth. (1991, 131)

Part Two

Wisdom of the Unconscious

Sometimes a word, an image, or an idea presents itself unbidden at the threshold of consciousness. At first its appearance seems strange, even bizarre, totally out of step with directed mental activity. Because it is so different, our impulse is to suppress it. Yet these visitations from the unconscious present opportunities for enhancing our lives.

Systematic and linear, the conscious mind carries on the day-to-day business of the world. Ideally the conscious should listen to the unconscious, a reservoir of feelings, attitudes, imaginings, and the other mental activities. But because of the Western habit of mind and the pressures of everyday life, the conscious relies more on itself, neglecting the knowledge that the unconscious may provide. As we reconcile the demands of both the conscious and the unconscious mind, we reach toward wholeness and the balanced life.

Writing has traditionally been envisioned as rational, sequential, effectively organized, and correctly spelled. Anne Mullin tells about writing that is not. A trace, Anne Mullin writes, is "a word that is left out, a substitution, a double-edged phrase, ambiguous punctuation, a jarring juxtaposition, contradiction, or sudden turning away from an idea in progress." Mullin describes traces in students' writing and explains how they connect to the unconscious elements in their lives.

39

Writing about rivers evokes the unconscious—stories rich in image and symbolism; significant situations; crossroad events; memories; mysteries; and personal metaphors. Dick Graves and Susan Becker invite young writers to come to the river and write from their own experience. Students' work growing out of their rivers reveals the breadth of ideas the unconscious can generate. That many civilizations have considered rivers sacred—the Ganges, the Nile, the Jordan—illustrates their universal appeal.

Elizabeth Holman draws on the work of British psychologist Tony Bastick to discuss the unconscious wisdom of intuition and "its dramatic counterparts, insight and inspiration." They cannot be called up at will but come of their own accord, on their own schedule. They wait and listen; they watch for just the right moment. Preconscious and preverbal, they are a powerful yet silent ally in composing. Little wonder writers welcome intuitive insights when they occur.

The unconscious speaks in many voices. And so we listen, drawn to what we perceive as wisdom just below the surface. Then we respond, like William Stafford (1977, 19) in the poem "Ask Me," confirming the wisdom of the unconscious: "What the river says, that is what I say."

4

Traces in Texts
Reading the Waters
Anne E. Mullin

We are standing on a weathered dock that extends about thirty feet out from the hemlock-crowded shore of a small, quiet pond. The pond's surface, winking under a slight breeze, gives back essentially our view: bright sky, dark green tree line, stony rim of shore.

If, however, our gaze rests on a shadow, say one that begins just where a dock piling breaks the pond's surface, we are introduced to a different world. We can follow our gaze down where the water is brown, where large moss-covered rocks push against the piling to hold it steady, where layers of silt-laden leaves have sunk on an ancient bough. Our eyes adjust to the amber light, recognize movements of shadows within shadows, and a flourish of S curves. Three sunfish just hang for a moment then weave into a wedge of reed stems beyond view. We blink, returned to the surface light. We find our way down again, when we wish, guided by ruptures and shadows.

Much the same gaze shifting is necessary when we respond to written language. We may experience a surface response which reflects back to us within our frame of reference, our expectations of genre, content, style, or standard usage. But when these expectations are jarred in some way, when the mirror is pocked or dark-streaked, we are invited into a different realm. Seeing pocks and streaks as invitations instead of blemishes open us to new ways of experiencing texts.

Derrida alerts us to the power of the "brisure" or "trace" to open a text's appearance and signification "to what is beyond it, or anterior to it in space/time" (1976, 65–68). He has also called us to view "trace" as a record of resistance, a clue to repression. "Writing is unthinkable

41

without repression" (1978, 226). A trace in a written text might be a word that is left out, a substitution, a double-edged phrase, ambiguous punctuation, a jarring juxtaposition, contradiction, or sudden turning away from an idea in progress. A trace is also "the erasure of self-hood, of one's own presence . . ." (1978, 230). A reader might notice this as an absence; perhaps a sentence has no clear subject, or personal pronouns (especially first person pronouns) are lacking or confused, or there is undue dependence on the passive voice.

We trust accomplished professional writers to create deliberately the traces that so surprise and tantalize us. But we assume that our student writers' cracks and fissures are accidents, not meant to introduce us to a treasure of lively possibilities. We expect that our writing students are attempting to render a relatively unblemished surface in order to reflect recognizable ideas in appropriate relationships and proportions—sky, tree line, and shore all balanced in the mirror pond.

I propose that for all writers the traces are often signals of unconscious activity—the teeming source of our most powerful creative impulses—and that gifted writers make use of their traces while inexperienced writers do not. If we are teaching writing, one most important thing we can teach is how to read our own work for its traces, as Mark Twain tells us how to read the surface of the river as a text whose full meaning lies below:

> The face of the river, in time, became a wonderful book . . . delivering its most cherished secrets as clearly as if it uttered them with a voice. (1903, 82)

Opening students to the possibilities that surface glitches reveal in their work may sound like a more psychoanalytic approach than many composition instructors comfortably embrace. Yet, if we believe that language use involves unconscious as well as conscious symbols, we may also believe that our students (and we) need an approach that does more than view errors as primarily cognitive lapses to be corrected or smoothed over (see, for example, Shaughnessy 1977; Kroll and Schafer 1978; Bartholomae 1980; Daiute 1981; Epes 1985).

Ever since Freud demonstrated how the language of dreams, jokes, and even everyday conversations can testify to unconscious or primary process mental activity, analysts have refined their techniques for interpreting such oral language events as ambiguities, lapses, contradictions, repetitions, surprises, and substitutions. Psychoanalyst Roy Schafer (1976) discusses patterns that clarify or obscure concepts of action and agency, thus expressing or denying responsibility. British therapist Charles Rycroft (1985) emphasizes that both primary and secondary process thinking processes need to be recognized as working in human expression. Indeed, Rycroft confirms philosopher Susanne Langer's (1957) thesis that both presentational or non-dis-

cursive as well as representational or discursive elements are fundamental to human mental activity. Analyst Hans Loewald's (1988)
treatment of symbols and "articulation" and Hanna Segal's (1986)
case studies expand our awareness of the noncognitive aspects of verbal expression. Reading these and other psychoanalysts does not make
us therapists, but it deepens our understanding of how language works
on more than one level. In our writing classrooms then, we are able to
shift our gaze from seeing "errors" as interference with the smooth
flow of ideas across a reflective surface to seeing them as glimpses of
ideas moving indirectly through amber-lit depths.

And then what? I suggest an approach that involves a two-step
process of observation and interpretation. We first observe the formal
characteristics of a piece of writing from a descriptive, not evaluative
perspective. Then we ask writers to associate, to interpret the observations—as reader-response and poststructuralist approaches recom-
mend (Bartholomae and Petrosky 1986; Anson 1989; Crowley 1989;
Lawson, Ryan and Winterowd 1990).

One instructive example of the approach is demonstrated by
British psychoanalyst Marion Milner, whose work with "free drawing" parallels that of Ken Macrorie and Peter Elbow. Milner (perhaps familiar to many by her pseudonym of Joanna Fields) explains in
On Not Being Able to Paint (1957) how her free drawing was first
"done on impulse" as a kind of doodling, but then required "will-
power" to "keep one's hand moving on the paper" and to

> maintain the kind of attention which created a gap ahead in time
> and a willingness to wait and see what was emerging to fill the
> gap. . . . one could not plan beforehand exactly what was to be pro-
> duced . . . but what one could do was plan the gap into which the
> new thing was to fit. (104)

But whereas most of us use freewriting as a process for generating
content for further drafting and editing, I think we can learn much
from Milner about how also to view the *forms* generated by the
process. For Milner is convinced that her free drawings provide a
way to observe "aspects of the difference between the inner world and
the outer one," between subject and object, between imagination and
reality (130).

In *The Hands of the Living God* (1969) she explains how client
Susan brought pages of drawings to her therapy sessions. Milner
responds to them as to her own drawings, first describing the formal
elements visible on the surface:

> She has brought three sheets of drawings. On one there is . . . a
> markedly plantlike form, with leaves shown springing up from a
> single focus or root at the bottom, the leaves spraying outward on

> each side; also above the second pair of leaves there emerge two
> strong budlike forms which are, however, shown cut right across by
> a bigger and smaller circle, seen in flattened perspective, and one
> above the other, suggesting to me that the vigorous budding plant
> has been cut clean across its double bud. (85)

She also tries to involve Susan in the interpretation: "What she says,
at first, about this drawing is that, 'It's nothing . . . it's mad.' But
when I ask her about the two flattened circles, she says, "There is no
life without opposites" (85).

Milner then interprets the material, going beneath the surface features to what might be moving in the realm below, part of which she
has already glimpsed in previous encounters:

> although she had first said that all these shapes she has drawn are
> devils, she now says that they are chrysalises. Thus it seemed to me
> that the deepest meaning must be that they are all to do with a grow-
> ing capacity once more to differentiate out her own feelings . . . she
> does know they must break through their fæcal shells and emerge
> into something different. (94)

Milner's work with non-verbal symbols offers a model for observing
and describing (but not judging or correcting) formal features of verbal symbols. She helps us see how the formal features of writing, like
drawing, present a readable surface between inner and outer reality.
Psychologist Marshall Edelson more specifically demonstrates observation and interpretation of the formal features of written language in
his treatment of Wallace Stevens' "The Snowman." Edelson first
observes the characteristic patterns of language in the poem, citing,
for example, in the 89 monosyllabic words out of 108, the predominance of three accent syllables per line, and characteristic sounds
and sound links. Then, noting that "[d]eviance of any kind is an
occasion for interpretation," he speculates on the significance of
deviant forms, such as the tri-syllable "misery" in the opening stanza
(1975, 157).

Great writers employ such deviance with great effect (and affect),
but there is no reason to assume that it has been cognitively calculated.
As Janet Emig (1964), William Stafford (1964), Barrett Mandel (1978,
1980), and Mimi Schwartz (1983) have noted, most published writers
apparently discover their best lines after they've written them.
Accomplished writers recognize—whether consciously or intuitively—
Derrida's "jouissance" or play of power in the way chosen patterns
work to evoke live forces beyond the text. For them, editing becomes a
matter of enhancing rather than smoothing away that evocation.

Student writers too can learn to recognize and respond to patterns and anomalies in their own texts, especially when we model the

process for them and with them. We are rarely at a loss for examples of departures from standard written English when encountering student writing, to be sure, as countless researchers are fond of pointing out (Connors and Lunsford 1988). But we all may be missing an important insight as long as we continue to analyze "errors" in terms of what they are not—appropriate forms according to standard usage—instead of what they are—departures from conventional forms which may signify important unconscious meaning. Instead of viewing anomalies as blemishes to be corrected, erased, smoothed over, we can see them as "occasions for interpretation," in the way Twain read "tumbling boils," slanted lines and circles in "slick water" that compromised his complacency as a riverboat pilot (1903, 84).

The following examples of texts collected from basic writing students at the University of Massachusetts during 1989-90 illustrate surface eruptions begging for interpretation rather than for correction. In each case, we tried to describe the formal elements of the "error," to determine the nature of its departure from writers' typical patterns, and to interpret its function as an expression of unarticulated material that writers might tap when revising. To facilitate our observations and interpretations, students and instructor used the same kind of reader response form (see below), modelled after Anthony Petrosky's (1982) adaptation of David Bleich's categories of Content, Affect, Form, and Expectations.

Responding To Writing

for_____ from_____ date_____

CONTENT
I think the writing is saying . . .

I think it is not saying . . .

AFFECT/ASSOCIATIONS
When I read . . . .

I feel . . . .

It reminds me of . . . .

FORM
  Here's what I notice about patterns of words or phrases or
  images . . . .

EXPECTATIONS
  Because the writing says . . . .

  I expect . . . .

  I am surprised when . . . .

  I would really like to know more about . . . .

Here is a final passage from one of Karim's papers:

> There was no way that he could have found money so quick,
> because I left around 8:30 p.m. and the concert had started at 9 p.m.
> I felt hateful; I didn't want to deal with this kind of cheating by a
> friend, but I missed him. He was a funny guy who makes me laugh.

We observe in this passage that Karim has negotiated his way through
no fewer than eight appropriate past or past perfect or conditional
past tense forms, no mean feat for a non-native speaker of English.
The final verb in the paper is a deviant, present-tense form—"who
makes me laugh." I jotted this on my response sheet to Karim, interpreting it as presenting an ongoing wish that the erstwhile friend
could be (*is*) still making Karim laugh. In fact, the paper's opening
line was "Friendships are always forever." That seemed to me related
to the way in which the ongoing present tense in the final phrase prevents closure; it prevents the incident described in the paper as well as
the friendship itself from ending. In conference, I asked if the relationship was reconciled yet. Karim stated:

> Well, it's not . . . It's not. But ahhhh, I wish it would . . . because he
> would still, like, you know, write to me now, and, you know, make
> still jokes, but it's not.

Ideas about maintaining relationships played through Karim's writing
once they were encouraged to surface. Perhaps they wouldn't have
had I simply marked the correction to "made me laugh" and commented (as I would have in my pre-Milner days) "Your ending seems
abrupt. Conclusion?" Karim himself became attuned to how the laps-

es in his written language might reveal deeper meanings. For his fourth paper he discussed his educational experiences since coming to America, including gaps and ambiguities in the language he used when corresponding with family and friends back in Somalia:

> I wrote them back and I told them all the great places that I had been to, New York City, Boston, and Amherst. I did not tell them that I had a rough time speaking English and that I had no friends. They asked me how exciting it is to be in America, not how hard it is to live.

Similarly, Mia's work also illustrates how form can be read as a trace, in Derrida's sense, of an underlying issue. On her self-response sheet to a paper based on Liliana Heker's short story, "The Stolen Party," Mia noted that she wanted to give "more examples where I myself have become more influenced by my place in society." Yet, in the paper itself, the only approximation to a "place in society" reference occurs in this paragraph (emphasis mine):

> Still, we will never be free of the social barriers that inhibit us from becoming equals. There will always be a line that separates us. *I realize that there never again will be a time in my life when I will not be in the least bit influenced by society to form friendships.*

The italicized sentence, with its two negatives deferring meaning, was the only awkward sentence in Mia's entire paper. I responded:

> This might be the place to ask yourself what other ideas are trying to break through? What stories, memories, deep-rooted feelings might you draw on here to enrich and clarify this writing?

We talked in conference about the indirect and negative phrasing in the sentence. Mia agreed. "Yeah, it's kind of hard. You have to figure out what the sentence is saying. Maybe it's 'cause I just didn't know how to say it." In her next two papers Mia wrote on racism and the myth of the American Dream, attitudes toward education, and the fact that most individuals fall somewhere between social and cultural extremes. She was indeed expressing her concern about her "place in society" in her subsequent writing, a concern that had made itself visible through irregularities in her earlier text.

Such irregularities may appear more readily in final or close-to-final drafts of writing, where they "mar" the otherwise orderly prose. We are less likely to appreciate them as traces at that point, however. We expect a smooth finish and the ripples and pits eliminated. In a kind of catch-22, however, we may also *seek* possibilities for development in still fluid freewriting or rough drafts, but not *see* them in their formal aspects. Since we expect the form to be rough at those stages, we don't follow the traces of broken sentences, pronoun shifts, repeated words and phrases. Instead we are likely to focus on the content. We ask, "What ideas could be more fully developed with examples?" or, "What about an opposing point of view?" But if we give them a second look, we are apt to find that formal clues abound in rough drafts, such as this one by Susan:

> When an individual is apart of a large institution such as an university many times the individual may feel that he can hear what is happening but may feel that they can not be heard, they may feel that they loose their identity because of being apart of a large institution and feel isolated. . . . Even in society culture and different find well let's call it a common ground, ground that one can feel where they can function and be the person they want to be where just as different cultures as I mentioned before have pressures placed on them by society and why they find a common ground of exceptances and get away from many of the prejudices, this same situation happens in a large institutions. there are prejudices and pressures just as there is in the outside community as there is with in institutions . . . in many ways I feel that there are ways to overcome the overwhelming feelings of the being apart of the University by joining a sector of a familiar group and meet friends.

Distinguishing deviance from nondeviance in a passage like this might tax even Marshall Edelson, but some formal patterns are discernible. Boundary definitions are quite thoroughly blurred at the paragraph and sentence levels (only three periods over a page and a half of text divided into just two paragraphs) and, even more intriguing to me, at the word level (*apart, with in*). The boundary confusion accurately represents Susan's subject, which is the confusion of a college student trying to negotiate boundaries for individual identity within the large institution. Further, each of the apparently misused words—*apart, exceptance, with in*—accurately expresses the writer's major concern. She does feel apart, isolated, afraid of not being accepted, of being an exception, perhaps a victim of prejudice and pressure. She is, I think, typical of writers that Mina Shaughnessy identifies as having problems because of "mature perceptions" and "rudimentary skills in writing"(1977, 66). On my response sheet to her draft, I pointed out how her tangled syntax was a perfect presentation of important but conflicting ideas of individuality and belongingness, common ground and diversity, and pressures from both inner and outer forces. I hoped to encourage her to clarify her thoughts and feelings when revising. She withdrew from school before completing the assignment; I cannot say I was surprised.

The writing that students do *in* their papers offers many occasions for interpretation; so also does the writing they do *about* their papers. Here is Jada's own comment about her paper on Liliana Heker's "The Stolen Party":

> The places where I am least satisfied are in the beginning where I tried to explain that the view of rich people is what really the outcome of this story as Senora handed her money.

The place referred to, the opening of the essay itself, reads as follows:

> "The Stolen Party" is a story that reflected the view of rich people toward the lower class. The view of the outcome of this story was how rich people thought that money would satisfy the lower class . . .

I wasn't sure when I read either of these passages what connection Jada was trying to make between "view" and "outcome," but something seemed to be troubling the syntax in each statement. In one, a verb was missing in the final relative clause. In the other, both repetition and displacement occurred: The "view of rich people" became the "view of the outcome." In conference I told Jada how, to me, the sentence actually implied several "views"—of the "rich people," that of Rosaura, the story's protagonist, of the author, Heker, and especially Jada's own view.

Interestingly, Jada had come close to elaborating her "view," not in the essay itself but, again, on the response sheet:

> I've really said what I want to say about the view of upper and lower class . . .

> There may still be more that I want to say about. . . . how I accepted myself treating Rosaura like Senora did . . . I think I'm worse than Senora when I lived in Thailand, having an employee who lived with me.

This comment surprised me when I read it, because of the self-recrimination ("I think I'm worse than Senora . . .") and the revelation about "having an employee who lived with me." I wrote a note in the margin: "Well, you could push this further if you want to in a revision." The response sheet statement made me doubt a passage in the essay itself which read as follows (emphasis mine):

> It is class discrimination but, somehow, people in the upper class were brought up with this idea by tradition for so long that it became an expected behavior. *I would accept myself treating her the way Senora did because I wouldn't know how Rosaura felt.* I would think that she would prefer to be paid since she could use the money to buy something she needed . . .

I noticed the denial ("I wouldn't know how Rosaura felt"). And I noticed that, since the essay dealt mainly with the Heker story, it had only two other sentences relating to upper class or lower class views, with no examples of either. My sense was that Jada had *not* said all she wanted to say about "the view of upper and lower class." Unstated, perhaps still unconscious, conflicting feelings about the treatment of servants seemed to need sorting out before Jada could state whether the prevailing views of upperclass Thai employers were truly her own. Thus, I saw a perfect expression of Jada's unclear feelings in the unclear syntax of those sentences about "views"—both in the essay and on her response sheet. I would also note that this muddled syntax contrasted sharply to her usually fastidious sentence structure.

Jada chose this essay for revision and described some of what she did in a process note:

> I tried to be clear on what my main ideas were. . . . but I felt like I didn't give a clear explanation on my last idea in the first paragraph . . . I added in the view of the employee . . .

In fact she completely reversed herself, demonstrating in her revision an ability to represent her "view" of employees and employers in general and her family and herself in particular. Here are the beginning, portions of the middle, and the conclusion of her revised essay:

> "The Stolen Party" makes me think of the different points of view existing between the two classes, the upper and the lower. This concept is familiar to me as I come from a country that is half poverty and half prosperity with very little in between. In Thailand, rich families have anywhere from one to five maids. An employee working as a maid is considered to be very low class, yet, they live with a very high class family. . . . a maid is expected to know that she can not walk past the employer, the owner of the house, without bowing. . . . When the owner and the guest are sitting in the living room, she must kneel down to walk slowly on her knees as she serves the food. . . .
>
> The lower class is somehow always aware of its status, as such there will always be a barrier. . . . Therefore, however nice or friendly the employer is, this does not mean that they can go beyond the limits of their status.
>
> . . . During my last summer vacation, I returned to Thailand finding that my family had a new maid. After three weeks, my parents scolded me and told me that I was being too strict on the maid. I guess I was too picky about the things that she was doing for me. When I finished reading "The Stolen Party," it made me think of how I treated my maid, and I realized that I had neglected her sensitivity as a person in the course of her service to my family.

This revision demonstrates the presence of ideas and feelings that were absent from the original essay. Although repressed, they were sufficiently powerful to exert tantalizing tugs on the text. The writer *did* know how a maid would feel. She *did* understand the various points of view of different classes in her society. Her syntax had betrayed her attempts in the first writing to gloss over contradictions inherent in denial.

Once we become accustomed to seeking traces in place of "errors," we are rewarded with ever more fascinating glimpses of how tenuous a surface exists between *im*-pressions and *ex*-pression. We notice, for example, an intriguing unintended double negative in Steve's paper: "The arguments never ceased to stop." In conference we discover that this wording, although Steve did not realize it consciously, actually expresses his underlying feelings that his stepfather always shut him up; the arguments did, in fact, never stop stopping. Or we share Joseph's realization, when he reads to his peer group, that a gap in his text ("My family was to go to the jungle") signals a painful memory ("My family was *forced* to go to the jungle"). We can read a subtext about a mother's identity being hidden from a child when that subtext reveals itself in pronoun confusion ("because the Lady is really my mother but not her and she had a right to do anything to me . . ."). And while we are initially puzzled by an attempted sentence of Tim's ("Two people so madly in love with each other is like losing someone so close but has not yet gone"), we rejoice with him when he re-views it and sees that both the ideas and the words he has been avoiding (separation, death) can be drawn on to make sense of what is yet inarticulate: "Separating two people so madly in love with each other is like losing someone close who is dying."

What happens when instructors' interpretations raise sensitive issues for student writers? What happens happens naturally. Asking students to read and respond to their own texts as readers initiates much of the process. Giving the same kinds of responses, instructors are then likely to build on their students' own beginnings. Conferences allow for elaboration, for further interpretation. Ultimately, of course, writers exercise author-ity by either pursuing these traces during revision—or not. Students often agree with an interpretation, but decide not to tackle, at least for the time being, the issue that may be circling in the depths. Certainly, as writing instructors we do not want to violate their right to privacy, but we can help students appreciate their writing as a surface on which more may be written than is read at first glance. We can help them see that though the surface tension is delicate—a gossamer damsel-fly wing can, after all, ripple the pond—it is strong enough to hold. Writers learn to value points of interpenetration as they write and read between their inner and outer worlds.

5

Let the River Run
Exploring Personal Archetypes Through Writing

Richard L. Graves and Susan M. Becker

For many years the field of literary criticism has drawn on Carl Jung's concept of archetypes as a way of understanding literature. Guerin and his colleagues (1979), for example, devote thirty-nine pages in their handbook of literary criticism to mythological and archetypal approaches. It is natural that literary criticism should embrace Jung's ideas since Jung himself frequently used fairy tales and myths to illustrate the presence of archetypes.

Although Jung's theories have been extended to literary texts, instructors of writing have not used archetypes as extensively as have instructors of literature. Writing instructors know that understanding a text and creating a text are related but distinctly different tasks. Many contemporary writing instructors encourage students to search for a worthy subject; freewrite about it; find a "center of gravity"; glimpse a vision or voice; draft for an emergent form from what was originally formless. For fear of subverting the process, instructors are reluctant to introduce what they perceive as extraneous elements, especially elements as complex as archetypes. All too familiar are those writing assignments that don't get off the ground because they demand a limited perspective. For example, when Carol Berkenkotter asked Donald M. Murray to explain death to young readers of *Jack and Jill* magazine, Murray produced only two lines of text: "Dear 11 year old. You're going to die. Sorry. Be seeing you. P. Muglump, Local Funeral Director" (159).

If it is true that writers must find their own subjects, and if it is also true that archetypes are alive in us all and represent the deepest level of our personalities, then an awareness of archetypes is a likely asset in the writing process. But in order to be successful, writing instructors cannot come to the question of archetypes the same way literature instructors do—by simply listing common archetypes or by analyzing a completed text.

What we present in this essay is an approach for letting individual archetypes emerge spontaneously during the composing process. That is, we attempt to provide a way in which the unconscious mind of writers is unlocked, thus becoming an ally during the act of composing. Our essay is divided into three parts. First is a summary of Jung's ideas about archetypes, especially those relevant to teaching writing. Second is a description of the techniques we use to help our students discover their own archetypes. Finally we provide illustrative student writing and their comments on the process.

Jung's Theory of Archetypes

In order to understand archetypes, we must first understand what Jung meant by the term *collective unconscious*. In his classic essay, "Archetypes of the Collective Unconscious," Jung hypothesized the presence of both a personal unconscious and a collective unconscious in the life of every person:

> A more or less superficial layer of the unconscious is undoubtedly personal. I call it the *personal unconscious*. But this personal unconscious rests upon a deeper layer, which does not derive from personal experience and is not a personal acquisition but is inborn. This deeper layer I call the *collective unconscious*. I have chosen the term "collective" because this part of the unconscious is not individual but universal; in contrast to the personal psyche, it has contents and modes of behavior that are more or less the same everywhere and in all individuals. It is, in other words, identical in all men and thus constitutes a common psychic substrate of a suprapersonal nature which is present in every one of us. (1968, 3–4)

The *personal* unconscious, consisting primarily of "repressed or forgotten contents," is different within the life experience of each individual. The *collective* unconscious, on the other hand, is universal and composed of archetypes, a term that Jung found occurred as early as the first century A.D. in the writings of Philo Judaeus, "with reference to the *Imago Dei* (God-image) in man." Some two hundred years later, Irenaus wrote, "The creator of the world did not fashion these things directly from himself but copied them from archetypes outside himself." The term *archetype* is almost identical to the term *représentations collective*, which Levy-Bruhl used to denote "symbolic figures in the primitive view of the world" (Jung 1968, 4–5). In this essay when we speak of personal archetypes, we mean individual manifestations of the collective unconscious.

Although the collective unconscious is universal, individual archetypes vary. We are all familiar with the common archetypes — the hero, the mother, the trickster — but personal manifestations of archetypes may include not only characters but "typical situations, places, ways and means" (1968, 48). An archetype, for example, may occur as color, music, a field of crows, or luminous light in a dream. Jung believed that it did no good merely to learn a list of archetypes, for "their immediate manifestation, as we encounter them in dreams and visions, is much more individual, less understandable, and more naive than in myths" (1968, 5). If our goal is to come face to face with our own living archetypes, then we must look to the fabric of our own life, not to some exterior source.

Archetypes, occurring just below the level of consciousness, manifest themselves as life themes, recurring images, numinous dreams, meaningful accidents, or coincidences. These manifestations, according to Jung, "are symbolic expressions of the inner drama of the psyche. . . . Even the best attempts at explanation are more or less successful translations into another language" (1968, 6). In other words, the archetypes themselves are metaphors of a psyche that ultimately remains inaccessible even though it lies at the base of all consciousness. We come closest to that reality by discovering our own archetypes, which are generated via some "crystalline lattice" deep within the body's structure.

> The uniqueness of the psyche can never enter wholly into reality, it can only be realized approximately, though it still remains the absolute basis of all consciousness. The deeper "layers" of the psyche lose their individual uniqueness as they retreat farther and farther into darkness. "Lower down," that is to say as they approach the autonomous functional systems, they become increasingly collective until they are universalized and extinguished in the body's materiality, i.e., in chemical substances. (Jung 1968, 173)

Even at their clearest, our archetypes remain shadowy and vague. We can see the surface of the river but can never fully know its depth. We can feel the pull of a current, but understanding its force reaches beyond the power of cognitive thinking. Despite the uncertainties, Jung envisioned the path to understanding when he stated, "The most we can do is to *dream the myth onwards* and give it a modern dress" (Jung 1968, 160). The pathway to one's own living archetypes is through "letting go": letting go of rational analysis, preconceived opinion, and personal prejudice, and then somehow finding a larger flow. The elusive flow is both personal and universal: personal in that it is bound up in the immediate fabric of life experience; universal in that it is composed of the historical experience of all mankind.

What purpose is served by attempting to make known the contents of the unconscious? If we pour our energy into our conscious life, the center of most of our life activities, do we not neglect the unconscious side, the center of our feelings, emotions, and values? Ignoring the deeper voices within, said Jung, exacts a price:

> Archetypes were, and still are, living psychic forces that demand to be taken seriously, and they have a strange way of making sure of their effect. Always they were bringers of protection and salvation, and their violation has as its consequence the "perils of the soul" known to us from the psychology of primitives. Moreover, they are unfailing causes of neurotic and even psychotic disorders, behaving exactly like rejected or maltreated physical organs or organic functional system. (1968, 156–57)

Jung called the process of bringing the conscious and the unconscious into harmony the process of individuation. "Wholeness," he insisted, "consists in the union of the conscious and the unconscious personality" (1968, 175). The attempt to understand the wellspring of life is a step toward wholeness, toward realizing the persons who we were intended to be, what we always were. Those who become involved in this process feel as though a "treasure lies in the depths of the water and will try to salvage it" (1968, 24). Individuation is a self-fulfilling process.

We suggest that it is also satisfying to write out of our own archetypal experiences because writing addresses the deepest level of the personality. But how can instructors help students uncover those topics of which even the students themselves are unaware? Is it possible for one person to help another tap into the unconscious? Jung provided a clue for gaining access to the unconscious when he suggested that water, a common symbol of the unconscious, occurs frequently in dreams and myths.

> Water is the commonest symbol for the unconscious. The lake in the valley is the unconscious, which lies, as it were, underneath consciousness, so that it is often referred to as the "subconscious," usually with the pejorative connotation of an inferior consciousness. Water is the "valley spirit," the water dragon of Tao, whose nature resembles water—a yang embraced in the yin. Psychologically, therefore, water means spirit that has become unconscious. (1968, 18-19)

As a basic element of life, water is common to everyone. In contrast with the cerebral, conscious mind, water represents instinct, the requirement of human existence itself.

> But water is earthy and tangible, it is also the fluid of the instinct-driven body, blood and the flowing of blood, the odour of the beast, carnality heavy with passion. The unconscious is the psyche that reaches down from the daylight of mentally and morally lucid consciousness into the nervous system that for ages has been known as the "sympathetic." (1968, 19)

In order to come to wholeness, we must "go the way of the waters." We must, so to speak, plunge into the water, though this is no easy task, for the conscious mind tends to resist the dark, the unknown. The urge of the conscious mind is to attain the heights, to spiral upward into greater levels of rationality. For those able to plunge in, however, the rewards are great; for "whoever looks into the mirror of the water will see first of all his own face" (Jung 1968, 20). Writing about water opens up the possibility of discovering the deeper layers of personality. By knowing ourselves, we become more connected, more universal.

We have used this idea of wholeness as the basis for developing a writing workshop which we call "Let the River Run." The workshop includes the presentation of poems, music, and art associated with rivers, as well as opportunities for writing. A description of our procedure appears in the next section.

The Workshop

"Let the River Run" works in a variety of circumstances. Participants have crossed all boundaries of age, sex, and ethnicity. They have included classroom instructors, college freshmen and juniors, high school sophomores, and adults at a church retreat. The length of time varies—from one hour with the church group to several class sessions with the college freshmen. The workshop seems especially effective over several sessions because the time between them permits reflection and revision. Consequently, what we describe here involves our work with college freshmen.

Students were enrolled in a freshman composition course in a conservative midwestern community college. Their English ability was average, and their backgrounds were rural or small town, although some had grown up on the outskirts of a large working-class city. What they shared was a large working river linking the St. Lawrence Seaway from the north to the Mississippi River flowing south.

This writing exercise was one of the group's first assignments. The rationale was to start with something they had in common: the physical river on which so much of the community's livelihood and recreation depended—the river with which they had grown up. We began at the end of class one day with a twenty-minute brainstorming session to acknowledge the actual physical river. In an oral give and take, students contributed words such as the following:

barge	dead bodies	coal
tug	sailboat	picnic
mud	riverbank	waves
bridge	swim	froghunt

Then we moved from the outer river to the inner, from the concrete to the abstract. This line of brainstorming resulted in words such as these:

life	death	undercurrent
floating	surface	spirits
dreams	moods	carrying
enduring	tranquil	mysteries

The students went home to think about rivers.

The next day we began with brief personal reminiscences of the river, which included the instructor's confession of having a lifelong, almost mystical attraction to flowing bodies of water. We questioned: Are others similarly affected? Do rivers run through the lives of other people?

The students were asked to reflect on their river as we listened to an audio-tape of Carly Simon singing "Let the River Run." Afterward we heard Langston Hughes' poem "The Negro Speaks of Rivers." More discussion followed, and, a reflective mood prevailing, we listened to another version of "Let the River Run" sung by the St. Thomas Boys' Choir. The room was still. Poised, we were ready to plunge deeper. The timing was perfect for a reading of "The River."

The River

There's a river flowing deep down inside of me,
A river of pure spirit.
I don't know its source, when it began or where.
I remember it from childhood—
It seems to have been there forever.
Maybe it's a strand connecting me with the past,
With shadowy faces, still voices, dark figures from long ago.

The river is deep and the current swift.
Sometimes it rages out of control, overflowing its banks.

Sometimes it goes underground, hidden from prying eyes,
But it's always there.
It runs through my waking hours and my dreams.
It is the best part of me.

Sometimes on this river of pure spirit
I float effortlessly downstream,
Buoyed up by the current.
I let go and it carries me along. . .
    Let go . . .
        And let go . . .
            And flow with the current . . .
What is the River telling me?
Listen to the voice of the River.

Teach me thy way, O Lord,
Teach me the way of the River,
Flowing deep down inside of me.
River, fill my being to overflowing,
So I can live fully.
Teach me to listen
and see
    and feel
        and know . . .
Teach me the way of the River,
Flowing deep down inside of me.

Richard L. Graves, 1992

The students were now ready to write about their own rivers. They needed no urging to open their journals, and they wrote without hesitation as the tape played background water music by Jarre. For twenty to thirty minutes they wrote—some without looking up, others pausing to gaze into space before finding the words to express what they already know. When class was over, students took their notebooks with them in case they wanted to add to or revise what they had written.

At the next class session most students said they were pleased with their work and felt they had written well. A number of students were eager to share their writing aloud with the others—who were clearly moved at the depth of the content. Unaccustomed to the self-revelation, however, most students moved to the word processor, preferring to share their ideas in print form.

The student writings revealed that the water archetype is indeed a powerful metaphor in our lives. Through writing about their rivers, these students reached inside themselves to discover meaning. For the instructor, reading the river essays was different from reading essays that students wrote merely to fulfill an assignment. Each piece embodied something real, something worth reading because it was written from the student's inner self. The students too came away from the river assignment feeling that what they had written was worthwhile.

This section includes samples of original writing by the freshmen as a part of the workshop. The examples are not presented as exemplary writing, although readers may note several passages that could indeed be considered so. What this section most vividly illustrates is the scope and variety of ways that the river may be perceived.

The River as Physical Entity

The passage below describes a specific river, in this case the Mississippi, as well as the role of that river in the life of the writer's family. Although the passage is brief, easily discernible is the presence of the river as archetype in the student's life.

> The river is a part of me. Every time I see it I am reminded of who I am and where I came from. I am reminded that my great-grandfather who came from Germany traveled up the Mississippi from New Orleans and settled in St. Louis. I am reminded of the time I walked across it in Minnesota. I am reminded that time means change but the river is constant.

The River as Confidante

The following passage first described a family member's fascination with the Columbia River in Oregon and then her own fascination with the Illinois River. Here the actual river provided a way of reflecting on the current direction of life, because the writer was talking "to the river and letting it take [her] worries down stream."

> I will never forget the time when I was about twelve years old and my Grandma and I took a cross country train trip to Oregon. When we got to Oregon, our train was traveling parallel to the Columbia River. My grandma was just looking and admiring the river. It was as if every memory she had ever had about this river came back all at once. My grandma had returned to her teenage years once again, for she had lived in Oregon as a teenager. She told me how the river used to be crystal clear and how you were able to see the river bottom.
>
> I also remember the times I drove up on Grandview Drive, by myself, to just look at the Illinois River and think. When I needed to talk, but I didn't feel comfortable talking to a person, it was as if I was talking to the river and letting it take my worries down stream. I would remember the trip with my grandmother and that in itself

would make me feel better. Also, I remember driving on Grandview at nighttime and seeing the moon's reflection on the water. How bright and shining and beautiful is the river.

The River as Healer

At a low moment in his life, this student found solace in the river. Its restorative and healing force was more stable than the shifting events of daily life.

> When I finally hit bottom, there was no way I could hurt anymore. The water was my escape. The physical river and my inner river meshed together to help me through those tough times. I knew I could trust the river. It would not turn its back on me like people so often do. The tranquility of the river trickled along in front of me, keeping me going and my soul flowing.

The River as Metaphor of Life

The demands of daily life required the following writer to bury her dreams, but she didn't give up. For a while she was "stuck in the shallows," unable to propel herself forward. But she pushed away from the marshes and tasted freedom.

> Sorting through my thoughts, I found that deep down in my soul I knew what I wanted out of life, but I didn't know how to go about attaining these wants. I felt as though I were standing in a maze of bulrushes and willows along a river, but I could not find the river. I could hear the water rushing by but I was stuck in the shallows unable to go with the flow of the river.
>
> By setting a few goals for myself I have been able to change the course of my life. Changing the course of my life was risky, sometimes creating a certain amount of turbulence along the way. However, the end result has created a renewal of love and respect between me and my husband. By allowing those undercurrents of discontent to surface has made our relationship more genuine.
>
> No longer am I stuck in the shallows along the river. I'm not free-floating yet, but I'm in the river cautiously. Sometimes I get scared, and I want to run back to the edges, to the shallows where I know what to expect. My curiosity tells me to stay in the flow of the river even though I am not sure what will be around the bend. The new positive undercurrents of my soul tell me that just around the bend I may find those little treasures that I have held in my daydreams all these years.

One student saw in the many faces of the river the shifting moods
of personality. Feelings such as anger or envy or tranquility are all
reflected by the river.

> The river inside of me is inconsistent.
> It may be bright red when tranquil waters become monstrous and
> angry or green when I am envious.
> Blue waters indicate sadness; black is depression.
> But most of my days my river runs white for peace . . . .

The River as Uncertainty

The flow of the river is not always smooth. Cross currents, hidden
forces, and unpredictable drifts pull in different directions. One writer
compared the uncertainty of the river to the uncertainty of life.

> After high school had ended, I realized that the pace of the river
> had increased, the current got rougher, and the water lost its clarity.
> All this happened when college started. The water is cloudy because
> I really do not know what I am going to do with my life. The water
> is rough because it is very difficult to go to college and to hold down
> a steady job.

The River as Teacher

We learn from the river, but this learning is not an easy process. In the
passage below the writer sensed that the ultimate goal of learning is
wholeness.

> A river may be an enemy, friend, or acquaintance. From each rela-
> tionship within ourselves we learn and this is what makes us whole.
>   Rivers make up our very being and they can be educational and
> make us strong. If we aren't cooperative with our rivers, they may
> make us become a stranger to our very selves. Hopefully, we will let
> the waves dance and reveal a peace and joy within ourselves that we
> have never realized.

The River as Universal Life

In the following passage, the author described an awareness of the
river of life, something larger than herself, touching all humankind. This river is old and possesses a haunting, mystical quality.
For a moment the writer touched the archetypal elements in her
unconscious.

My river has been flowing for centuries. Its still, calm waters have touched many emotions. I'm not sure exactly when it began or where, but I can feel its wisdom running through me constantly. Sometimes it's an eerie feeling, as though its darkness has haunted many a soul. Other times it's a tranquil feeling, bringing me peace and calm. When I become angry, the river becomes quite turbulent, splashing against the rocks of my skin. However, when I'm happy, the river begins to flow steadily, pushing life quickly through me, warming me. The river becomes quite foggy when I'm sad and slowly escapes my eyes, guiding the tears down my cheeks, cold and wet. The river serves one great purpose—it protects me. When I am in danger, it becomes dirty, muddy and polluted. It warns of something evil, something bad. It may even cause illness or pain. For when I die, the river dies. Then, the river ceases to flow in me. However, the river is always reborn somewhere else, giving life to another.

The River as Confluence of Two Lives

Just as the river is composed of many smaller streams, so may two people come together to form a union, two lives but "one water."

But any moment that we reunite is as natural as the streams joining the rivers. Like a river with large islands, our lives have become really one stream, which can look like two. But we are of one water.

And the river doesn't wander or doubt. It knows its course and destiny. The river knows the answer. The river is a strong, firm, gentle hand, moving and placing us and asking only our surrender. Lie atop the water. It will carry you. Trust it. Trust the river of life.

Teach that river of life. Tell someone else about it. Share. Flow. Let go. Float. Ah! Carry me, sweet river of life! Carry me on, and on, and over again, till we return to the source and begin again.

Student Responses to Rivers

Following their writing about rivers, students were asked to react to their assignment. Their responses were informative. Several students remarked that this kind of writing was different from traditional school writing. They noted that they seldom had the opportunity to explore their imagination:

Rivers—different from any writing I've ever done. Made me think and use my imagination, which I hardly ever have the opportunity to do.

At first I thought the river assignment might be dumb like other English teachers' assignments, but as I wrote, I discovered that the river has a deeper meaning. Writing what you feel helps you become more confident about yourself.

Music was introduced to create a reflective atmosphere. Some students noted that it helped the writing process by making them more relaxed.

The way the music flowed made my pen flow. The words just seemed to be written down exactly as they should. There was hardly any contemplation of how something needed to be said.

I thought that the assignment enabled each individual student to express himself in a way that most assignments do not allow. A more relaxed atmosphere in the classroom motivates the student.

One student stated that the best part of the workshop was the time spent writing and writing from the heart—one of our goals from the outset.

My best time with rivers came during the actual writing process— more so than during the brainstorming, music, and poetry, but they set me up for the meaningful part: writing from my heart.

We believe that our general approach opens up new horizons in the teaching of writing. The assignment is specific enough to provide some direction, but more important, broad enough to encourage deeply personal individual response. Our purpose is to encourage writers to discover their own topics. And as we listen to what they find, we stand in awe at the depth and intensity of the work. We have no expectations. Sometimes a poem occurs, sometimes a narrative, sometimes a note of personal history. But in almost every case there is intense involvement in the subject because the subject represents the writer's experience and perspective.

Some Rivers

Some rivers are inevitable,
Like the morning sun or
Mist in the winter woods,
Coming unannounced but coming just the same,
Natural and easy,
Familiar as morning slippers or
The shape of your own breath.
Watch the surface of the river,
Feel the current with your hand,
　but remember:
Some rivers—some rivers are inevitable.

Richard L. Graves, 1992

6

Behind the Screen of Consciousness
Intuition, Insight, and Inspiration in the Writing Process

Elizabeth Holman

For months developmental psychologist and writer David Feldman experienced a strange dream dominated by an octopus-like object revolving around a central source. Puzzled by its meaning, he drew a picture of the image for his colleagues, hoping that they could help him determine its significance. They couldn't.

One morning when Feldman was taking a shower in his hotel room and thinking of nothing in particular, the meaning of the object suddenly became clear to him. It was a conceptual model of the human developmental process he had been trying to formulate. The solution so startled him in its "full, blazing impact and dazzling effect" (1988, 271) that he ran naked across the hall to share the experience with his colleague. Feldman experienced similar, though less dramatic, instances in which new knowledge suddenly appeared without conscious effort when he least expected it. While such events are often difficult to articulate and explain, all profoundly affected him and made his thinking "clearer and better organized than ever before" (282).

Feldman's experiences represent the entire intuitive spectrum, from the subtle "hunch" or feeling of certainty that accompanies intuition to the fanfare and fireworks of sudden discovery that accompanies an insight or moment of inspiration. Many of us who write have similar experiences. Frequently a new idea or the solution to a perplexing writing problem pops into our minds when we are relaxed or thinking of something else. We wonder what causes us to have these kinds of perceptions. And we cannot help but agree with Mandel's suggestion that what goes on "behind the screen of consciousness" may have more to do with composing than rational thinking does (1980, 371).

For centuries great minds have been intrigued by intuition, insight, and inspiration: our ability to apprehend immediately and directly some knowledge or truth without any apparent reasoning. Ancient Greeks and Romans, for example, believed that knowledge coming from such sources was at least as important as that presented by the external world. Such knowledge was particularly valued because it was considered a message from the gods (Noddings and Shore 1984, 3). Aristotle's inquiries into the nature of knowledge led him to believe that either an intuitively known truth or an inductive-empirical one was needed to begin inductive reasoning. His *Posterior Analytics* postulated that "no genus of knowledge exists which is more accurate than scientific knowledge except intuition," and he believed intuitive knowledge to be the starting point of all scientific discovery (1981, 72–73). Locke (1632–1704) and Kant (1724–1804) also considered knowledge derived from reason subordinate to that intuited. Both philosophers bifurcated knowledge into the demonstrative and intuitive—that which could be reasoned through and that which could not. Of the two, intuition was the more direct, fundamental, and unequivocal (Langer 1967, 128–29).

Intuition is thus not only the objective validity of judgments made without reasoning. It is positive knowledge of things in and of themselves without the *intervention* or *impurities* of the conscious mind. Intuitive knowledge is the direct and obvious possession of the apparent "not mediated by any formulating (and hence *deforming*) symbol[s]" (Bergson in Langer 1957, 98). The operative attributes of intuition are its immediacy and its direct access between person and entity also without conceptual or discursive mediation. Intuition is therefore not cognitive in the usual sense of the term. Nor is it the product of any "logical" machinery.

Furthermore, intuition is not voluntary. It is an involuntary act; it comes upon us. But it can be "selectively evoked, blocked, or modified" (Langer 1967, 146), depending on various external or internal circumstances instead of on acts of judgment. Like rational thought, intuition may be accompanied by relief. Although we now know that intuitive knowledge is not always accurate, we recognize that even our most elusive intuitions are invariably accompanied by a "subjective sense of correctness" (Bastick 1982, 25).

Jung was one of the first contemporary psychologists to recognize the complex and elusive qualities of intuition:

> Intuition is, according to my view, a basic psychological function. It is that psychological function which transmits perceptions *in an unconscious way*. . . . Intuition has this peculiar quality: it is neither sensation, nor feeling, nor intellectual conclusion, although it may appear in any of these forms. Intuition is a kind of instinctive apprehension, irrespective of the nature of its contents. Like sensation it is an *irrational* function. (Jung 1933, 568)

Jung explained that his term "irrational" does not denote something contrary to reason, but something outside of its province. Intuition is an irrational (i.e., perceiving) function, "represented in conscious by an attitude of expectancy, by vision and penetration" (Campbell 1976, 220). When interpreted by Isabel Briggs Myers and Peter Myers (1990, 57), Jungian intuition became focused not so much on possibilities as on personality. The predominance of one or two ego functions over the others constituted regularities in the way individuals responded to experience (Campbell 1976). The "intuitive" type is one such ego function or dominant personality trait. Here, the definition of intuition does not change but its application does.

From Intuition to Insight

In Jungian type terminology the domain of intuition is the unconscious. Intuition is the perception of the result of one's own unconscious processes, *from which insights emerge* (Myers and Myers 1990, 131). It is here that we cross the border from intuition into insight. Both are non-propositional concepts. Both are pre-rational. Their rules are not those of formal logic. Intuition does not always lead to insight. But when it does, it is called an intuitive leap. From this vantage point insight may be considered a special case of intuition.

Because writers are grouped with other artists, the link between insight and intuition becomes especially important in creativity research. The most widely accepted role for insight appears in the model of the creative process as articulated by Helmholtz, Poincare, and Wallas (Vernon 1970):

1. *Preparation* or *Saturation* with the subject. In the first stage individuals collect and organize data relevant to a particular problem. The phase is marked by concentrated, conscious, and structured efforts to solve it.

2. *Incubation* or *Inactivity*. During this phase individuals are relaxed and not knowingly involved with the problem. Consciousness is

directed elsewhere—but progress is being made at the unconscious (or preconscious, according to Lawrence Kubie (1958)) level. Possible solutions to the problem are generated free of reasoning, language, and social constraints.

3. *Insight* or *Illumination*. The most intimate coupling of intuition and insight occurs at this stage of the creative act and is called insight or, more traditionally, illumination. It is during this third stage that the correct solution, association, or new idea is revealed in a brief and unexpected Eureka! or Aha! or Click! experience. This final inspiration or revelation is "the product of that presentational symbolism which the mind reads in a flash" (Langer 1957, 98), giving this very expression the earmarks of insight.[1]

4. *Verification*. The new idea, insight, or solution is articulated, tested, and evaluated (Robert T. Brown 1989, 6).

Unfortunately, the linearity and product orientation of this paradigm does little to explain what causes creative ideas and insights. For example, why does intuition often occur without an obvious period of incubation? Why does intuition occur when data are incomplete? How can solutions occur without reasoning? What happens in the mind behind the screen of consciousness (Norman 1986, 385)? Neurologists like Richard Restak and Joseph LeDoux now recognize how a richer understanding of the brain deepens and refines our thinking about the creative act.

Intuition is Innate

Many of us believe that intuitive and inspired discoveries occur only to accomplished writers, artists, or scientists—particularly if we subscribe to Jungian-type theory. But neural sources identified by Langer (1967, 130) and others suggest that all people have the rudiments of intuition. British psychologist Tony Bastick's research also supports intuition as an "innate, instinctive knowledge or ability" available to us all (1982, 25). He explains that intuition is both "preconscious" and "preverbal"; intuition is felt and its meaning is "known" before the mind is able to form the concept into words. What has not been conscious becomes conscious. What is at first unverbalized becomes verbalized. Or maybe not. Intuitions may also overlap with felt sense, as they do with insight. Whatever the case, the experience is no less intuitive.

[1]Cognitivists explain that this insight "constitutes a shift from the subject's previous way of representing the phenomenon," and usually results in a breakthrough which may be explained via ordinary reasoning processes (Clement 1989, 369).

In fact, intuition may well be an evolutionary remnant before the left side of the brain became sufficiently developed to support language (Gazzaniga 1985, 155). Some primitive abilities continue to be part of our biology even though they now coexist with language, a relatively recent evolutionary development. Our capacity for language, however, does not exclude our prelinguistic ways of knowing ourselves and our world:

> These relatively primitive systems, which are also capable of registering experiences and regulating purposeful behaviors, operate largely outside of conscious awareness. The conscious self thus only comes to know and understand these hidden mental dimensions when they are expressed in behavior. (LeDoux 1985, 198)

Brain researchers now realize that much of our knowledge involves dynamic, evolving patterns that are stored at multiple levels in the brain and nervous system and are inaccessible until they are combined with emotions or "analogical representations" at which point the knowledge erupts into consciousness as intuition, insight, or inspiration (Langley and Jones 1988, 177; Restak 1991, 153). We label the process intuition when it is slow. We label the process insight or inspiration when its results appear in a flash.

Research on unconscious processing conducted by Robert Zajonc (1980, 170) demonstrates that exposure to nonsense shapes influences the development of preferences for these shapes even though they were presented to subjects too rapidly to be processed consciously. Zajonc concludes that such reactions are based not only on the properties of the stimuli, but also on individuals' internal states (see also Bower 1981). These states develop in the absence of conscious awareness of the stimuli. Moreover, they may bypass cognition, and may even increase cognitive efficiency.

Researchers also understand the importance of emotion in unconscious processing. For example, the emotionally laden word, *fear*, subliminally flashed on a screen too fast for a subject to perceive it consciously produces a sharp burst of activity. However, when the word is flashed slowly enough for conscious perception, the brain takes twice as long to react (Restak 1988, 15). Medical researcher Howard Shevrin (in Restak 1988, 15–16) concludes that all messages to the brain are selectively transmitted to the unconscious for "filtering," and this process causes the delay. Only after "filtering" does the conscious mind become aware of the stimuli to be used at any particular time. The brain apparently has the ability to recognize, sort through, and then store information in the unconscious without our conscious awareness, particularly if that information is emotionally laden. Undoubtedly, our capacity to store information prevents our minds from being overwhelmed with sensory stimuli. It explains how information may be stockpiled by the brain and nervous system until it breaks into consciousness as intuition, insight, or an inspired moment.

Intuition and Insights:
Collaborations of Body and Mind

Insofar as it is "the indirect perception of things beyond the reach of the senses," the process of intuition deals in "meanings, relationships, and possibilities" (Myers and Myers 1990, 192). Langer herself stated that the extent to which "we detect qualities not correlated with...a specific sense organ" engenders a discussion of intuition (1967, 128). However, at the same time that logical thinking generally takes place in the mind, the intuitive process depends on "global knowledge," which comes from *all the senses simultaneously* (Bastick 52). Intuition in consciousness is often brought there by emotional memory hooks—a sight, a sound, or an odor that awakens earlier impressions.

Bastick asserts that the unexpected knowledge resulting from the collaboration between body and mind is also reflected in the language we use about it. We say that we have a "hunch" or a "gut feeling." The intuition becomes an insight or an inspired moment because it is felt in that "flash" or we may suddenly "see" the solution in our mind's eye. Researchers now find that the metaphors we use to describe these events may actually have molecular underpinnings. They have found powerful neurochemicals called "information molecules" that regulate, modulate, and convey information from cell to cell and that have receptors in the stomach and areas of the brain associated with touch, sight, smell, sound, and taste (Hall 1989, 64).

Researchers theorize that body and mind constantly chatter back and forth biochemically. Therefore, although intuitive knowledge cannot always be explained or articulated clearly, "gut feelings" may result from the biochemical chatter that is "heard" physically and emotionally. Although physical reactions to intuitions can now be detected by electroencephalograph and galvanic skin response monitors, brain researchers look forward to the day when they can trace with imaging machines what happens in the brain at the moment of an intuitive breakthrough or insight.

We already know that such breakthroughs have palpable physical reactions that make them memorable to people who have written about them. A. E. Housman, for example, wrote that when a line of poetry unexpectedly strayed into his mind as he was shaving, his skin would bristle, his throat constrict, and a feeling would pierce his stomach "like a spear" (1933, 46). Rollo May described how "a special translucence enveloped the world," his vision cleared, and a "strange lightness" came to his step when the solution to his dissertation dilemma appeared (1975, 58-61). In contrast to the relief writers experience at deriving a solution cognitively, the element of surprise and unexpectedness of insights and inspiration seems to increase their physiological effects.

Intuition, inspiration, and insight are not only accompanied by physical reactions, they are often stimulated by physical activity. Joan C. Gondola's[2] research with physical education students indicates that insights often occur during and after vigorous exercise. Many writers in fact find that insights and inspired moments occur when they are jogging, walking, or swimming. That individuals become receptive to creative ideas occurring during or after physical activity has a biochemical basis; chemicals in the brain are apparently released that seem to produce a euphoric state of mind analogous to a "runner's high" (Restak 1984, 309).

On the other hand, intuition, insight, and inspiration also emerge when writers' mental states are quiescent. Bastick (1982) explains that during periods of "hypnogogic reverie" when writers' mental states hover between wakefulness and sleep, egos are sufficiently relaxed so that seemingly "chaotic association of images and ideas" produce unexpected insights (342). Brain researchers find that during these less vigilant periods chemicals are released in the brain that are responsible for the reverie in which intuitions and insights are apt to emerge (Restak 1984, 309). Although we must not oversimplify the results of biochemical research, the dichotomy between body and mind surely begins to blur.

Intuition, Inspiration, and Emotion

Not only do our bodies and minds collaborate in forming intuition, but "emotional involvement is central to all aspects of intuition" (Bastick 84). Intuition, Bastick finds, is the result of a "complex interplay of sensory input, level of arousal, and central mediating process-

[2]Telephone interview of September 24, 1990.

es in emotion," often producing our "most effective high-level think-
ing" (86; see also LeDoux). Reports from intuitive individuals illus-
trate their intense involvement and concern for their work. In her
Notebooks of the Mind, for example, John-Steiner describes Thomas
Mann's passion for writing, and physicists who were close to Einstein
saw in him a similar intensity. In the words of Einstein's associate
Dennis Gabor, "No one has ever enjoyed science as much as
Einstein" (John-Steiner 1985, 67).

Bastick emphasizes as fundamental to the intuitive process the
felt "grasp of the real psychic state of another person or object"
(280), in other words, empathic projection. Put another way, writers'
development of audience awareness is not simply a logical process.
Empathy is intuitive to the extent that, in order to evaluate their
work, good writers stand outside of themselves, empathize with their
audience, and temporarily "become" their audience. Research
(Bastick 1982; Teich 1992) indicates that the ability to wear the
shoes of other persons and take on their feelings, may be the emotion
most essential to developing intuition. Chilean author Isabel Allende
goes further. She connects empathic projection with her *moments of
insight,* calling it compassion—"the ability to become the other person, be in somebody else's skin and think and feel what *they* do.
Compassion can lead to acts of mercy and to acts of inspiration"
(Szerlip 1993, 50). Such empathy, like intuition, is postulated to be
an innate ability by which primitive humans communicated their
needs and shared emotions before human speech development
(Restak 1986, 212).

Brain studies with adults also indicate that the right hemisphere is most active when subjects respond emotionally, particularly the negative emotions such as fear, anxiety, or disgust
(Restak 1984, 263; see also Brand 1989a). Negative emotions are
especially considered "memory hooks" that help bring nonverbal
knowledge from the right hemisphere of the brain to consciousness
in the form of intuition, insight, or inspired moments. Moreover,
the right hemisphere encodes emotional knowledge in a form not
available to the verbal search processes of the left hemisphere
(Restak 1984, 256).

Individuals writing about their intuitive experiences note that
their insights occurred when they were perplexed or feeling anxious
about a problem they had been unable to solve. David Feldman had
been unable to decipher his strange dream image. Rollo May had
reached an impasse in his doctoral dissertation when an insight
occurred. Rick Gebhardt writes of the time he had almost given up the
search for an elusive transitional sentence when it suddenly appeared
while he was showering, and he dripped from tub to desk to write it

down (Gebhardt 1982, 622). Student writers also find that insights occur when they have been "stuck" on some aspect of writing or have procrastinated to the point of panic.

Developing Intuition, Insight, and Inspiration in Classrooms

Like many other natural abilities, intuition must be used or it weakens. Some psychologists believe that we, as educators, tend to drive intuitive impulses "underground" when we convince students that these impulses are an inappropriate way to approach formal subject matter (Clinchy 1975, 36). Because intuition and its dramatic counterparts, insight and inspiration, tend to occur in comfortable, nonthreatening atmospheres, instructors who value intuitive thought can transfer that value to their students. They share their own intuitive experiences and discuss how other writers use and depend on them. Furthermore, when students read and describe accounts of the insights and inspired moments of professional writers and thinkers, they promote awareness of their own inner promptings. Recording ideas and intuitions helps students remember the activities and situations that stimulated them. When students understand that feelings may signal valuable intuitions, they begin to pay attention to the slight sensations they have previously ignored. They can explore the written "pool of knowledge" that psychologists say we hold in our unconscious in order to articulate images, emotions, symbols, or to sketch pictures and ideas, and thereby free intuitions.

Because writers' intuitions, insights, and inspirations are based on nonverbal sensory information, cross-modal physical activities such as dancing, drawing, and role-playing encourage subtle sensory discriminations and develop intuitive awareness (Bruner and Clinchy 1966, 78). The pedagogy of Maria Montessori, for example, was developed specifically to include the widest number of sensory and imaginal activities to strengthen intuitive perception and thinking (Edwards 1986). Visual representations such as mapping, diagramming, and clustering clear the way for insights and inspiration. Chilean author Isabel Allende improves her potential for inspiration by exercising a "playfulness" in areas other than the writing with which she directly and normally relates to the world. Her moments of revelation come from "doing something else — make drawings, put on a play, dance" (Szerlip 1993, 50). The writers in my research composed at the computer. However, those reporting the most insights sketched in the margins, drew arrows from page to page, or scrawled ideas between the lines of their rough drafts (113–17). Brain researchers studying hemisphericity speculate that such activities allow the verbal, analytical left hemisphere of the brain to rest while the intuitive and visual right hemisphere takes over.

As we learn more about the intuitive process, we can help our students depend on their intuitions and make their intuitions more dependable. As scholar and researcher Philip Goldberg indicates, we need to recognize the "intricate, mutually enhancing relationship between intuition and rationality. We need not just more intuition, but *better* intuition" (1983, 28). A dynamic collaboration of body and mind, our intuitions can then become truly inspired.

Part Three

Wisdom of the Body

Sometimes the body knows before the mind knows. Ask a potter about the wisdom of the hands, about the feel of clay, its moisture and texture, about the form emerging from raw clay. Ask the dancer about movement and balance and spontaneity, about arms and feet, about uncanny physical awareness at any given second. Our understanding of such events is so limited that the term *body wisdom* is indeed a metaphor. But we know its reality. We have experienced its presence, even if we do not quite understand it.

"What happens when we write is not only a mental phenomenon but also a bodily one," states Sondra Perl. Basing her work on the writings of psychologist Eugene Gendlin, Perl suggests "that it is our felt sense that guides us both in choosing words and knowing whether those words capture their intended meaning." In the lead essay of this section, Perl provides an approach for eliciting the felt sense during composing. Her insights have been affirmed by others who understand their writing process in terms of both body and mind.

Employing specific bodily activities to parallel and reinforce rhetorical elements, Karen Klein and Linda Hecker exploit the idea of "learn-by-doing," by "cross-fertilizing students' linguistic abilities with spatial kinesthetic intelligences." Their work argues for the primacy of the physical body in the learning process, the flesh as a way of coming to the word. Combining verbal constructs with body awareness holds considerable promise in the teaching of writing.

Who is the more effective instructor, lecturer or listener? Current models of teaching emphasize the role of instructor as listener, someone who hears learners' needs and responds appropriately. As a way of perceiving the world, generous listening, as Trudelle Thomas calls it, encourages "a greater intimacy between the knower and the object of knowing." This kind of listening approaches a realm of awareness in which opposites are reconciled and diverse elements find harmony and union. The way of the writer is the way of generous listening.

7

A Writer's Way of Knowing
Guidelines for Composing

Sondra Perl

Have we ever written the last word? When we look, don't we inevitably see more to say and write? How do we know this "more"? And what does such knowing suggest about the ways we write and the ways we teach writing?

These questions ask us to watch closely as we write, to notice, for example, that we often begin to compose with nothing more than hunches, inspirations, intuitive pulls, pushes, and leanings. We head in a certain direction, somehow knowing what comes next, but not certain until it comes whether or not it will work. If skilled in this process, we know to trust what comes and to reserve for later the question of whether or not to make changes. What matters first is to allow the words to come as they do. Sometimes, though, we need to stop and change the words before we can go forward. We must reread, pause, and listen to what's on the page to see if it makes the sense we want it to. If it does, we know we're on track and continue. If not, we rework a phrase, a paragraph, a page, or more and only when we sense it is beginning to work do we move on easily.

Each act in this process involves a way of knowing that brings out from what is unformed a greater clarity, a fresh articulation, and at times a creative surprise. Such acts do not lend themselves to models of information processing or pre-programmed procedures, because

I am grateful for the thoughtful and supportive readings of early drafts of this essay from Ann E. Berthoff, Mickey Bolmer, Peter Elbow, and Nancy Wilson. I am indebted to Arthur Egendorf whose dialogues with me about philosophies of teaching and living continually help shape my own.

they deliver completed expressions from what is not itself ever complete. But how, precisely, do we access this resource in ourselves?
And what do we thereby come into contact with?

First, we draw on such knowing deliberately only to the extent
that we interrupt our more customary preoccupation with already
finished thoughts and expressions. It is a matter of paying attention to
what is not yet articulated or structured. To this end, almost any form
of exercise in relaxation and concentration is helpful, at least as a
first step. Second, what we seek to contact is not abstract. Our goal is
to reach out to the immediate sense of what opens to us directly, what
is present that we can feel bodily. The feeling is nascent meaningfulness, usually more subtle than ordinary emotions and certainly more
intricately textured.

In an earlier article (Perl 1980) I used the term "felt sense" to
refer to what we attend to when we work in this manner. This term
was originally coined by Eugene Gendlin, who built on the works of
Dilthey, Merleau-Ponty, Heidegger, and others in his extensive explorations of "thinking beyond patterns" (1962; 1991).

Our felt sense of anything relevant is vibrant, open, ever evolving
(see also descriptions by Elbow and Belanoff 1989; Gendlin 1981;
Perl and Wilson 1986). Working with this sense is intrinsically creative, and nothing about it stays still. Delving into it does not simply
yield a discovery of something already formed yet hidden from view,
the way an archaeologist unearths an artifact on a dig. The very "delving in" helps shape what emerges and may shape and reshape the
very manner in which we "delve." This way of working is alive and
lives, as we do, in our bodies.

Cultivating this approach brings us to a kind of riddle: on one
hand, words have particular meanings; on another, there is no end to
the new uses to which they can be put. Similarly, in the best writing
words are chosen precisely, as if something very specific needs to be
said. But no writing ever says the last word; every expression, including this one, opens possibilities for more, much, much more.

By the same token, tuning in to felt sense reveals an observable
ground that is at once precise and boundless. Our felt sense of something is always quite specific. The sense you have at this moment is
unquestionably *this* sense and no other. But to write what you sense
may take some doing. The first problem is that you can't just throw
words down and be satisfied. Only certain words will say what you
sense; and these may only come by a careful process of slowing down
and listening, of paying attention to those hunches, leanings, and subtle pulls. The second difficulty comes in realizing that this sense is
vast, actually endless. Like vision in an open field, it goes on and on.
And the more fully and richly we sense something, the harder it may

be to do justice to it in speech or text. At each step along the way, we need to consult our felt sense as to what we are trying to say. For it is this evolving touchstone that tells us whether the words on the page do in fact say what is just now wanting to be said.

Guidelines for Composing

This way of knowing has implications for the classroom. In order to help students locate and draw on this knowledge, I created the Guidelines for Composing. They are tools that invite writers to work directly with felt sense, to use it to discover what they want to write and to rely on it as a guide, both in choosing words and knowing whether those words capture their intended meanings. More often than not, they lead to writing that is powerfully connected to the writer and powerful in its own right.

Over the past fifteen years I have used the Guidelines with students from middle school through graduate studies. I have introduced them to hundreds of teachers. Many have reported that they use them regularly with their students and have applied them to specific topics and exam questions.

The Guidelines for Composing are, essentially, a series of questions intended to call up and draw out writers' felt sense. They invite writers to stop, relax, pause, and listen quietly so they hear not only their usual thoughts but the silences between them. The questions have an order intended, at times, to interrupt writers, to invite them to look more closely at what has begun to emerge on the page. The idea is to generate on paper valuable musings and richly evocative phrases, not a finished product. The usual result is a series of notes that writers make to themselves. They are not meant to be shared, unless someone chooses to share them.

What is shared is the process itself. Writers often experience deep emotion or emotional release. Or they end up excited about the direction they discover or are touched by an image that emerges. Whatever their experience, they need to express what has occurred and hear from others. Although there are similarities, no two people experience precisely the same process.

The Instructor's Stance

Respect. Trust. Caring. Patience. This is not a process that works effectively when any one of these qualities is missing. It is not easy to determine whether sufficient trust exists in the classroom, or whether students feel sufficiently cared for and respected, or whether the classroom climate itself is sufficiently open to allow for such deep work. I would not begin a course using the Guidelines; I would wait instead until the students and I had established certain routines, including frequent sharing of writing-in-progress, and until enough rapport signaled that it was worth a try.

I say a "try" because I never know if implementing these Guidelines will work. It always feels a bit risky. I'm never sure how things will turn out, if everyone will find something valuable to write about, if someone will feel overwhelmed. But I want to stress here that good writing is risky; to say what we haven't said before, to discover and articulate what we don't yet know we know, can shake the ground from under us.

Instructors using these Guidelines then embody a particular stance about writing and knowing. One part of this stance is knowing that facing the blank page may be a frightening experience, and that what instructors are about to do is to hold someone's hand (or 18 or 28 or 39 hands depending on class size) as he or she is about to write. Instructors may then ease the panic that often accompanies composing, the anxiety or fear of not-knowing that hits us just before we begin to create something. This is perhaps the most valuable aspect of the process: that another person is there to accompany us along a path that initially appears daunting.

Another part of this stance is knowing that as we invite others to look inward and then write what comes, we act on the belief that everyone in that room is capable of writing, that everyone has something to say, that each and every student is a writer who can and will make meaning of experience.

The Introduction

First, I tell participants that we are about to engage in a process that takes approximately forty minutes. I will ask them questions which they then repeat silently. When they begin to hear themselves answering, they begin to write. I tell them that their writing is private — no one sees it; they do not hand it in; it is for themselves only. Sometimes, I say, they may begin to see a direction for a piece of writing. If the urge to begin the piece is strong, I tell them to ignore the rest of my questions and start. Generally, though, I ask them to stay with me through the process and let them know that we will discuss their experiences with the Guidelines when we have finished.

I talk briefly about the purpose of the Guidelines: to help people discover topics they are interested in writing about. Often, when students are asked to write, they respond: "About what?" Rather than provide a range of topics that may not connect with their interests, I offer the Guidelines. By looking inward at what's not yet said, students often discover ideas, issues, memories, images, people, and themes that hold within them valuable material for writing. If people come with topics already in mind, I tell them that's fine. The Guidelines help them deepen their sense of the topic, or they may find ways to change the topic to make it even more meaningful.

Finally, I talk briefly about felt sense. I often use the example of writing itself. I describe how, when we write and the writing is going well, we can tell by how we feel. This is not a purely mental or logical knowing, but a bodily one. It is not about grammatically correct sentences or accurately spelled words. It's a knowing that says, "Yes, for me, these words are the ones that are right. They work. They get me closer to where I'm trying to go." At such times we may feel a quickening and a sense of expansion or relief. But the reverse is equally true. When the writing is not going well, we know it. We don't like how the words sound. We feel stuck. We sometimes move around uncomfortably. Again, it is a bodily awareness. Many writers have had some corresponding experience and nod knowingly as I talk. Even if they haven't, the process seems to work for them. I tell them that at times during the process, they will look for this felt sense in relation to what they have written.[1]

The Opening: Getting Quiet

Once the group is seated quietly and expectantly, I say:

> If it's true that writing involves our bodies as much as our minds, then let's relax our bodies and breathe deeply before we write.

Most people accept this. Sometimes I see a frown. I continue.

> Sit quietly. Know that you are about to begin a journey. You are about to do some writing. Take a deep breath and close your eyes. This helps you relax. If you don't want to close your eyes, then just lower your gaze to your desk or the floor.
>
> Use this time to listen to yourself rather than to me or others in the room. Now, breathe in slowly. As you exhale, see how much you can let go of any tension in your neck or your arms. Breathe in again. Shake out your hands. Notice if you can feel yourself sitting

[1]This introduction need not take more than five minutes. The last instructions I give before we begin are to move into comfortable positions, to change desks if necessary for private space, to hold any questions until the end, and to go easily with whatever changes occur. I often write with the group, finding it improves my pacing. I also tell the group that for some, I may move too slowly and they need to wait for me; for others, it may feel too fast and they need to pace themselves. It's okay, if people are writing, to miss a question. I hand out copies of the Guidelines at the end so that participants do not have to concern themselves with writing down everything I say.

on your chair. If there is any discomfort, breathe into it and again, as you exhale, see how much you can release whatever tension or discomfort you are feeling.

I continue quietly, pausing after each direction, inhaling and exhaling slowly myself. This takes about four minutes. My goal is to have people sitting quietly, meditatively, in their chairs, not dozing or sleeping. If there are distractions in the building, noise coming from outside or from another room, I mention it:

Notice that there is some laughter next door, and then bring your attention back to yourself.

When everyone seems quiet and relaxed, I move on to the questions that lead to writing.

The First Questions: Making An Inventory

I say once again:

I am now going to ask you some questions that you can silently ask yourself. Once you hear yourself answering, make a list. Do not delve into any one item on the list. Just keep compiling as if you were making an inventory. Now, ask yourself, How am I right now? What's going on within me? What comes to mind? When you begin to get some answers, jot them down.

I pause for about a minute.

I'll ask again. What's on my mind? What am I thinking about these days? Again, when you hear yourself answering, add these to your list.

Another short pause. I continue:

Now that you have a list, long or short, I want you to look again, and ask yourself: What else is on my mind? Is there anything I'm overlooking? Maybe a person I like, a place, an event, something I might write about at some future time? Add these to your list.

I pause again for a minute or two. Then, usually one last time I say:

Look one more time. Remember to continue breathing deeply, and ask yourself: Is there anything else—a color, a memory, a dream—anything at all that I might want to add to this list? If there is, jot it down.

At this point, even if I, too, am writing, I check to see if everyone has a list. In case someone is stuck or someone came with a topic already in mind, I say:

If nothing comes to you at all, write down "nothing," and if you
came with a topic in mind and it's not on your list, add it now.

The only time I change the opening questions is if I notice a lot of
tension or if several individuals seem unruly or if a difficult or upset-
ting event has occurred in the community in which I am working. At
those times I begin with this opening:

> Is there anything in the way of my writing today? Is there anything
> that will get in the way of my composing? If so, jot that down. Put
> whatever is in the way down on paper.

I wait usually less than a minute.

> Now, put that aside. It will stay there and you can come back to it
> when we have completed today's work.

If I start here, after people have written, I ask them to use a clean
sheet of paper and then begin with the usual opening questions.

A Turning Question: Focusing In

I continue:

> Now that you have a list, look it over. As you do, ask yourself:
> Which one of these items stands out? Which one asks for attention?
> Which one says: "Me. Pay attention to me"?

I pause briefly, maybe thirty seconds.

> See if something jumps off the page at you. See if one item or a
> group of related items draws you in. If so, circle or star it or mark it
> in some way.

This is a good moment to watch. If the process is working,
participants are circling items and you know you are on track. Then
I say:

> Be sure you choose something that has some real interest for you,
> that speaks or calls to you. But if something feels just too big or
> overwhelming, let it be. Don't necessarily pick the heaviest or the
> hardest item on your list. And if nothing stands out for you, just
> pick something for the sake of the assignment.

A momentary pause. I continue:

> Take this item and write it at the top of a new page. Save all your
> earlier writing. You can come back to it for topics at any time. But

right now we are going to focus on the one item or issue that you
selected (or that selected you).

The Middle Questions: Getting Deeper

Once the students have written the single issue or item on the top of a
new page, I continue.

> If you think about it, you already know a lot about the issue you
> have chosen. What I'd like you to do now is to ask yourself: What
> are all the things I already know about this? What are all the associ-
> ations, names, people, questions that come to mind? Spend some
> time now briefly writing down all your associations to this topic.
> Don't go into any one association too deeply. Just collect them and
> write them down. This writing may take the form of a list or some
> phrases, some notes to yourself, or a stream-of-consciousness. Just
> write whatever comes.

I allow about four to five minutes and often sense that individuals
are becoming more deeply engaged with their topics.

At this point many people are writing. This is the time when some
may choose to ignore me because they have already found what they
want to write. But I try to get everyone's attention. I say in a deliberately louder voice:

> I am now going to interrupt you. I want you to set aside all that you
> already know about the topic, all your ideas and associations and
> take a fresh look.

I pause. Then more slowly I say:

> I want you to set aside all the bits and pieces and picture yourself
> holding the topic or issue in your palm. Stay there and just picture the
> whole topic right there, stretched out in front of you. I want you to
> look now at the whole of it, not the bits and pieces that are so familiar
> to you, and ask yourself the following questions: What makes this
> topic or issue so compelling or important? What is at the heart of this
> issue for me?

Brief pause.

> Now wait until you get a word, or a phrase, or an image that captures
> your sense of the whole topic. Once you get it, write it down and
> begin exploring it. See what it says to you. As you write, remember
> to breathe deeply and evenly.

Since this is a long series of instructions, I often repeat them, varying
them occasionally.

At this point some writers may look puzzled or distressed. I continue:

> If nothing has come, look again at the whole issue and gently ask yourself: What makes this topic so hard for me? What makes it so difficult or uncomfortable?

Brief pause.

> Again, wait until a felt sense forms. See if you get a word or a phrase or an image that captures your sense of the difficulty.

Usually, after this question, everyone is writing again.

By now individuals may be writing intently or they may be slowing down. I provide several more opportunities for writers to keep looking and working with their own sense of their topics. I say:

> As you write, let your felt sense deepen. See if it says you are on the right track. Notice what else it may be telling you. Can you experience the shift in your body that says: "Yes, this feels right. This begins to say it"?
>
> If at any time you feel yourself slowing down, you can ask: What's missing? Is there anything I've left out? Again, look to your felt sense. You can continue now, moving between "Is this right?" "Does this begin to say it?" and "What's missing?" until you feel yourself nearing the end.

I leave between 10 and 15 minutes for this series of questions and writing.

The Final Questions: Coming Out and Making Sense

Now I say:

> You may have anywhere from one or two pages of notes to several pages of writing. Ask yourself: Where's this all leading? What's the point I'm trying to make? And write again whatever comes to you.

Brief pause.

> Once you feel you're near or at the end, ask yourself: Does this feel complete? If so, write down your answer. If not, ask, again: What's missing? And, again, look to your felt sense of the topic for some guidance.
>
> Once you have a sense of where this is leading, ask yourself: What form might this be written in? Is this a poem? A play? A narrative? Is it a dialogue or a story or an essay? What form would work best for what I'm trying to say? Then ask: Who's speaking? Whose point of view is this? Would another point of view be useful?

> Can someone else tell this story? Make some notes to yourself about
> what forms you might use or from whose point of view you might
> work as you compose your piece.

I provide between three to five minutes here.

When everyone has finished, I invite participants to reflect on and
write about the process.

> Now that we've finished, I'd like you to go back, look at your initial
> list, then briefly look at what you've written. Write a short descrip-
> tion of what this process was like for you. Where did you start?
> What happened? Where are you now? Although the specifics of
> what you wrote are private, I will ask you to share your description
> of this process with the entire group.

I allot at least five minutes for this writing and at least ten minutes for discussion. With more time I invite people to begin their
drafts right then, advising them not to distract themselves by talking
to others, and we discuss the process later in the day. If we are
rushed, I skip writing about the process in favor of individuals' verbal reports.[2]

Conducting a Process Discussion

It is valuable to invite participants to discuss the process. Frequently,
powerful emotions are evoked and people are surprised. Often they
are embarrassed. Some may be angry. A few may be frightened. It is
the responsibility of instructors to find out how participants feel, to
encourage them to speak and to assure them that strong feelings about
the process are appropriate and acceptable. Having completed the
Guidelines, participants may decide that the process is useful but that
what they produced is "too personal" to share. That is fine. They can
return to their original list and see if they would like to explore something else. With encouragement, some find that they really want to try
writing something "risky," and this wish often leads naturally into a
discussion of the types of responses writers ask of their readers. After
such discussions, writers often look forward to sharing their emerging
drafts. Still others see that a shift in point of view enables them to
compose a piece that is important to them but from which they can
also establish some distance. And some writers occasionally report
that the process did not work for them. Since our writing is connected
to us in ways we don't often suspect, it should not be surprising that
at times the process is unsuccessful. Some are just not "ready" to
look deeply and write.

[2]The timing is approximate. The Guidelines can be completed in forty minutes or more leisure-
ly, allowing a full hour for writing and fifteen or twenty minutes for discussing the process.

But whatever writers report or choose to do, they have now had an opportunity to be guided through a particular way of composing. Some look forward to being led through it again. Others find these questions enter naturally into their thinking and later on report: "You know the Guidelines we did? I ask them now of myself, whenever I'm writing."

Toward an Understanding of Composing

When the Guidelines are effective, what works is not so much a technique as a philosophy. As instructors we are granted the power to shape learning. When using the Guidelines, we do so by directing attention to our students' ability to make sense and to share that sense in speech and text. This is a use of instructional leadership that values and cultivates *explicitly* the authentic and varying voices unique to each person.

A great deal is also conveyed *implicitly* through the vast subtext communicated in the Guidelines and the instructor's stance. One key idea is that our individual ways of being are also, intrinsically, ways of being with others. Genuine voices can be forged, against all odds, in the most adverse circumstances. But individual authenticity flourishes when such authenticity is also valued by the group. When using the Guidelines, we do not *tell* students they have something valuable to say. We *show* them. We say, in effect, that there is more to each person present than he or she is usually aware of. In fact, we show that what individuals are already living and coming to know is enough to generate valuable raw material for further shaping. Nobody has to struggle or dissemble. But it takes being quiet together and some discipline to grant ourselves and each other the time and attention that fresh thinking requires.

The Guidelines show further that the path toward authentic expression cannot be programmed in advance. But neither is it haphazard, ad hoc, or fuzzy. We proceed according to a precise understanding that meaningfulness is not something stored and retrieved, but created. And what we work with when articulating meaning creatively is a sensate knowing that we can refer to and draw upon, even though it may never be fully said. To uncover this sense and to let what we thereby contact speak through us is no mere deciphering or decoding. It deserves to be called a higher literacy, for we "read" the hitherto unwritten and "hear" what is not yet spoken. Such an intricate process, forever rich and unfolding, reveals how being and knowing are interwoven in the ways we compose.

8

The Write Moves
Cultivating Kinesthetic and Spatial Intelligences in the Writing Process

Karen Klein and Linda Hecker

Tinkertoys in a college classroom? Choreographing an essay instead of outlining it on paper? We recently developed these strategies for writing for two different student populations, Karen Klein for visual thinkers at Brandeis University and Linda Hecker for high-potential dyslexic students at Landmark College. Both of us were influenced by reading about the Multiple Intelligences Theory in Howard Gardner's book *Frames of Mind* and devised ways to use spatial and kinesthetic intelligences to facilitate writing.

Our strategies exploit the ideas of "learn-by-doing," cross-fertilizing students' linguistic abilities with spatial or kinesthetic intelligences. By working directly with students and observing their writing difficulties, we found that many individuals struggling to express their ideas on paper could build models of how ideas relate using colored pipe cleaners, Legos, or Tinkertoys, or they could walk those ideas across a room, changing direction to indicate changes in logical structure. These techniques are mutually reinforcing, sharing the qualities of three-dimensionality and concreteness. They also bring together the writing process and mobility, emphasizing the notion that essays are composed of parts that can be shaped, moved, rearranged, and moved again. Furthermore, both strategies help students generate language as well as organize it. Holding or touching an object or moving our bodies through space appears to stimulate the flow of language, even for those who may be halting or dysfluent in their speech or who have difficulties with word retrieval. Our work bears out Thomas West's suggestion in *In the Mind's Eye* that "systematic experimentation with a range of emerging, visually oriented tools and processes might prove to be especially fruitful for many different kinds of students with different talents and different brains" (42). This chapter details each strategy, first "walking the structure" and then "hands-on manipulatives."

Walking the Structure

Thinking about writing kinesthetically involves imagining an essay as if it were a three-dimensional map moving in different directions. The classroom floor is the place on which the essay is walked. Using whole body movement, students walk the large pattern of an essay, following the changing direction of its thoughts. This strategy can be used both to generate ideas and to understand something already written. Whether a student needs to think through an argument in order to write, or to understand a first draft or a published essay, actually moving through space makes concrete the structure of the logic and shows the strength—or weakness—of the essay's connections. Here's how it works.

Students begin at one part of the room and imagine that the goal or end of the essay is at some other point in the room. To begin, students speak an idea, a piece of information, or, as Peter Elbow puts it, a "felt problem or itch" (1985, 297). Or, if an assignment is given, it may be discussed and the direction of the essay explored verbally. Then, working with either a group of students or the instructor or both, the individual walking the structure begins to move forward if new information is being added. If the line of thought is not a directly forward movement, students must—by walking in different directions, marking time in place, moving laterally, turning to the side or back— indicate through these physical movements the relationship of subsequent ideas. Students ask questions throughout the walking: Where do I want to go? How do I get from here to there? What information or ideas do I need to express to get from where I am to where I want to go? All questions are formulated in spatial terms to keep students focused on the concrete movement of the essay as they track their own body movements. Either the instructor or a student makes notations on paper or the chalkboard.

Walking the structure enables students physically to map the experience of setting out in one direction, finding dead ends or new paths, probing an argument from all sides. Instructors do not set up an imaginary straight line as the ideal development. Doing so can be as detrimental as old, rigid outlines were. If, however, students don't know how to develop an idea, they must stand in place. At that point, other students and the instructor ask questions, or offer suggestions to get the walker unstuck and moving again. Getting unstuck is both a physical and an intellectual liberation.

Although this technique was originally designed for the large structure of the essay, students can use it at the paragraph level or even to clarify relationships among ideas in a unit as small as a sentence. Our language has code words, directional signals, as it were, that tip us off as to the way we should go physically and mentally. These words, and the logic that each word represents, can be encoded in symbols and written down, as in using shorthand, or made tangible in three-dimensional, movable forms such as pipe cleaners. Essentially, the physical movements dramatize the logical relationships of addition, contradiction, causality, comparison, and dependence. Each change of direction or physical movement of a walker indicates a difference in logic or in the direction of the essay.

Our students use the following walking directions and symbolic transcriptions to track the logic of their essays or those they read:

1. All new information enables students to walk forward. "And," "further," "in addition" are all represented by + and keep us going in the same direction.

2. "For example" belongs to the logic of "and," which is simple addition or juxtaposition. But this connective involves walking in a side line, putting a foot or hand out in the same space along an imaginary line, since examples essentially do not move an argument forward, but stay in the same place and expand on that space. Or, walkers' arm movements can indicate the use of examples by making a "T" shape with their hands; the lower hand moves and touches the outstretched upper palm at a number of places representing the number of examples. The visual notation for examples is a horizontal line with verticals beneath. If the examples are all of equal significance, the vertical lines are equal: ⊓⊓ . If the examples increase in importance, the line length indicates this: ⌐⊤⊐ ; if they decrease, the reverse paradigm applies: ⊓⊓ .

3. Unlike "and" which keeps us walking forward, words like "but" and "however" make us reverse direction because they involve contradicting. These words signal a change in direction and the visual sign our students use is ⟶↙⟵ . One Brandeis student explained it this way: "It means you were going one way, but now you have to go another."

4. Sometimes directional signals indicating contradiction also main-
    tain connection or indicate only partial contradiction, as in the
    cases of "despite" or "yet." In those instances, writers do not
    completely reverse direction, but rather make a partial reverse;
    and this sign is used, $\Longleftarrow\!\!\!\Longrightarrow$, indicating both contradiction and
    connection.

5. The directional signals for simple causation—"because," "due
    to," "on account of," which are visually represented as $>$, also
    move an argument forward. So when they appear, walkers take
    another step in the same direction and hold their hands in a V
    shape in front of them.

6. Some causation is more complex. For example, "although" or
    "even though" indicate reservation or qualification before cau-
    sation takes place. In these instances, writers lean back first
    and then walk forward with their hands in a V shape; the nota-
    tion is $\curvearrowright\!\!>$.

7. Sometimes possibilities need to be expressed before causation
    happens, as in "if..., then." Our sign for "if" is the infinity sign,
    ∞ and it is followed by a "greater than sign" $>$ for causation.
    The physical movement for "if..., then" is for writers to raise their
    hands with palms open and then make the V shape.

    However, causation can also be complex and sequencing it—
    what to say first, what next?—can be problematic. The use of
    before and after signals such as "prior to" and "subsequently" or
    simple numeration, "first, second, and so on" sometimes helps
    sort things out and move walkers forward as new information is
    added. In revising the written draft, many of these signals can be
    removed.

8. The directional signals for results, for closure and conclusions—
    "finally," "in sum," "consequently," "therefore"—can be visually
    represented by a funnel-like shape. The walker can simply stop or
    hold his or her arms up in a funnel shape to represent all ideas
    funnelling to the conclusion $\searrow\!\!\nearrow$.

When composing an essay, students must be alert as to how the
material they add connects to what they've already said. This awareness also helps them understand the logic of someone else's essay.
These three sentences from the first paragraph of "Growing Up
Expressive" by Carol Bly provide a good example for representing
connections in the movement of the argument:

> Love, death, the cruelty of power, and time's curve past the stars are
> what children want to look at. For convenience's sake, let's say

these are the four most vitally touching things in life. Little children ask questions about them with relish. (201)

Sentence One is an assertion made in a sequence of additive concepts, so students walk forward on each one. The visual notation, on a blackboard or in the margin of the text, for the sequence is a series of "plus" signs, + , the sign of simple addition, new information, or juxtaposition. Sentence Two brings the four items of the sequence together under a single definition, "the four most vitally touching things in life"; students take one step forward while sweeping backward with one arm, then bringing the arm forward. This indicates that material from the previous sentence is being brought along in the argument. The visual sign for this movement is a loop which indicates connection: ℓℓ; the size of the loop is determined by the distance of the new statement from the place where the material was initially presented. Sentence Three adds new information about what children want to do with the sequence, now referred to as "them." This moves the argument in the same direction, so walkers take a step forward. There can be two repeated arm sweeps, as both subjects, children and the sequence, are being brought forward.

The sequence in the Bly example shows simple juxtaposition in a single sentence, but the principle of the sequence can structure paragraphs, even whole essays. Refinements in the sequence range from the "even" sequence, when each item is of equal importance (a zigzag line), to the "uneven" sequence, when items vary in importance— that is, build (visually shown as steps ascending to the right) or diminish (steps descending to the right) in value. Visual signs for each are: even sequence ∧∧∧ ; building sequence ┌┌ ; diminishing sequence ┐┐ . The visual image of steps underlines the principle of sequences; i.e., items remain connected while separated.

Remaining connected while separate is at the heart of the rhetorical process of repetition with variation, a process that structures musical and visual compositions as well. Unlike a sequence of terms, repetition and variation apply to a single term whose separate variations throughout an entire piece continue the connections. This process of repetition and variation is indicated by walkers' arm movements. The exact shape of the movement is arbitrary; it must simply preserve the logic of sameness with a difference. Walkers move their hands horizontally to the right along an imaginary line and then move their hands vertically up and down. Or they can draw a large circle in space with their finger and then a series of smaller circles. Visual representations are: ‾/ / / ‾ ⊂⊃‾ oooo .

Sometimes continuous connections in a paragraph mean simply the way the argument links itself to the preceding material sentence

by sentence through repetitions of key words, phrases, and ideas. To
indicate this kind of connected logic, students walking a paragraph
hold one hand in the other in front of them, making a kind of double
fist. The graphic for this is less like a loop, our sign for sweeping
back to connections, and more like a chain: ⚬-⚬-⚬-⚬. If these con-
tinuing connections are not felt, students hold their hands open and
out. We have found -○- to be a useful graphic to indicate the
absence of connection, especially on compositions in which the logic
demands coherence between sentences or between paragraphs.

Sometimes connections seem to have no function because the
writers are simply repeating material without adding any new
information. Such sentences are usually pure "filler"; they weaken
an essay, make it sound repetitive, and are easily omitted. Walking
the structure quickly alerts students to these kinds of sentences
because they have to stand in place and literally "mark time" with
their feet. Lacking new information, they can't move forward, and
the essay feels as kinesthetically redundant or stagnant as it is sub-
stantively.

Connections are also made through contrasts. But these involve
the logic of "either...or," giving choices and alternatives, and not just
adding information or examples. With "and" walkers move forward;
with "or" or "either...or," walkers take one step forward on a diagonal
and then bring the other foot forward on the opposite diagonal so that
a V shape is made. The graphic essentially represents the logic of
dual structures and can be used for "or" and even for "and" when
"and" connects two contrasting things. Sometimes writers set up a
dual structure, implying that two things are opposites. Students walking this structure and trying to understand how these things are opposite, may find that the two are, in fact, similar and that an author's
logic is faulty.

Another way to represent duality is through "on the one hand,"
and "on the other hand," an effective image through which to structure essays requiring contrasting two ideas, authors, texts, and so on.
The image operates as students walk to one side of the room then to
the other and gesture alternatively with each hand while making contrasting points. The hand gestures remind students of two sides of the
topic. Walking back and forth forces them to be attentive to both
sides of the issue and to avoid overdeveloping only one side. The
crisscrossing movement also shows the points of connection, where
the two ideas under consideration are similar; there students move
only slightly to one side, then the other, or stand in place and gesture
with one hand, then the other. Similarly, when the contrasts between
two points are extreme, students move very far to one side, then to the
other. Subtle degrees of similarity and dissimilarity are indicated by

how far in each direction students move. New comparisons and contrasts may evolve from this exercise, and the entire essay may ultimately be restructured around them, rather than around the authors or texts of the first walking draft. These comparisons then become the focal points for moving the essay forward.

The walking structure is unique to each essay, and instructors and students trying to use it should not worry about memorizing formal moves then rigidly applying them. The true utility of this technique is not in learning a specific set of moves to apply to logical structures (in fact, individual students are encouraged to invent their own sets of moves, if that feels more comfortable to them) but in the actual, physical movement itself. It is the gross motor movement of arms and legs, hands and feet that makes the abstract both concrete and tactile.

In *Hand and Mind: What Gestures Reveal About Thought*, David McNeill provides theoretical support for what we have been doing in practice. He argues that "gestures are an integral part of language as much as are words, phrases, and sentences" and that "gesture itself has an impact on thought" (2). Asserting that "gestures and speech really are parts of one process" (245), he postulates an ongoing dialectic between the gesture side that is idiosyncratic and constructed at the moment of speech and the linguistic side that uses the formal grammatical patterns and hierarchical structures of language. This dialectic, he proposes, constitutes a continuous transformation of thought. Further, the timing of the gestural stroke during utterance is significant. Because it foreshadows speech by a brief interval, "the breaking edge of our internal narrative may be the gesture itself; the words follow." If, as he hypothesizes, "gesture...can reflect the mind's own narrative structure" (266), then these walking and gesture exercises may help students both access and verbally express that structure. Particularly for those students at Landmark, walking increased the expressive fluency of those with halting speech or word retrieval difficulties.

Because walking the structure of an essay is not something students do instinctively, before getting them up and walking, instructors should model the process the first few times, doing both the walking and the visual notations. Doing an entire essay, however, is tedious and unnecessary. Enough can be learned from a single paragraph. And after a few times, students internalize the process of thinking kinesthetically about the way an essay develops.

At this stage, the three-dimensional representations of the visual signs can be used. Brandeis students made portable models from different colored pipe cleaners which they can manipulate while composing at a desk or reading an essay. Their three-dimensionality provides a constant reminder of the concrete, constructed nature of writing. Returning at any point to walk the structure is also useful should students get stuck.

Hands-On Manipulatives

Walking the structure locates language in motor skills. More hands-on is the use of manipulatives. These rely on visual-spatial and tactile means to generate and organize language. Manipulatives may be used in conjunction with walking the structure, as we've described, or by themselves. The remainder of our chapter addresses this latter strategy. This involves taking Cuisenaire rods, Tinkertoys, pipe cleaners, or other colorful manipulatives right out of the primary classroom where Piaget's theories of cognitive development first placed them by virtue of his emphasis on concrete experience. While Piaget's work suggests that developmentally children outgrow their need for direct sensorimotor experience as they develop their ability to think abstractly and hypothetically, in fact Piaget calls for both concrete, practical experiences and the verbal exercises of "discussion and disputation" in educating adolescents (McNally 1977, 168). Our observations suggest that for many learners, adults and children, an efficient and memorable way to develop new concepts, especially language abstractions such as sentence structure or paragraph organization, may be via a return to sensorimotor experience with concrete objects.

We've found that these strategies seem to work best with students who are strongly associational rather than sequential in their thinking, and especially well with students who have Attention Deficit Disorders. These students often present original, even brilliant insights and new approaches, especially in discussions. But they have difficulty focusing, isolating, and organizing their ideas into the complex sequences demanded by college-level writing tasks. Visual schema or flow charts of an essay form may not help because they fail to express relationships among ideas with enough complexity. They are also limited by being two-dimensional and impalpable. The three-dimensionality of our process is significant. One student said, "It satisfies the right side of my brain," while another commented, "In my head I have so many thoughts, they paralyze me. I can't quiet them, so I get all mixed up. But if I can touch it, it's real." Students with Attention Deficit Disorder, in particular, report that having a concrete object to see, touch, and move helps focus their concentration and thinking.

How does this strategy work? After students have chosen a topic and generated some ideas by brainstorming or freewriting, instead of organizing these ideas into an outline—the traditional next step—students select a set of manipulatives. We ask students to "show" how the essay ideas are related. Typically, students build a model of pieces

of different sizes, shapes, and colors. This model represents their intuitions about structure. Some students create something akin to a three-
dimensional essay outline with the main pieces representing the introduction, thesis, major points and conclusion, all connected by linking
pieces that express the sequencing of those parts. For instance, one of
Hecker's students built a Tinkertoy model for a paper on the role of
modern China in contemporary world politics and explained how it
helped her. "With this model I see what fits and what's tangential. I
could never follow a flow chart or someone else's structure because
they don't express the way I see the connections between ideas. In
building the model I found that thinking about the size, color, and
shape of the pieces helped me make decisions about where the pieces
belong in the overall structure." At the top of her paper she wrote:
"Tinkertoys: There is nothing playschool about them."

Other students create more pictoral or symbolic representations.
A Landmark student writing an essay about the three stages of
Malcolm X's life built a complicated and artistic structure from colored pipe cleaners that had three main parts each in a different color
and a large black X in the center. A Brandeis student used a large tube
that she had marked with different colors and writing to show the
emotional progressions and connections in an essay. Because many
students are unable to complete essays because they have no overall
sense of how ideas fit together or of how one idea leads to the next,
tactile models help reify them. Ideas can't "fly away" as students try
to form them into sentences, and they can literally see where to go
after they've discussed one point. Using a model, a student observed:
"I used not to really know where I was going with my ideas. But now
the organization was so clear that I knew how to write transitions
because I could see what came next. Also, I didn't wind up writing
pages and pages that were off-topic. I knew what process I would
use to develop structure. That was a big relief in itself."

The next step in the process entails talking about the model.
Students name each part of the model and explain how the parts connect. This crucial step translates the image into words and bridges
the gap between the visual-spatial and linguistic domains. At this
point students generally sketch the model on paper and write down
the names of each part as a mnemonic aid. Finally, students decide on
a logical order for the explanation and number each of its parts. This
sequenced structure is now a working three-dimensional blueprint for
the essay. As with the walking structures, these strategies are used to
foster understanding as well as writing. If students are struggling to
understand the structure of an essay or another piece of text, they can
represent its ideas with colored blocks or pipe cleaners and experientially observe how the pieces work together.

Students adapt the general strategy of model building to their individual learning styles and the demands of their papers. One student doing a research paper comparing the effects of ozone depletion to those of global warming created a set of nesting boxes to show levels of organization in his information. The student explained that when he dealt with lots of information, he got confused. So he wrote each piece of information on a slip of paper and placed the slips into different tape cassette boxes, labeled according to the topic each explained. All the cassette boxes fit into a shoe box which represented the overall subject. When he wrote on a particular topic, he pulled out the relevant box and dealt only with the information on its set of paper slips. This not only clarified which information went into which paragraph, but it also enabled him to stay focused on one set of ideas at a time and not get lost in irrelevant data. While this approach is not radically different from the traditional one-idea-per-file-card approach to writing research papers, the dimensionality of the nesting boxes conveyed to the writer a sense of structure that piles of flat file cards never could. Both student and instructor noticed a significant improvement in the organization of this research paper compared to his earlier papers.

Most of our college students enthusiastically embraced these strategies. No one refused outright to try them, though perhaps some may have privately thought them offbeat or childish to begin with. The strategies worked particularly well for both LD students and non-LD students; however, they do not work for everyone. Verbally adept students may, in fact, be slowed down by this technique. Ultimately students employing it are self-selected. Many experienced relief from the frustrations of composing in a strictly language-based process and were willing to apply the strategies to other writing projects, modifying them to suit their learning styles. Students found that after constructing models or walking several papers, they needed only to imagine performing the strategies in order to achieve the desired organizational clarity. They all internalized a strong sense of language structure in a way that was not possible when we explained language by using more language.

Finally, we want to emphasize the centrality of students in this technique. These are not recipes for churning out essays. As instructors, we learned how to modify the strategies by observing our students in action. We encourage composition teachers in various settings, not just college classrooms, to experiment with similar strategies, to be candid about their exploratory nature, and to respect students' individual discoveries.

9

Generous Listening
A Deeper Way of Knowing

Trudelle H. Thomas

About a hundred of us were gathered in a rented hall to learn about "Adoption and the Trans-Cultural/Trans-Racial Family." As an audience, we had much in common: all of us were parents or prospective parents of children adopted from developing countries and/or across racial lines. The daylong workshop was organized around the stages of children's development from infancy to adolescence, with a focus on the special challenges faced at each stage by adopted children of color. The workshop leader was herself an adoptive parent and a respected social scientist and adoption specialist, so that many examples were drawn from firsthand involvement.

She spoke of the sense of loss that many adopted children feel, even in early childhood. Her own daughter had been adopted from India in infancy; born to a destitute woman, minutes after birth she had been abandoned for dead. It was little wonder that this young girl would periodically battle grief for years to come—grief at the separation from her first parents and grief over feeling rejected by her own country. In addition to the grief of adoption, children of color adopted by Caucasian parents feel loss at having a skin color different from their parents'. The workshop leader offered practical guidance as to how we as parents can help our adopted children come to terms with this lifelong sense of loss.

I found myself listening intently, trying to take in everything the workshop leader said. In newscasts and documentaries, I had heard

The seeds of this essay may be found in the article, "Connected Teaching: An Exploration of the Classroom Enterprise," (*The Journal on Excellence in College Teaching*, Fall 1992).

statistics about the millions of hungry or homeless children in the world. But today's workshop made the statistics real. Poverty and racism and sorrow — familiar concepts — took on new meaning when presented in terms of living children. I gained a wealth of information about homeless children in addition to practical skills for parenting. But more important, I gained a deepening compassion.

Months later, while researching teaching styles, I thought back to that workshop. What made it such a powerful learning experience? It followed a traditional lecture format. The leader wasn't particularly charismatic. And the subject matter was largely familiar. Yet the workshop was a powerful experience for me, one whose impact endured. How could I, as an instructor myself, learn from it?

What distinguished the adoption workshop was the quality of listening. The highly motivated group of parents was listening attentively. The workshop leader herself modeled a distinctive kind of listening. She spoke from a grounding in firsthand, thoroughly felt experience that reached far beyond studying texts on attachment theory or racism. And much of what she talked about was indeed listening: listening to your children, listening to your internal experience.

The theme of listening echoes ideas set forth by Peter Elbow in *Embracing Contraries*. Elbow describes the importance of writers (and others) practicing "the believing game," whereby individuals seek understanding by deliberately and temporarily taking on viewpoints other than their own. In other words, the believing game asks people actively to embrace or enter into a belief (or belief system) that does not come naturally to them and, for the sake of learning, pretend to believe it for a time. With practice, the believing game becomes a way of broadening experience and deepening understanding by freeing people from a fixed and narrow perspective. In order to take on someone's viewpoint, we must first learn it — and a key tool is listening.

In contrast to the believing game is critical thinking or, in Elbow's words, "the doubting game" which is at the heart of our Western intellectual tradition; the doubting game pursues truth through detachment, doubt, and impersonal analysis. Ideally, Elbow believes that the believing game and the doubting game, practiced in a sort of yin/yang balance, leads participants to a richer and more complete understanding of truth. Neither "game" used alone accomplishes this.

Recent scholarship substantiates Elbow's notion of the believing game. Researching the learning styles of female college students and adult women, Belenky and her associates (1986) discovered a distinction between what they call "separate knowing" and "connected knowing." Separate knowing, like the doubting game, relies on questions, critiques, and detachment. In contrast, connected knowing seeks truth by trying to understand another person's truth—that is, by believing, accepting, and trying to understand a version of reality remote from one's own.

But connected knowing goes further. In the believing game, Elbow emphasizes the intellectual or cognitive dimension of believing—believing a proposition or taking on a point of view. Connected knowing also involves cognition, but it recruits feelings and imagination as well. It grows out of caring and intimacy and presumes a relationship of interest and empathy between the knower and the object (or subject) of knowing. Descriptions of connected knowing include feeling and imagining as well as believing:

> Connected knowers develop procedures for gaining access to other people's knowledge. At the heart of these procedures is the capacity for empathy. Since knowledge comes from experience, the only way they can hope to understand another person's ideas is to try to share the experience that has led the person to form the idea. . . . [Connected knowers] act as connected rather than separate selves, seeing the other not in their own terms but in the other's terms. (Belenky, et al. 1986, 113)

To describe connected knowing Belenky and her colleagues use terms such as "genuine care," "grounded in firsthand experience," and "learning through empathy" (113–15).

In our Western intellectual tradition, we tend to privilege separate knowing as the only true thinking, and to disparage connected knowing as subjective, undisciplined, and misleading. Yet Belenky found that both separate knowing and connected knowing are deliberate procedures for seeking truth. Both "ways of knowing" are learned; neither is an inborn or "natural" response, though either response can occur more spontaneously with practice, and individuals may have a natural proclivity toward one or the other. Similar to separate knowing, connected knowing can be cultivated over time through learning, guidance, and practice.

One exercise for cultivating connected knowing is what I call "generous listening." Generous listening invites instructors and students to take on an unfamiliar belief system or experience and then respond to it. That is, listeners temporarily identify with speakers, trying to see and feel the world from their vantage points, and then mirror their insights back. For example, the leader of the adoption workshop urged parents to practice active listening with children. When children encounter racial prejudice or express grief, parents can try to "enter their world," to see and feel the experience as fully as possible, even physically getting on children's eye level. Through such listening parents grow in understanding and compassion; in the process they help their children come to terms with the thoughts and feelings stirred by prejudice or loss.

One quality that distinguishes generous listening from other kinds of learning is that it requires reciprocity. Generous listeners cannot be passive receptacles. As we consider and integrate new ideas and experiences with our own, we must also respond to or interact with the subject or object. We traditionally describe learning in terms of the metaphor of seeing—as in "seeing the light," "seeing with the mind's eye," and "having vision." Such metaphors fail to capture the kind of learning I am describing. "Seeing" involves looking at or taking in information or ideas, yet it places on the viewer (or seer) no demand to respond. The metaphor of seeing is essentially passive and nonrelational; students can "take in" visually and yet remain aloof, detached, and passive.

As an alternative to the metaphor of vision, Belenky advocates "finding a voice" as a more accurate way to speak of learning:

> We adopted the metaphor of voice and silence as our own. It has become the unifying theme that links the chapters in our story of women's ways of knowing and of the long journey they must make if they are to *put the knower back into the known* [emphasis mine] and claim the power of their own minds and voices. (Belenky, et al. 1986, 19)

Participants in their study spoke of "gaining a voice," having a "different voice," "speaking up," and "being heard." Many of us in composition studies have long been familiar with the concept of "voice."

The metaphor of voice is superior to the metaphor of vision in several ways. As Belenky suggests, it validates personal experience and empowers students by allowing them to "put the knower back into the known and claim the power of their own minds and voices." It suggests greater participation in learning and a greater intimacy between the knower and the object of knowing—a back-and-forth exchange, a dialogue with the subject. Unlike "seeing," "voice" places demands on students. Voice does not allow them to be passive receptacles. And the metaphor of voice carries with it, as Elbow (1992) points out, the possibility of growth in authority and authenticity.

Yet voice presumes a listener just as listening presumes a voice. If we accept the metaphor of "finding a voice" to speak of teaching and learning, close listening becomes central to the process; through generous listening, we create a climate conducive for students to "find a voice"—for them to speak up and trust their own authority. Both instructors and students must learn to listen with what one writer has called the "delicate balance of a quiet meditative mind and an open loving heart" (Dass 1982, ix). We set the tone for generous listening by first becoming listening teachers.

Listening Teaching

As writing instructors, we expect from our students a degree of emotional and intellectual engagement seldom required in other course work. We ask students to listen to their own experience as well as to the voices of experts, often requiring them to weave various voices together. And because so many students believe their writing is an expression of the self, we ask them to become vulnerable, to open themselves in ways that many instructors do not expect. For these reasons, it is all the more important that we try to create listening classrooms—environments of trust and receptivity where both instructor and students listen generously (see also Thomas 1992).

"Listening teaching" is largely a matter of attitude. I find helpful Martin Buber's conception of "I and Thou"—a relationship where two individuals meet in a spirit of receptivity (1970). The "Thou" is regarded with an attitude of reverence for his or her "other-ness." Listening teachers regard their students with this respect and anticipation. Expecting to learn new things from their students and their subjects, they resist imposing their own interpretation or direction. When responding to drafts of students' essays, for example, they refrain from imposing their own ideas, instead letting students steer their own course. Listening teachers are also willing to set aside carefully planned lessons when they sense the class is moving in different and more fruitful directions. And such instructors bring to classrooms each day (and to their meeting rooms and offices and studies) their willingness to listen generously.

One way to improve our own listening skills is to make a point of standing back and observing how we listen, and how our colleagues listen. Family gatherings or visits to the in-laws or simply eavesdropping in the student union or a public restaurant provide opportunities for taking stock of the quality of listening around us. Even more instructive is to take a week (or even a day) in which we stand back and observe the exchanges that occur in the faculty lounge, in the hallways, in departmental meetings, in our own classrooms. Who is speaking? And who is genuinely listening? When genuine listening does not occur, what is blocking it?

I recently experienced such a "standing back" during a departmental hiring meeting. We had completed the arduous process of screening dossiers and interviewing several candidates for a position;

now was the time to rank them and make an offer. As we gathered around the conference table, my colleagues and I attempted to show our openmindedness and goodwill. Minutes into the meeting, however, it became clear that the veneer of cooperation was thin. Most of us had made up our minds regarding who should be hired; indeed, many had been on the phone for days before, marshaling votes for a favored candidate. What might appear to an outsider as a rational and open-minded discussion was in fact a lengthy exercise in nonlistening. Is it any surprise that many of us come away from such meetings feeling dishonest and alienated?

It is also fruitful to reflect on the obstacles that prevent listening. In my professional life, over-busyness and lack of privacy often prevent me from listening as generously as I would like. Conversations on-the-run, in the mail room, hallway, or shared office space, may not foster real listening. Other barriers are more subtle. For example, we may feel distrust, vulnerability, anger, pride, or contempt toward students or colleagues. To new faculty members we may communicate a lack of acceptance. And because they do not want to appear incompetent, they are reluctant to express the struggle of adjusting to new courses and students. Harsh judgment by colleagues (or fear of harsh judgment) prevent a candid exchange, and true listening is blocked. Inward barriers to listening are especially insidious because they are often not recognized as barriers. What started out as a disagreement with a colleague may, as the years pass, harden into smug contempt that admits no possibility of genuine discussion. Impatience with slow students may evolve into a rigid and isolating arrogance by professors.

"Listening teaching" affects not just how we treat our students but also the way in which we prepare for our classes or conduct our own research. We can bring the same spirit of anticipation and receptivity to the time we spend preparing for class or pursuing our own research. Educator Parker Palmer suggests that we let the subject we are studying speak to us:

> We need to find ways to give [the] subject a voice of its own, a voice that can speak and resist our tendency to reduce it to our terms. . . . [T]he autonomy of the subject's voice grows as I move my students beyond *"looking at" the subject into personal dialogue* [emphasis mine], with it. . . . When we interview the subject instead of just viewing it, then we find the subject speaking back to us in ways surprisingly independent of our own preconceptions. (1983, 98–99)

George Washington Carver spoke of such a "dialogue with the subject" in regard to his agricultural research:

I knew the world needed the things the little peanut could provide so I asked God to help me find them. I went to my laboratory to see if I could find milk in the peanut because not everyone can afford regular milk. I talked to the peanut and through the peanut God talked to me. I found milk and butter . . .[and] soap, creosote, instant coffee, cooking oil . . . and at least three hundred other products. (Brown 1978, 199)

Similarly, in a novel by Gail Godwin, fictional professor Stannard advises a young scholar, Hilda, on how to approach her research into a medieval Abbess named Hilda:

[A]pply the empathy that I consider to be your gift. You'd use your respectful imagination. . . . After apprising yourself of what is known about her world and her circumstances, you'd look *into* Hilda and it's my feeling that the Abbess herself would look back at you across thirteen centuries, take an instant liking to you, and reveal herself. (1991, 151–52)

In his thoughtful book, *To Know as We Are Known*, Palmer offers additional examples of "letting the subject speak" from various disciplines.

I am best able to "let the subject speak" when I build space for silence or meditation into my life, be it breathing meditation, Zen meditation, or simply long quiet walks. Palmer offers additional observations about the value of meditation and silence in academic life as well as in specific class activities that "let the subject speak." To promote the attitude of openness that "listening teaching" requires, Palmer suggests that instructors regularly study (or even teach) in fields beyond their own. By becoming students again, we recall what it is like to approach a subject without the "delusion of mastery." This is practice especially instructive when I attempt a subject for which I have no natural talent. Courses in art history or educational theory come easily to me; more difficult is learning about financial planning or basic home repair.

A few years ago, for example, I reluctantly received instruction in electrical wiring. Having just purchased an older home, I needed a grounded electrical outlet for my computer. A friend offered to show me how to install one, insisting that all new homeowners should learn basic wiring. Lying in the flower bed with sawdust in my eyes, I drilled holes into floorboards and wrangled an electrical cable into the space between the walls. Later, my friend at my side, I routed cables through floor joists in the basement and connected individual conductors to the circuit breakers in the house panel board. Throughout this process, I was terrified of instant death by electrocution and/or permanent disgrace by my friend. A patient teacher, he drew diagrams, offered explanations, and heaped praise on my timid efforts. Still, my fear and embarrassment undermined my learning. Then it hit me: Was this the way students in the Writing Center feel when faced with the mysteries of essay organization? Was this the frame of mind of students in developmental English on the first day of class? Such unfamiliar learning—venturing beyond our expertise—forces us to set aside our "delusion of mastery" and practice the humility necessary for effective teaching.

Palmer comments on the understandings that can arise from such learning experiences, as uncomfortable as they may be:

> [By becoming a student again] the teacher is forced to see the world from the student's point of view, to deepen the capacity for empathetic [sic] identification. . . . The result is more than new knowledge. It is the enlargement of our capacity for community, of our ability to receive the personhood of our students. (114–15)

Becoming a student again strengthens the attitudes of humility and receptivity that are needed for listening attentively. Such listening is also central to the "clearness committee," a process growing out of the Quaker tradition. The clearness committee is used by individuals seeking insight regarding decisions in their lives. Originally used by couples contemplating marriage or by individuals entering an intentional community, it has been adapted for use by those facing other decisions such as career change or marital separation.

An individual undertaking the clearness process begins by enlisting a group of thoughtful friends from various spheres of life. He or she then concisely presents the decision to be made, listing the pros and cons of various options, and perhaps describing an intuitive sense of direction. The "clearness committee" is then invited to make observations and, most important, to *ask questions* regarding the decision. One ground rule is scrupulously observed: none of the group members is to give advice. The belief is that through posing questions from many different angles, the group enables the individual to come to a sense of "clearness" regarding the path to be taken. Often several meetings spread over time are needed to gain this clarity.

The value of this process is that it brings multiple perspectives to a decision, and it allows intuition and feelings as well as reason and expediency to influence decision-making. As an alternative to listening to the voice of the larger culture, individuals are able to "let the subject speak" from deeper sources. Clearness committees helped me make both a career decision and, later, a child-rearing decision; the same kind of listening can serve writing response groups (see Woodrow 1976 and Fischer 1988).

Listening teaching can also be promoted by a distinctive approach to classroom discussion. Too often class discussions are adversarial proceedings in which students and instructors spar or, as one of my students put it, "tear one another's ideas apart." A more receptive way of leading discussion is to encourage students to put forward ideas, not as fixed opinions, but as they are thinking them through. We can do this by asking questions and inviting elaboration through comments like: "I think I understand what you mean—could you expand on it some more?"; "What you're saying seems really important. Let me make sure I'm following you" (followed by a summary of the student's comment); "Who can build on what Alex is saying?" Such questions and comments set the tone for generous listening by creating a climate of trust that invites students to stretch intellectually as well as take risks. I am not suggesting that ideas should go unchallenged, only that our first effort should be to build on students' insights rather than "tear them apart."

Finally, a "listening teacher" provides opportunities for students to offer candid feedback about the class itself. I periodically ask students to hand in anonymous "comment cards" on which they respond to any aspect of the class they wish—be it content, assignments, class dynamics, etc. Asking students to write regularly in a collaborative class journal is another way to invite such comments. Teacher Jean Graybeal, for example, keeps a class journal on reserve in the library where students write at leisure. Another instructor asks a committee of three or four class members to meet with him regularly as liaisons between him and the class as a whole. Similarly, Jane Tompkins (1990) recommends that instructors practice what she calls "the good sex directive," believing that the most satisfying relationships require frank talk ("How was it for you?"). She exhorts teachers to "talk about the class with the class." At the beginning or end of each class, Tompkins checks in with students to see how they think it is going so that problems can be addressed before they become overwhelming (659). Whatever the format, instructors need to invite honest, anonymous responses from students regarding not just content of the class but also the emotions associated with it.

Teaching Listening

Listening teaching is just one aspect of the classroom I try to create. Just as important is teaching students themselves to listen well, to develop "connecting muscles" that will serve them in *all* their classes and in their personal lives as well. Two ways I have found useful for teaching generous listening to students are interview-based research assignments and guided journal exercises. Interview projects (specifically, oral history projects) require students to tape community or family members on a topic of interest. These are often historical topics (such as the Depression, World War II, the Civil Rights Movement, and the 1960s counterculture), but they may also be contemporary issues such as teenage runaways, gay rights, and single parenting. Other students interview adults about particular careers, in the manner of Studs Terkel's *Working*, or interview international students about American culture versus that of their home countries.

After one or more taped interviews with their person of choice, students write research papers that combine the material from the interviews with information from print sources. Sample research papers in Donald Murray's text *Write to Learn* serve as models, as does Ken Macrorie's concept of the "I-search paper." In addition to, or in place of, research papers, students may write feature stories, personality profiles, and edited oral histories, like those published by Terkel, where interviewees speak directly to readers without intervention from the writer.

Such interviews are often more challenging than students anticipate. To conduct an effective interview students need to prepare thoroughly and then to "connect" with interviewees. This means imaginatively entering the world of the interviewee, listening attentively while offering feedback, and keeping the interview on track without dominating it. To help students do this, we discuss the interviewing styles of media figures such as Bill Moyers, Barbara Walters, and Oprah Winfrey. We talk about obstacles encountered and we role play. Students conduct library research and draft and practice interview questions (see Brown 1988 and Neuenschwander 1976). I myself also conduct sample interviews, so that I have firsthand awareness of the problems students face. As my students and I grow in our interviewing skills, we grow also in our capacity for empathy and generous listening.

A second way to teach generous listening is through guided journal exercises that invite students to "enter into" or "believe in" a way of life or way of thinking that does not come naturally to them. These exercises may, of course, be assigned as reaction papers or dramatic sketches rather than as journal entries. The three types of exercises that help my students become more empathic listeners are venting, empathy, and dialogue entries.

1. *Venting entries* invite students to express strong emotions regarding the class, what they are reading, their own or other students' writing, the instructor, and so on. By encouraging students to be aware of and to express their feelings, "venting entries" make them more responsive to someone else's, whether the person be an interviewee, a character in a book, or another student (see Staton 1987). To become comfortable doing this, students may need

prompts and repeated reassurance that negative emotions will not be held against them. And I protect their privacy: entries are not shared with the class without a students' permission, and students have the option of stapling shut confidential portions of the journal (see Staton on the value of "venting" in dialogue journals).

2. *Empathy entries* are those in which students temporarily take on the identity of another person and write *as if they were that person.* In a literature course this might be a character from a novel, or in a fiction-writing course, it might be a character the student is trying to develop. They might take on, for example, the identities of Nick Adams or Nora Helmer and explore important experiences or relationships drawn from their lives. Sometimes I assign a particular type of character, while other times students create their own. Such practice in empathizing is particularly instructive when students choose characters for whom they feel little natural sympathy, such as Dr. Flint in Jacobs's "Incidents in the Life of a Slave Girl" (1990).

3. *Dialogue entries,* an approach originating with psychologist Ira Progoff (1975), are imaginary written conversations between individuals and another person or entity. A dialogue might occur between one student and another, between students and someone from their earlier lives (such as a childhood friend or a relative), a character in a book or movie, or even between two imaginary characters. The point is that students practice their ability to move between two very different points of view. First, they write as if they were one person. Then they write as if they were someone entirely different, imagining the language these persons would use, the emotions they might feel, how their minds would work. To help students write such dialogues, local actors visit my class and describe how they go about identifying with their theatrical roles.

When I think back to the adoption workshop, the honest expression of opinion and the empathic exchange among participants was as important as the information presented. Powerful learning is possible when generous listening is part of the curriculum. If we are to prepare our students for the human challenges beyond the classroom, we need to take this counsel seriously:

> For us . . . to profit from our own rich intuitive wisdom, we must cultivate [a] deeper way of knowing. We do this by learning to listen: listen to what the Quakers, for example, call "the still small voice within"; listen to the patterns, laws, and harmonies of the cosmos of which we are a part; listen with a delicate balance of a quiet meditative mind and an open loving, heart. This work of listening must be done by all of us. . . . Our service to each other must be rooted in just this work on ourselves. (Dass 1982, ix)

Part Four

Images

When reading a text, readers create images. The same text can create as many images as there are readers. Writing consists of words, not pictures. But for many individuals, the act of writing itself creates images, too.

Hildy Miller found that images occur frequently when college students write, and that these images push the writing forward. Writing is not a "virtually disembodied skill practiced in response to external rhetorical situations" but an act replete with emotions, images, and other elements of the human drama. Images arise from bodily sensations—directly and spontaneously, almost magically.

Imagery interacts with feelings, both positive and negative, and this interaction plays a complex role in the writing process. In a study of underprepared college writers Kristie Fleckenstein found a positive correlation between high imagers and high engagement with their texts. For those classified as low imagers and low engagers, however, the correlation between imagery and engagement was negative. Fleckenstein suggests that high engagement is correlated with self-sponsored writing.

In view of the unpredictable nature of images, the question arises as to whether individuals can consciously improve their ability to visualize. Researcher Demetrice Worley devised exercises involving three kinds of visualization—perceptual, mental, and graphic—and taught them to students enrolled in technical writing classes. She found that those students performed significantly better than untrained students in using details, in applying overall problem-solving strategies, and in the overall quality of writing.

Image improves writing, sharpens it. When detail weaves in and out of the printed page, when image and word work together in a text, writing takes on richness and texture, rhythm and scene.

10

Sites of Inspiration
Where Writing Is Embodied in Image and Emotion

Hildy Miller

> Close your eyes and don't let yourself write down any words until you can actually see and hear and touch what you are writing about.
>
> To hell with words, see something.
>
> Elbow, 1981

Such practical advice suggests that emotion and image are processes through which writers actually experience their ideas. Even the most ordinary piece of writing is often produced by dynamic processes in which writers react to emerging text subjectively and physically. Thoughts feel inspired when they are embodied and animated at cognitive levels so fleeting that they are often inaccessible to study. Historically, this quality of writing stems from the long-standing but suppressed tradition of rhetoric as magic (Romilly 1975), driven by "divinely inspired enchantment," "unreason," or "irrational disruption."

More recently, philosophers, linguists, and critical theorists have focused on ways in which language is grounded in bodily experience. In most accounts, ideas are said to spring from immediate perceptions, then extend metaphorically until their figurative qualities are concealed by an apparent abstractness (Barfield 1928; Cassirer 1946;

Johnson 1987; Lakoff 1987; Langer 1957). For example, a compara-
tively neutral expression such as "I suppressed my anger" is really a
vestigial representation of underlying physiological reactions to anger
that include heat, agitation, and internal pressure (Lakoff 1987, 385).
Metaphorically, anger is envisioned as a hot fluid for which the body
acts as a container. Thus, anger that is "suppressed" will not "boil
over." As a result of linguistic transformation in which that which is
concrete becomes abstract, much of the color in language is effectively "whited out" (Derrida 1974). Yet these rich layers, drenched
with emotion and image, persist in thought as linguistic substrata,
sites of inspiration for writers.

Those composition specialists who follow the expressivist tradition wherein elements of rhetoric as magic are preserved (Berthoff
1981; Elbow 1981; Murray 1978; Rico 1983) have emphasized this
locus of inspiration rather than that of techne, wherein writing skills
are acquired and displayed. Some encourage writers to access this
magical site by having them intentionally regress into concrete and
experiential ways of thinking. Such a process is necessary because in
both our individual and cultural development, a split between concrete experience and abstract thought widens over time. For many of
us the realms of the abstract and concrete are so dichotomized that to
bridge the gap means we must strive to recover experiential awareness. As Elbow has said:

> For the magic used to be there. It was there for earlier societies and
> for each of us as children. Words were once connected in a more pri-
> mary way with experience or things. (1981, 359)

In the same vein French feminists Cixous and Clement (1975/1986)
as well as Kristeva (1979/1981) note the suppression of experiential
substrata by phallocentric traditions of thought. Their refrain to "write
the body" in order to recover "jouissance" or joy in writing suggests a
similar process of regression that allows us to rediscover sites of bodily pleasure in language. For many expressivists and feminists, then, it
is not simply a matter of gaining access to experiential substrata but
of recovering somatically that lost access.

Other theorists assume that considerable vestiges are still in place
and readily available to writers. In experiential substrata we can
already be said to "write the body" from the site that Johnson (1987)
refers to as the "body in the mind." The ruminative language of this
inner realm is traditionally set in opposition to the presentational form
of final texts. As typically characterized, this language is "the associative, idiosyncratic, self-referential language that writers use to talk
to themselves," unlike the "autonomous texts that supply the interpretive contexts, logical connections, and explicit meanings readers

expect of public discourse" (Trimbur 1987, 211). At this experiential site where inner thought takes place, emotions and images have somatic connections. Sondra Perl has described the writing processes located here in terms of Gendlin's "felt sense":

> When writers are given a topic, the topic itself evokes a felt sense in them. This topic calls forth images, words, ideas, and vague fuzzy feelings that are anchored in the writer's body. . . . When writers pause, when they go back and repeat key words, what they seem to be doing is waiting, paying attention to what is still vague and unclear. They are looking to their felt experience, and waiting for an image, a word, or a phrase to emerge that captures the sense they embody. (1980, 365)

Still, though such processes have been theorized, we seldom see glimpses of them as they engage writers. In the past work on cognitive processes in writing has generally focused on what is verbal, easily articulated, and most directly converted into text. Many theorists have assumed, as Flower and Hayes once declared, that words were "where most of the work gets done. . . ." (1984, 124). It was Flower and Hayes, however, who noticed so many figurative schemata appearing in their protocol data that they felt compelled at one point to illustrate some of the recurring images in writers' thoughts. In accounting for experiential representations, they commented:

> Concepts—the power and glory of verbal thought and the hallmarks of precise analytical prose—are themselves abstractions, often mentally represented by generalized prototypes . . . by image, by buried metaphors, or by schemata. (142)

Even so, we have few descriptions of these processes at work. What little research is available on emotion in writing has also focused on the way it helps engage writers with their material. Generally, writers experience fluctuating emotions throughout a writing task, which result in bodily sensations (Brand and Powell 1986, Brand 1989a; McLeod 1987). Some emotions such as boredom inhibit writing (Brand 1989a), while other emotions such as enjoyment generate and sustain writing (Brand 1989a; Larson 1985; McLeod 1987, 1991). Positive emotion, generally conducive to writing, has been associated with a variety of factors, including whether the writing task is interesting (Brand 1989a), whether it is school- or self-sponsored, and whether the writer is skilled (Brand 1987). Yet much of this work has focused on identifying emotions connected with attitudes toward particular writing tasks and toward writing in general. As Brand has pointed out, we have seen few glimpses of the role of emotion where ideas are generated in experiential substrata:

What composition research really needs is an account of how much was lost in a protocol, through data reduction, where it occurred, and what it was. Such an account would undoubtedly include a lot of grunts and groans. But it would also reveal imagistic and free associative thinking and connotative commentary. This is precisely where differences in cognitive style and personality may be observed. This is where emotions happen. Without that information, can we really say that we have an accurate description of the mental activities that underlie writing? (1987, 439-40)

Thus far, a clear view of suppressed magical sources of inspiration in writing has been largely obscured.

In my study I try to illuminate this experiential realm in writers by providing examples of ways that images—hidden or not—inspire writers emotionally: interest them, motivate them, sustain and disrupt their work, lead to private purposes and private approaches to rhetorical situations. Writing is embodied in many ways for these writers: ideas are bodied forth as images; writers see themselves and others as projected bodily into imagined, remembered, or current rhetorical situations; and writers reveal a range of bodily sensations stimulated by their writing. This is what "writing the body" may actually look like.

Method

Participating in the study were 148 upper and lower division students enrolled at a large midwestern university in writing courses in business, science, social sciences, the technical fields, and the humanities. The study was organized in two stages: In the first part students produced writing samples during which they were stopped three times and asked to fill out written "thought-sample" questionnaires, after which they completed a "post-sample" questionnaire. In the second part representative students were interviewed.

Part I

First, students were trained to provide accurate verbal reports. Then they wrote for forty-five minutes about how they learn best. Throughout the writing task they were interrupted three times at intervals approximately eleven to thirteen minutes apart and asked to complete written thought-sample questionnaires. Based on standard techniques for image assessment (Sheehan, Ashton, and White 1983), scaled questions identified dimensions of imagery such as vividness and detail, and two narrative questions captured the overall image (A: "What was the last thought you had in your mind just before you

were interrupted? Be as detailed and accurate as you can; work back-
wards to other thoughts if you want to." B: "What, if any, connections
do you think the thought had to your piece of writing?").

So that I could compare reported thought with text, writers
were also asked to mark the places in their texts at which they had
been interrupted. After completing the writing samples, students
reflected on their processes on a post-sample questionnaire. One
item on the questionnaire determined the role of image in larger
rhetorical aims ("Were there any ideas that really stood out for you
as you wrote? What were they? Were they mostly in the form of
words or images?").

The thought-sampling method should be explained. It is a self-
report technique for capturing near concurrent thought with minimal
interference. While writing, subjects respond to a prompt by stopping writing, immediately completing a written questionnaire reporting the last few seconds of thought, and then resuming writing.
Thought sampling has been used extensively to study mental images
(Anderson 1981; Klinger 1978), particularly by Eric Klinger whose
instruments and procedures have been adapted here. In composition
studies think-aloud protocols have been used more often to study cognitive processes (Flower and Hayes 1981). Yet, as ongoing oral
reports of thought, their narrative structure makes them less likely to
capture imagistic thought, especially the simultaneous mix of nonverbal and verbal thought. Thus, as a method, written thought samples
are better suited for capturing glimpses of image and emotion in writers' thoughts.

Part II

Twenty-nine writers were interviewed within two weeks of the writing session, after being selected by type and amount of imagistic
activity reported on their questionnaires. The standardized interviews
were extensive, lasting about 1 1/2 hours each, with identical questions asked of all writers, including their writing history, general attitudes and habits, samples of their writing, and thought-sample and
post-sample questionnaire responses. The questionnaire served to
ground the retrospective accounts for accuracy (Tomlinson 1984).

Images and Emotions in Writing Processes

Overall, images were plentiful in participants' thoughts throughout
writing: While in approximately half the written thought samples,
thinking occurred mostly in words, in nearly one-fourth, thinking was
mostly in images. In an additional fourth, thinking occurred both in

Figure 1
Types of Thoughts at Interruption

Thoughts (n = 444)	TS 1	TS 2	TS 3	Mean
1. Mostly words	71 (48.0)	66 (44.6)	74 (50.0)	70.3 (50.2)
2. Mostly images	31 (20.9)	38 (25.7)	32 (21.6)	33.7 (22.7)
3. Both at same time	44 (29.7)	42 (28.4)	35 (23.6)	40.3 (27.2)
4. Can't remember	2 (1.4)	2 (1.4)	6 (4.1)	3.0 (2.3)
5. Indeterminate	—	—	1 (0.7)	—

Note. The three thought samples are referred to as TS1, TS2, TS3. The values in each vertical column represent frequencies of types of thoughts with equivalent percentages indicated in parentheses.

words and images. The table in Figure 1 details the types of thoughts captured during the three thought-sample interruptions (abbreviated as TS1, TS2, and TS3).

As shown in the table, in fully half the random thought samples, some visual activity was reported. Finding so many images in expository writing processes is perhaps surprising, given our emphasis on verbal data. However, this result is consistent with the number of images found when daily thoughts are sampled (Klinger 1978). The sheer quantity of images captured by the thought samples suggests that the visual dimension in writing is more important than we have believed. Moreover, forty-one percent of all the images reported in the written thought samples did not appear in corresponding places in texts where the writers were interrupted. Thus, a significant amount of generative imagistic processes exposed by the thought samples remain hidden from view.

Images also varied throughout the writing sample. The table shows overall image use peaking midway through writing, increasing nearly five percent at the second thought sample (TS2) before dropping back to its former level[1]. Such an increase suggests that, as writers warmed to their task, thinking became increasingly imagistic. While some images appeared hazy and sketchy, others were strikingly vivid and intense. In nearly two-thirds of the written thought samples students reported some degree of detail, while in about one-third, images seemed vague. Participants confirmed in interviews that at particular points in writing, they experienced a succession of images, with individual images changing from detailed to vague as new images arose to replace them. A closer look at specific images and emotions suggests ways that they embody ideas and inspire writers.

Images and Interests

Writers often dramatize ideas when they are either especially interested or trying to muster some interest in a topic. Ideas can be quite literally embodied as characters in a dramatic rhetorical situation. One student, Gena, explained her imaging processes: "It inspires me. It's a way of making sense, making it concrete. If I can see it in my mind, it makes it interesting. If I didn't have it, I wouldn't write as creatively. Something about them triggers something." Bette commented: "Writing comes alive. . . . I think that I don't like the subject. Then if I start to get some images, I start to like the subject." Other students recounted specific instances of dramatizing material, stressing always the rhetorical need this process fulfilled. They felt they had to experience what they were writing about, even though the images and emotions might never actually appear in their texts. Mark, for example, described how he actually pictured Michelangelo as he wrote about the artist: "I had to have an image of him doing something before I could say, 'He did this.'" While Mark focused on one character, Cindy, in writing about the Chicago Seven trial, had to imagine the entire shifting courtroom scene: ". . . what the trial looked like, the people, and the characters they were, how they talked and carried themselves."

In this study many participants reported such dramatizations in written thought samples. A typical image occurred when Gregg was interrupted:

> Again I was about to make a point about the seemingly useless nature of a learning experience. I was visualizing an exam from the

[1]The tendency demonstrated here parallels the hill and valley pattern that Brand ("Composing Styles" 1989b) found when tapping particular emotions during composing. In both studies image and emotion peaked as writers presumably became more engaged in the task, then decreased thereafter.

class in order to write an example of how far removed from real life
the material was.

The detailed image was a fairly simple depiction of his idea about
learning. Other dramatizations, however, varied in complexity, with
the most elaborate and detailed representations consisting of multiple
minidramas that played out simultaneously. As such examples suggest, mental images seldom take the form of static snapshots but are
more often characterized by ongoing activity.

   We have long suspected that writers probably use images to
imagine themselves and their audiences in actual rhetorical situations
(Flower and Hayes 1984; Murray 1978). Indeed, some students in
this study were caught during written thought samples seeing themselves making a convincing point or speculating on audience reactions. But, given the current emphasis in composition studies on
social context, we might expect to find more of these immediate
rhetorical concerns manifested visually. Instead, writers were more
likely to dramatize the material itself, thereby engaging themselves
emotionally with embodied ideas.

Controlling Images and Interests

While the students visualized several thoughts throughout writing,
one or more ideas were often most compelling. In a post-sample question, the students were asked to reflect on what ideas stood out for
them, and to indicate whether they were mostly images or words. We
usually assume that a key idea for an essay would be a conventional
thesis in words. Yet only ten percent named a thought in words that
could be identified as their thesis. Key ideas occurred in images over
half the time (51.4 percent), with ideas in both words and images
adding another 10.1 percent. What often interested students most,
then, were imagistic thoughts not readily apparent from the abstract
ideas presented in their texts.

   Some underlying images functioned as both source and sustainer.
Memorable experiences in students' schooling, for example, seemed
to contain the essence of what they were currently expressing. In two
typical responses, though the incidents were never actually described
in the texts, the thought-sample responses showed writers imagining
the scene of their original insight. From Doug:

> What kept going through my mind was a composition class taught
> by Dr. Okray in Wisconsin. He was more organized and deliberate
> in his presentations than any Professor I've had since. But at the
> time I didn't realize this! I was trying to think of what he did that
> was so special.

From Eric:

> I kept seeing an image of my sister-in-law who has a Ph.D and our conversations about the failing of most colleges to consider practical experiences important as compared to theory in most every discipline taught.

During interviews students commented that such images recurred—as if returning them physically to the initial jolt of insight and then sustaining their purpose throughout writing.

Recurring images seem to motivate writers to discover a private sense of purpose apart from the extrinsic purpose of the task itself. The strongest writers, in fact, are often those who can retain ownership of their work by developing their own motives for writing (Miller and Ashcroft, in press). Motivation, in general, is far more powerful when it is generated intrinsically rather than extrinsically (Atkinson 1977; Murray 1964). Yet, as this study shows, such purposes are not always evident from the task or text but more often are bodied forth as covert controlling images.

Images, Emotions, and Current Concerns

In some cases, thought samples revealed that what drove an essay was an image underlying a significant personal problem. By working out issues often tangential to the topic, the rhetorical situation became therapeutic. For instance, Beth, was enraged throughout her essay, as she admitted in a post-sample response:

> I really don't have much organization, because I started to get angry when I was writing and the next thing I knew my pen couldn't stop.

Indeed, in her text she ranted about unnecessary courses, the pressure of grades, and the dim prospects of succeeding in her profession. At one point she even grimly predicted that she might remain a waitress all her life. It was, in fact, this image that she identified as her key idea:

> Yes, the idea of making money kept popping in my head. I saw visions of me 50 years old and waiting on tables.

Her negative feelings about this idea in fact inspired her purpose for writing, namely, to protest educational injustices.

Whereas Beth's anger was evident throughout her text, Rick's problems were well concealed. He indicated in a post-sample question that while writing he saw recurring images related to a recent breakup with his girlfriend:

> I kept thinking about my girlfriend and how I don't remember things
> she says—and how we fight on this subject.

After completing his essay, Rick reported feeling relieved because
the writing task helped him come to terms with the failed relationship.
Yet only a trace of this private purpose surfaced in his text.

Cases like these show how, for some writers, the extrinsic purpose of writing can be subverted successfully into ways to resolve
intensely personal problems (Brand 1980, 1985). Yet images and
emotions engendered by such thoughts may be almost completely
concealed. Studies of imaging activity in everyday thought have
shown people often preoccupied with visualizing their current concerns (Klinger 1978). Thus, it is not surprising that images and emotions around personal problems would also emerge during writing.

Fluctuating Images and Interests

Sometimes interest peaked with other emotions and images elicited
by issues raised in the essay. Mark was stopped while referring briefly
to a boring biology class he once took. When interviewed, he commented that he had found himself beset with a visual "flood of all the
confusion and anxiety" associated with that time of his life. In a written thought sample he reported:

> I had the image of this awkward man trying to communicate difficult
> ideas to generally apathetic freshmen. I also saw myself walking
> around the campus trying to figure out what the hell was going
> on. . . . Images of confusion kept coming in.

Mark, seeking strong feelings as he worked, seemed able to manage
the discomfort evoked by the images. Other students, like Michelle,
found these extraneous images and emotions distracting. She commented on a post-sample question:

> As I was writing—I saw repeated images from high school and
> junior high—flashbacks which distracted me—I therefore could not
> obtain clear, concise thoughts.

While Michelle struggled to concentrate, Andrew, in contrast, became
most animated at the point at which he expressed his key idea. In his
post-sample response he revealed the pleasant associations that
engaged him:

> The thing that stood out most was my intro about my grade school
> comic writing. I had some vivid pictures of some of my old friends
> laughing.

Indeed, he opened his essay with a humorous story about grade school
before moving on to education. Both image and interest levels
dropped off thereafter.

Recalling an instructor during her first thought sample, Stacey got so carried away that she wound up refocusing her whole piece in order to reflect on what she had learned about hard work. But her ideas were visual and emotional, as indicated by her thought sample: "I was thinking about my dance teacher in high school and how wonderful she was." Not surprisingly, in her post-sample response it was the images and emotions about the dance instructor that proved most significant:

> My dance teacher's image really stood out. I could picture my classes, times we spent together, and certain things she said to me. I think I'll write her a letter tonight.

In fact during the interview she remembered feeling so strongly that she laughed aloud and right then resolved to contact the instructor.

Fluctuating emotions that students experience at visually and emotionally charged moments may account for some unevenness of their texts. Students go off on private emotional tangents that seem to overtake their papers, or they produce pieces of writing alternately enervated and energetic. The ability to generate positive emotions, so important to successful writing (Brand and Powell 1986; Larson 1985), can stem from underlying images that are personally meaningful.

Overwhelming Emotions and Images

In a few cases images and emotions became overwhelming; students re-experienced intense feelings that actually induced bodily sensations. David, a student able to hold intricately detailed images in mind, recounted such an incident when writing about mountain climbing. Though the paper was organized as an instruction manual for climbing, he recalled that while writing it he began involuntarily visualizing a particular climb during which he became ill. To his surprise, he found himself again feeling so nauseated and lightheaded he had to stop writing.

Not all writers respond to such strong sensations the same way. Those inclined to seek out emotion as they write enjoy bodily reactions, while others who prefer to remain detached find such responses disturbing. Two students in the study were among those sampled at these moments. Ellen, a highly imaginative writer, sought out the stimulation of emotion and image as she worked. During one thought-sample interruption, she visualized an incident that had left her feeling alienated and misunderstood:

> I was thinking about the physical and mental feelings I had experienced when the professor mentioned 'the real world.'

As an older student she felt nowhere near as naive as his remark implied she was. Later in our interview she stated that at the time of the interruption, she had literally re-experienced the physical shock she had felt in the original situation. While such feelings were not particularly pleasant, she enjoyed these moments best since it made writing "come alive" for her. Christine, on the other hand, was a controlled writer who avoided emotion but continually visualized elaborate outlines as she worked. She typically wrote methodically from her plan, allowing nothing to disturb her. Yet, during her second thought sample she visualized a time that a friend was unfairly expelled from class:

> I was picturing the day a fellow student was kicked out of lectures for disagreeing with the professor.

Later she commented, "The image brought back all of the resentment and shock I had felt at the time." As a result of this sudden disturbing emotion, she found to her dismay that her visual outline was completely obliterated.

Writers so extraordinarily sensitive to image may be called "high imagers," individuals distinguished by their ability to create and react to mental images (Katz 1983). Certainly, not all participants registered this degree of sensitivity. But such examples suggest the spectrum of emotions stimulated by imaging during writing, ranging from mild interest to bodily reactions of shock or illness.

Writing the Body

Recent studies of writing have emphasized its most tangible features, that is, writing as a virtually disembodied skill practiced in response to external rhetorical situations. Yet, the glimpses of experiential thought processes uncovered here indicate that what is most compelling is both created and nourished in embodied ideas. Such findings suggest that we need to reconsider and perhaps retheorize the magic of embodied processes at work.

In addition to systematic models of image and emotion, we need richer descriptions that take into account individual differences in imaging ability, writing ability, and emotionality. As instructors, we need to encourage students to become aware of the imagistic-emotional components of writing. At the same time, writers need to learn how to manage the sometimes unmanageable jumble of images and emotion—to use them, enjoy them—but not be overwhelmed by them. For writing is a physical activity, located not just in motor movements with keyboard or pen, but in the bodily experience of our thoughts.

11

Mental Imagery,
Text Engagement,
and Underprepared Writers

Kristie S. Fleckenstein

While few writers enjoy anxiety-free or problem-free composing, many experience compensating moments of text engagement: a sense of immersion with their evolving meaning when they are absorbed emotionally and intellectually by what they are creating. In a study of such pleasure pursuits as music composing, chess playing, and rock climbing, Csikszentmihalyi (1975) defines these moments of absorption as *flow*, "the wholistic sensation present when we act with total involvement" (43). During flow, actions and decisions proceed as if guided by an internal if not unconscious logic, where our sense of self and "outside" environment disappears into the activity. For writers, flow manifests itself in the moments when their texts seem to create themselves.

Like all writers, underprepared writers must also contend with anxiety and frustration. But the composing of basic writers is more acutely fraught with such difficulties as anxiety (Reigstad 1985), truncated analytical thinking (Petrie 1976), and sporadic progress (Shaughnessy 1977). Moreover, these frustrations are rarely balanced by compensating moments of engagement.

These limited instances of text engagement hold serious implications for the improvement of underprepared writers. Text engagement indicates that writers have committed themselves to their evolv-

Support for this study was provided by a research grant from the School of Liberal Arts and Sciences, Purdue University Calumet.

ing meaning and to their readers. Such commitment contributes to student discovery of writing as a fruitful enterprise. However, without these compensating experiences of flow, the transition from reluctant underprepared writer to involved and proficient writer is more difficult to effect. To help students develop such commitment, we must first understand the phenomenon of text engagement. This study examines one aspect of text flow by investigating a correlation between the ability of underprepared writers to evoke vivid mental images and to engage with their evolving meaning.

Throughout *Flow: The Psychology of Optimal Experience,* Csikszentmihalyi (1990) only indirectly connects mental imagery, flow, and the pleasures of thinking. But researchers in related disciplines have more directly connected imagery to two factors—goals and emotions—that Csikszentmihalyi specifically cites as important elements of any experience of flow. For instance, work in linguistics (Beaugrande 1984), psychology (Paivio 1989), and composition (Flower and Hayes 1984) suggests that goals and imagery may function in tandem. Goals, both in writing and in life, are frequently envisioned imagistically. Imagery also functions as an anchor for ideas, for plans (Flower and Hayes 1984), for information from disparate forms of knowledge (Bartlett 1932; Paivio 1989), and as a means by which a variety of ideas and emotions can be held (Sadoski 1983).

Goals and images also embrace a powerful emotional element, a central property of flow (Csikszentmihalyi 1990). First, Beaugrande (1984) hypothesizes a strong link between the formulation of goals and emotion. Writers construct and evaluate their goals according to the desirability (physiological, emotional, social, and personality-based) of the goal state (107). Second, imagery has been connected to the evocation of emotion (Aylwin 1985). Third, work with text engagement in reading highlights the role of imagery in emotional involvement (Sadoski 1983; Sadoski, Goetz, and Kangiser 1988).

Finally, the limited research on text engagement among students in regular composition courses suggests that the ability to incorporate personal goals (Langston 1989) and to create vivid mental images (Fleckenstein 1991b) contributes to flow. These factors may also contribute to the text engagement of basic writers, given the similar ways in which all writers organize their composing processes (Perl 1979).

Project Design

To test this connection, I examined the writing engagement and imaging abilities of students enrolled in a basic writing program. The study involved two days of testing of eighty-two student volunteers, all of whom were enrolled in a writing course designed for underprepared writers.[1] On the first day of the study, students completed a five-item questionnaire soliciting information about their writing history. They also completed Sheehan's (1967) shortened version of Bett's (1909) Questionnaire Upon Mental Imagery (QMI). The QMI is a thirty-five–item form requiring subjects to assess their ability to evoke seven types of mental images (visual, auditory, cutaneous, kinesthetic, gustatory, olfactory, and organic). Students created images in response to written prompts and rated the vividness of those images according to a seven-point scale (with one as most vivid and seven as no images present at all).

The second day of the study was scheduled approximately six weeks after the first day to ensure that the students were not unduly influenced by the prior completion of the imagery questionnaires. At this point students produced a personal journal entry in response to the following prompt: "Write about something that has recently pleased or disturbed you." Previous research (Fleckenstein 1991b) indicates that expressive writing, as defined by Britton, et al. (1975), offers greater opportunity for text engagement than does more public transactional writing. After students completed their entries, they reread their text and informally wrote down what they were thinking as they composed.

Results

The writing-habits questionnaires were examined for three factors: evidence of self-sponsored writing, types of self-sponsored writing, and type of subject matter. Types of self-sponsored writing fell into two categories: expressive (personal letters, journals) and poetic (poetry, song lyrics, short stories, etc.) as defined by Britton, et al. (1975). Details of subject matter were examined for explicit reference to emotion (Example: "I write about my true feelings") and/or implicit references to imagery (spatial, scenario descriptions, concrete analogies, visually metaphoric language, etc.). Informal retrospective reports were examined for explicit references to emotion and imagery.

Scores for the QMI were computed. Composite scores were tallied and means calculated for all imagery tasks with separate totals for visual and kinesthetic imagery tasks. Students with scores below the mean were classified as high imagers, those above the mean as low imagers. The decision to examine visual and kinesthetic imagery sep-

---

[1]Students were registered in English 020, Fundamentals of Composition, on the basis of a composite score, made up of class rank, SAT scores, and types of classes taken in high school. When composite scores were unavailable, in the case of returning students, an English placement score from the Test of Standard Written English was used.

arately was based on research indicating the strong relationships between visual imagery and emotion and between kinesthetic imagery and emotion (Aylwin 1985).

The degree of text engagement was determined by examining the students' writing samples according to five criteria based on Berlyne's (1960) work on emotional intensity. In *Conflict, Arousal, and Curiosity,* Berlyne contends that the intensity of an affective response or engagement is determined by five characteristics of an individual's situation: conflict, intensity, incongruity, complexity, and uncertainty.

Conflict, the principal source of emotion, occurs when we want to respond in different ways to the same event. Intensity, or the level of unexpectedness, occurs when we react to an event by preparing a response to what we expect will ensue; then, something unexpected intervenes. Incongruity occurs when an event leads us to an expectation that is subsequently unfulfilled. Complexity depends on the amount of diversity we perceive in a situation. And, finally, uncertainty occurs when possible events each have an equal chance of materializing (or not materializing). According to Berlyne (1960), the more these variables play into a situation, the greater our emotional intensity is.

Three readers examined the writing samples for evidence of these five characteristics and judged the degree of engagement according to a five-point scale (1—high engagement, 5—low to no engagement). Students scoring below the mean were identified as high engagers, those above the mean as low engagers, with interrater agreement at eighty-nine percent.

Imagery and engagement scores were analyzed in two ways. First, the data were examined among high and low engagers for correlations between engagement, QMI composite scores, visual imagery and kinesthetic imagery. Second, the data were examined among high and low engagers and high/low QMI, visual scores, and kinesthetic scores.

Links Between Engagement, Emotion, and Imagery

Results of the various analyses indicated both positive and negative relationships between the degree of text engagement and the degree of imagery vividness. First, data provided by the writing-habits questionnaire and retrospective reports tended to reinforce the raters' assessment of writing engagement. For instance, there was a statistical trend among students classified as high engagers to pursue some frequent and regular form of self-sponsored writing, usually personal letters (see also Brand 1989a). Eighty-two percent of the high engagers stated that they wrote voluntarily and frequently (weekly to bi-weekly). On the other hand, sixty-seven percent of all students who said they pursued no voluntary writing produced text classified as low engagement. This parallel indicates that basic writers with difficulty experiencing writing flow avoid writing whenever possible.

Based on the writing-history questionnaire, the relationship between imagery, emotion, and engagement was positive among high engagers. They tended to write about emotionally-based or imagery-based subject matter. As one student redundantly noted, he wrote "because of the emotional feelings I felt."[2] Another high engager also identified as a high imager described an amusing experience, concluding with the comment that "while I wrote this I could see it just like it was happening." High engagers also cited a repeated reliance on feelings and interests as the motivation for and the subject matter of self-sponsored writing (see also Brand 1989a).

Imagery appeared to play an important role in the subject matter of regular self-sponsored writing. Many of these underprepared writers said that they frequently described their daily lives, experiences, and events in their personal letters and solicited such descriptions in return. Aylwin (1985) and Paivio (1989) contend that such descriptions are reconstructed by means of static and active imagistic representations that include several modalities.

Retrospective reports again support the tentative correlation between imagery and engagement among some of the writers. For example, one high engager and high imager used imagery to project a picture of his future success on a math test in order to comfort himself about a recent failure. Others explained that as they described various experiences, usually unhappy ones, they evoked fragmentary pictures that accompanied reanimated emotions.

In addition, high engagers and high imagers consistently elaborated their retrospective reports. Besides adding details not present in the original text, these students analyzed the motivations of the "participants" in their original text. As they explained what they were feeling or thinking when writing, they also explained why (linguistically cued by "because") they acted as they did, why their "participants" acted as they did, even why they chose to write about that particular subject. On the other hand, low imagers and engagers tended merely to repeat their original entry, sometimes literally saying "same as above" throughout the report. Such elaborations suggest that writing a retrospective report, a process with which most of the students were unfamiliar, was used as an occasion to engage meaning.

The statistical analyses also found that imagery for students identified as high imagers might be associated with increased

---

[2]Spelling and punctuation have been regularized for all excerpts from the respective reports and writing-habits questionnaires.

instances of text engagement. A positive, statistically suggestive correlation was found between visual imagery (p=.06), kinesthetic imagery (p=.07), and high engagement. Thus, for writers evoking vivid mental imagery, levels of text engagement increased with levels of vividness.

On the other hand, for writers classified as low engagers and low imagers, the correlation between imagery and engagement was negative. Regardless of modality, as the degree of imagery increased, the degree of engagement decreased. This negative correlation was especially significant (p=.003) for the composite score on the Questionnaire of Mental Imagery, which measured imagery vividness in seven modalities. As students' mental representations gained depth through a range of senses, their engagement with their text decreased sharply. A similar relationship between visual (p=.010) and kinesthetic (p=.07) imagery and engagement underscored this negative correlation. These almost contradictory results suggest that mental imagery can correlate both negatively and positively to text engagement, depending on the writer. Three reasons for these paradoxical relationships suggest themselves.

First, the strong emotion evoked by especially vivid mental images may overwhelm the writing processes for underprepared writers. The very act of writing may intensify writers' emotions to the point where they are unable to continue (see Yerkes and Dodson 1908). Psychologists Gordon Bower (1981) and Dolf Zillman (1988) confirm that stimuli can reinforce or modify a person's mood. Exposure to a sad movie or a sad book can reinforce an individual's sad mood. On the other hand, exposure to a happy movie or happy book may change the viewer's or reader's sad mood. Likewise, writing about an agitating incident may reinforce an unpleasant emotion to the extent of disrupting the composing process. Just as people in highly agitated states tend to choose stimuli that relieve the unpleasant mood, writers would also stop writing as a means of controlling unpleasant feelings. One student in her retrospective report noted that she recalled "the pain and tears" to the point that writing made her "feel hostile." She just didn't want to "think about it anymore," she explained.

In the same vein, the evoked imagery may distract basic writers from the writing process by pulling them into daydreams, thereby dividing their attention and mental resources. This seems more frequent when the image is a pleasant one. Daydreaming about a pleasant experience is one way of reinforcing that enjoyable sensation without the distraction of verbal expression. In explaining a very short entry about a pleasant memory, one student wrote that "every now and then I would daydream in class about winning the gold medal," suggesting that he may have been happily engaged in just such a daydream.

Second, basic writers fear revealing too much of themselves in their writing. As one student responded to her questionnaire, "I feel myself tightening up when I have to write for someone else,—especially a teacher." Personal revelations add to writers' sense of vulnerability. Mental images are intensely personal, especially those that simultaneously evoke deeply felt emotions. Thus, to protect against such self-disclosure underprepared writers may transform into language as little of the image and emotion as possible. Beaugrande (1984) claims that a variety of affective factors can adversely affect the composition process, and fear is one powerful factor.

Third, the difficulty of mapping images on to linguistic structures (Beaugrande 1984; Flower and Hayes 1984) may be overwhelming, especially to those uncomfortable with the writing process in the first place. Although Allan Paivio (1989) in his dual coding theory posits the transformation of imagistically encoded into linguistically encoded information, the process can be particularly difficult. The layered nature of imagery (Paivio 1989) prevents an easy transformation into the sequential, linear form of language.

Imagery and Teaching Writing

For these eighty-two underprepared writers engagement and imagery exist in complex interaction. According to their anecdotal accounts, incidents of self-sponsored writing are related to clearly imagined and highly emotional evocations. The same data suggest that the ability to engage with one's evolving meaning is also connected to the frequency of voluntary writing. Statistical analyses indicate that students identified as high imagers experience text engagement to a greater degree than those writers assessed as low imagers. In fact, vivid imagery may relate adversely to text engagement, perhaps contributing to a kind of writer's block.

The double-edged nature of this relationship also suggests that we proceed cautiously in our research and our teaching. While underlining the importance of feelings and internal visions to text engagement, this study leaves us with an array of questions. For instance, how might we use mental imagery to enhance our students' writing fluency and confidence? Given the concrete and layered nature of imagery (Paivio 1989), could imagery serve as the basis of assignment making? Or could images in a variety of senses serve as an invention strategy, perhaps brainstorming images instead of ideas? Also, how might imagery contribute to our students' concept of audience? Haas and Flower (1988) contend that more proficient readers construct rhetorical scenarios in which reader, writer, and others participate in conversations cued by ideas in the text. Might underprepared writers find valuable the creation of similar scenarios with peers, instructors, tutors, and intended readers?

But as we ask these questions about the potential of imagery, this study also demonstrates that we must ask questions about its limitations. Susan Aylwin (1985) contends that we represent knowledge in three distinct ways: linguistically, visually, and enactively. Each person has a preferred mode of representation. If so, would requiring our students to use visual or enactive imagery prove detrimental to linguistically-oriented students? Or would underprepared writers have difficulty moving between linguistic and imagistic representations? Given preferred modes of representation, how might imagery interfere with invention, reader-based revising, even engagement itself?

At this point we are left questions, not answers. But the questions suggest the contribution that studies of imagery might make to our teaching and understanding of writing, especially the exhilarating experience of text engagement.

12

Visual Imagery Training and College Writing Students

Demetrice A. Worley

Writing instructors have been challenged by psychologists and composition specialists to develop their students' analytical or and holistic abilities (Weis 1983). Jerome S. Bruner (1962) advocates instruction that combines writing strategies with inspiration (23). However, rarely do these specialists provide information on *how* students' analytical abilities work with those holistic abilities. Nor do they provide specific "creative" pedagogies in the academic writing class.

One way in which writing instructors develop students' analytical and visual abilities is through visual/verbal exercises. However, when some of us think of visual imagery[1] in the writing classroom, we think only of the mapping strategies associated with inventing. Moreover, research on students' imaging abilities tend to focus on how they use external images, not their own mental images. Combining the process of selecting and/or creating visual images with translating those images into text draws on both students' analytical and creative abilities. Developing these abilities allows students to fortify their critical thinking with creative and intuitive insights. In addition, students learn to analyze their images and uncover the reasons they created them. Ann Berthoff (1983) maintains that when students improve their abilities to act on their visual images, they also develop their natural abilities to generate text (194).

Let me start with some definitions. An image is a sign, picture, or symbol that can be represented mentally or on paper, chalkboard,

[1]Students' imaging abilities are not limited to visual imagery but include auditory imagery, tactile imagery, and pictorial imagery—which students also have at their disposal while composing.

computer, and so on. As used here, visual imagery (visualization) is defined as mental projections created in the absence of appropriate visual stimuli (Kosslyn 1985, 24). These mental projections share many of the properties of physical objects or pictures of them. These images "may act as if they were actual, rigid spatial objects that can be looked at, manipulated and touched" (Kosslyn 1985, 24). As a result, after individuals construct a mental image, they draw on voluntary or involuntary perceptual skills to scan the mental image. Furthermore, the term, visual thinking, refers to how and when images are used. Visual thinking parallels all the processes associated with verbal cognition: "active exploration, selection, grasping of essentials, simplification, problem-solving, as well as combining, separating, putting in context" (Arnheim 1969, 13). The ability to create images that simulate situations or act as symbols allows us to envision familiar things in new combinations so as to see how they would interact and to use the image as a notation, a visual aid to abstract thinking" (Kosslyn 1985, 178–79).

Visual Imagery Study

I investigated the effects of visual imagery training on the use of details, on problem-solving strategies, and on overall writing quality of thirty-six college students. A quasi-experimental study[2] compared two upper-division technical writing classes. One group received ten weeks of sequential training in perceptual, mental, and graphic imagery; the other did not. Pre- and post-test expressive and problem-solving writing samples were collected and rated holistically by trained readers. Analysis of co-variance was performed to test the following hypotheses: A statistically significant difference (at the .05 level) was expected in the 1) use of details, 2) use of problem-solving strategies, and 3) overall quality of writing ability between students receiving the imagery training and those not receiving it. The statistical analysis indicated that the main effect was significant beyond the .05 level: hypothesis one (F=8.67, p=.004), hypothesis two (F=15.51, p=.000), and hypothesis three (F=10.49, p=.003) (Worley 1991).

Put plainly, the results of the study found that visual imagery training positively affected the use of detailed information (anecdotes, illustrations, or figurative language), problem-solving skills (the ability to see a situation from a variety of viewpoints; to create and recall detail-rich images; and to play out different scenarios such as determining "if this happens, then what else will happen"), and overall

[2]The study involved the direct manipulation of specific conditions, but there was no random assignment of subjects.

textual quality. Students participating in the visual imagery training grew more aware of their visual and verbal processes than did their nonparticipating counterparts. They felt comfortable with it and tapped into it as they wrote their posttest. According to the post-test results, the training apparently helped them connect their visual and verbal abilities, something they had not been doing before.

Visual and Verbal Connections

The selection and sequence of the perceptual, mental, and graphic imagery exercises were initially piloted over three semesters. During the study the classroom activities were composed of those imagery exercises and discussion.

Perceptual Imagery

One of the major problems inexperienced writers have with perception is saturation. Perceptual saturation occurs because instead of seeing the object in front of them, inexperienced writers impose their stereotypical image on top of the object they are seeing (Adams 1986, 13–21). For example, when writing students are asked to describe an object in front of them, say an ink pen, they are likely to describe it as "just a pen," a composite of all other ink pens they have seen, instead of the particular pen that is in front of them. In order to move beyond such perceptions, students need practice in actually "seeing" objects. In *Experiences in Visual Thinking*, Robert McKim (1980) states:

> Far more than the full participation of the senses is involved in analytical seeing. The intellect, with all of its store of knowledge, is also involved. . . . And because much knowledge is most usually stored in relation to language, words can powerfully catalyze seeing. (68)

Verbalization influences visualization. Words evoke mental images. Students should also use visualization to evoke words. The interaction between perceiving an object and describing it develops both processes. Visualization feeds into verbalization which feeds back into visualization: a visualization-verbalization loop.

Exercises

As future professionals, technical writing students are expected to provide full descriptions of objects or locations for readers unfamiliar with them. These exercises gave the students practice in seeing objects and describing what they saw. During the first and second week of the perceptual imagery exercises, students described small objects they actually held in their hands—a shell, a pine cone, and a button. They were asked to provide as much detail about them as possible, such as their size, shape, color, texture. During the third and fourth weeks of the perceptual imagery activities, students described black-and-white photographs. These exercises moved students beyond merely seeing the photographs as objects to seeing relationships within them. Students first looked at and wrote descriptions of photographs *as* objects. Next, the students worked with black-and-white photographs of the campus. They first looked at a whole scene and wrote a description of it. They then were asked to determine how all the elements in the picture created a unified scene (Hergenhahn 1986, 284).

After that, students described the "figure-ground" relationships. By figure-ground is meant "the division of the perceptual field into two parts: the figure, which is clear and unified and is the object of attention, and the ground, which is diffused and consists of everything that is not being attended to" (Hergenhahn 1986, 292–93). This exercise helped develop students' abilities to focus on the main object in a scene. So too in creating text. Students need to be able to eliminate background "noise" in their writing when they want to concentrate on their main points.

Finally, students determined how the environment in a photograph affected the way the main object appeared to them. For example, in one photograph only the top of an academic building was visible from behind a clump of trees. I asked the students: *If* they could see the academic building *without* the trees around it, would it change their view of the building and its place in the photograph? This task encouraged students to distinguish between element relationships. In their writing students need to become aware of how presenting one piece of information influences all other pieces of information.

Mental Imagery

Mental imagery is constructed in the mind itself and uses information recorded perceptually. The mental imagery activities were intended to help students progress from Visual Recall (remembering objects they have seen), to Manipulation of Mental Images (rotating or changing images) to Projection of Mental Images (predicting alternative situations) (McKim 1980, 94–119). The ability to experience clear mental images is not shared equally by all students. Although some students felt as though they could not create mental images, they seemed better able to do so after practicing these exercises. Again, the ability to create and manipulate mental images is precisely what we do when composing: manipulate ideas, rearrange information, and envision where ideas are headed.

Exercises

For the first visual recall exercise, students were asked to recall in their mind's eye the shell they had seen several weeks before during the perceptual imagery sequence. The written description of the mental image gave students practice in using images as a reference while creating text. Unlike the first exercise in which they recalled an object they had recently seen under the prescribed classroom conditions, the second exercise appeared more difficult because students were recreating images from their distant pasts—their childhood bedroom.

Then students performed mental manipulations in order to imagine the parts of objects that were not readily visible. Remembering the image of the button they had seen previously, students mentally rotated it so that they could first see the edge and then the back of the button. After this, they described the image they had created. They repeated the manipulation with a childhood toy.

During the last week students created mental scenarios. First, they remembered a goal they had achieved. They then described the image of that goal. Second, they created mental scenarios of themselves at their college graduation. They described those images as well. These exercises encouraged students to "play-out potential scenes" in order to project possibilities for themselves. In other words, they were practicing creating and modifying their future actions.

Text that changes as writers make choices is known as a fluid text. Students need encouragement to view their writing as "fluid," that their text is always evolving while they are working on it. When students are skilled at imagining mental scenarios, they seem reassured that if they do not like where their images (or text) is going, they can always change them.

Graphic Imagery

Graphic imagery, making up the last element of the instruction, refers to imagery that is "sketched, doodled, drawn, or otherwise put down in a written communicable form" (Adams 1986, 89), either to help us think or communicate with others. The exercises focused on what McKim (1980) calls the developmental mode of graphic ideation: simple drawn images. The students' objectives were to create drawings that allowed them to talk to themselves visually (18–19). They were told not to worry about creating "true to life" forms. Rather, they were encouraged to use the drawings as writer-based text. For some students simple, drawn images meant stick people and basic geometric shapes. To others it meant elaborately drawn people and figures.

Whatever the quality of the drawing, students were able to "read" their own graphic symbols. Understanding pictures is

> analogous to reading the printed word, where, in each case, the 'reader' must transform a set of symbols or signs from one system to another. It is only through a process of transformation that comprehension can begin. (Sigel 1978, 94)

In these graphic exercises students focused *only* on creating drawings that *they* had to interpret, thereby eliminating the problem of creating a drawing that someone else might "misread."

Exercises

During the first week of the graphic imagery activities, students drew representations of relationships with family and friends and then explained them in writing (McKim 1980, 166). The next week students received writing prompts describing particular situations to which they *drew* a response, which then became "outlines" for writing. The first prompt asked students to describe what they would do if all campus classes were filled before they could register. A second prompt asked students to describe their worst day in high school for their high school yearbook. Class discussion confirmed that having students write about a situation after creating a drawing of it encouraged them to refer to the drawing for more information. In the final week students created drawings as a prewriting activity. They drew themselves at a job they wanted and wrote a letter of application for it.

Class Discussion

After each exercise students briefly shared their imaging processes in small groups or as a class. Some students reported having difficulty generating mental images at the beginning of the semester. However, by the end of the semester almost every participant was to some extent able to create images. One student said that she could not "see" any images in her mind, but that her drawings were symbolic of the emotions she experienced when she was asked to remember a specific image. Throughout the semester students commented on the relationships between their mental and graphic images and the organization and detail in their written texts. Some students remarked that their mental images revealed themselves as "stories" that were easier to think about than to write. Other students stated that their drawings contained more description than their written outlines or that their drawings helped them recall more details about the original situation. One student reported that the visualization techniques helped her mind "flow." Thus, informal and formal class discussions provided students with an opportunity not only to analyze their own visual skills but also to develop metacognitive skills, that is, to analyze the images they created and to speculate on the reasons they created them.

The Window of Visual Experience

Though composition specialists acknowledge the importance of visual imagery in the writing class, they have not fully specified how to put it into practice. This is undoubtedly because, from about the third or fourth grade on, verbalization is privileged over visualization (Gardner 1980; Edwards 1979).

If students are not encouraged to exercise their visual imaging skills in school, where will they learn to develop their mind beyond passive visual reception? From the movies? From magazine advertisements? From the Music Television videos (MTV) that wash over them? One way students can strengthen their visual thinking is to use their own images as reference points during composing. Visual images can guide the texts they create, which, in turn, can guide the images they create — in instructive reciprocity.

Another way to develop students' visual and verbal abilities is to strengthen that relationship in reading assignments. Instead of glossing over diagrams, photographs, pictures, and objects, students can be encouraged to analyze visual material, describe their analyses, and discuss how graphic images enrich and explain written texts. Finally, when students read texts, imagery bridges "affect and cognition, affect and text world, text world and real world" (Fleckenstein 1989, 253). This connection is particularly important for instructors basing their classroom practices on reader-response theory. In a reading journal combinations of drawings and writing can serve to explain students' interpretations of textual material.

Students envision written language, Berthoff (1984) laments, "as a window which keeps [them] from enjoying immediate vision" (27). Their words fail to convey the ideas they want to express. Words, in effect, get in the way of seeing. Part of the problem is that our students are trained to think of writing primarily in analytical terms. Integrating holistic and verbal activities allows students to open the window, temporarily bypass words for images, and then return to them with a fullness and immediacy not experienced before.

Part Five

Emotions

How do emotions enter into the teaching of writing? The best answer is: "In almost every way imaginable." We speak of motivation and wonder how to elicit it. We suspect that writing is at its best when writer and writing are bonded in some sort of satisfying emotional experience. But we also know that enabling or disabling feelings occur throughout composing.

Drawing on the work of Carl Rogers, Nathaniel Teich begins his essay by exploring the role of empathy during the Holocaust. Those who were rescuers or who refused to participate in Nazi activities identified in some way with their victims. Can schools instill values such as compassion, caring, and empathy? Arguing that "reading and writing already engage the empathic process," Teich describes classroom techniques that result in such understanding.

Alice Brand envisions part of our psychic life as a continuum: at one end is the emotional (or hot) function; at the other end of the continuum is the cognitive (or cool) function. Between these two polar positions are infinite combinations of the cognitive—emotional mix. Brand's term *Valuative System* places a "full range of emotionally based mental experience" along the continuum—arousal, emotion, mood, preference, attitude, belief, and value. Brand concludes

141

with a call for a more explicit understanding of our emotional life during writing. Information alone is rarely enough. "The most important human values are emotional, not intellectual." Emotions are markers. Emotions lend significance to situations. What we feel is a measure of our personal truths.

13

Teaching Empathy Through Cooperative Learning

Nathaniel Teich

My initial plan for this essay was, first, to discuss in a detached manner some connections between cognition and emotion in order for empathy to be useful in our teaching. Next, I planned to describe practical examples of teaching for empathy in assignments calling for dialogue and consensus, in strategies for understanding the views of others, and even in the reading process itself. But when I started to write, I could not ignore what I had recently read about empathy and its horrifying opposites during the Holocaust. Because I believe that expressions of empathy must be situated in real-world contexts, not just in our imaginations or in linguistic constructions of the world, I could not avoid beginning with one historical location of empathy.

Empathy and Altruism as Affect

In *Ordinary Men: Reserve Police Battalion 101 and the Final Solution in Poland*, historian Christopher R. Browning presented a detailed account of the actions and attitudes of men in the German Order Police who contributed to the roundup, mass killings, or shipment to concentration camps of thousands of Jews. One of the most chilling themes Browning developed is how these men, most in their thirties and forties and too old for conscription into the regular army, learned and kept up their work. At the outset of the mass shootings, when about fifteen hundred Jews from one village were trucked to a forest and shot, a few reservists were too sickened to continue, a few walked away, but about eighty percent kept shooting as each truckload arrived.

143

Years later when some of these men were questioned, they hardly mentioned ethical or humane values in their decision whether or not to participate in the killings. Most stressed that they were following orders and conforming to the behavior of the group. Yet others described their refusal or struggle to kill Jews who spoke German or were deportees from the Hamburg area where the reservists themselves lived. For these specific reasons, some of the police ignored the peer pressure to follow orders and the anti-semitic propaganda of the final solution. How do we explain why some people refrain from or seek to prevent atrocities that their countrymen inflict on others, including helpless women, children, and the elderly?

One answer is empathy, which refers to the compassionate and caring psychological processes and social behaviors that link one individual to another, and, thus, link the family and group to the larger society.[1] Recent research on the Holocaust corrects long-established misconceptions about the limited extent of resistance to the Nazis and of rescuing victims (Oliner and Oliner 1988). Throughout Europe, hundreds of thousands of Christians risked their own and their families' lives to hide Jews or help them escape. How did these rescuers differ from their neighbors who did not help?

According to researcher Samuel Oliner, who as a teen was saved from the Nazis by a Polish farm woman, the personal and family values of rescuers were "predominantly rooted in care" and expressed by attitudes of social inclusiveness, responsibility for the welfare of society, and compassion. In short, empathy. Some rescuers had lived and worked among people of different religions and cultures. Rescuers' parents more commonly accepted others as equals and opposed the persecution of minorities than did the parents of non-rescuers (1988, 163–78, 183–86).

Parental discipline was also influential. Parents who reasoned with their children rather than resorted to violence were more common in the upbringing of rescuers than in that of non-rescuers (Oliner and Oliner 1988, 178–83). These findings agree with current research on child abuse and violence. Children who are abused tend to become abusers, thus perpetuating the violence to which they were subjected.

Today, confronted by increasing divisiveness and violence in schools and beyond, can our teaching model and instill values like

---

[1]In their broadest definitions, *compassion* and *care* represent the positive applications of empathy. Compassion represents not just pity, but sympathy, commiseration, tender responsiveness, and ultimately benevolence. Hunt describes the connections between altruism and empathy (1990, 169–84). Caring, to Mayeroff (1971) and Oliner and Oliner (1988), means paying attention to, taking an interest in, thinking about, or feeling concern for another. I am not including here empirical research on the connection between affect and cognition (e.g., Hoffman 1984).

compassion, caring, and empathy? Some established practices of cooperative learning, from dialogue and active listening to collaborative problem solving, directly or indirectly involve empathic understanding. Thus, as we teach reading and writing, we can teach for and about empathy as a human response to interpersonal and larger social problems.

Analytical Definitions of Empathy

The most familiar images of empathy are those of walking in another's shoes or putting ourselves in another's skin. These bodily and participatory images evoke the psychological activities of identification and projection. These in turn reflect the kinesthetic and aesthetic origins of empathy from the metaphysical psychology of Theodor Lipps in the late nineteenth and early twentieth centuries. Since that time the term has accrued a range of contradictory meanings and applications (see Teich 1992, 237–47). While some conceptions of empathy range from the intuitive and emotional to the mystical, most psychologists recognize some form of empathy as integral to therapy. In psychotherapy the concept of empathy embraces both the emotional and cognitive aspects of the communication between therapist and client.

The theory and practice of empathic understanding applies as well to composition studies. Practitioners in both fields best employ empathy when it is understood in the following ways: as a "mode of analytic listening," as a balance between "rational understanding" and "emotional and sympathetic affective attunement," and "as a special mode of affective communication" (Bornstein 1984, 111). In other words, empathy involves tuning our emotions to the thoughts and feelings of other individuals as well as rationally understanding and articulating those thoughts and feelings.

The metaphor of empathy as "attunement" suggests sensations of hearing sound and being in harmony, which I relate below to "analytic listening" or "active listening." But first, three brief examples from the psychological literature illustrate some similarities in defining empathy cognitively and affectively. In 1983 psychoanalyst Michael F. Basch investigated the etymology of empathy and its original German form, *einfuhlung*. He concluded that empathy is appropriate in psychoanalytic theory and practice if it is not limited to the "affective resonance" of the therapist and the client's feelings. Rather, it should lead the therapist to "a reasoned, though not necessarily conscious, interpretation," which is "then subjected to validation or disconfirmation . . . through further reflection, observation, or experiment" (111).

Psychoanalyst Heinz Kohut was the first to postulate empathy as the chief "observational method" of psychological studies, defining empathy as "vicarious introspection" (1959/1978, 209). Kohut combined both introspection and empathy as the first step of the "two-step procedure . . . that characterizes depth psychology." Within the first step there is an emotional and intellectual "understanding." The second step is the "explaining" of that understanding (1977, 142). Another of Kohut's descriptions of empathy as "the expansion of the self to include the other" (1973/1978, 705) avoids negative connotations of empathy as passive reception of or active intrusion into the mental states of another person (Teich 1992, 259–63).

Psychologist Carl Rogers, whose theory and practice extended empathy from clinical to broader social settings, stressed that empathy did not entail simple identification with another person. Rather

> empathy, or being empathic, is to perceive the internal frame of reference of another with accuracy and with the emotional components and meanings which pertain thereto as if one were the person, but without ever losing the "as if" condition. . . . If this "as if" quality is lost, then the state is one of identification. (1959/1980, 140–41)

For the purposes of therapeutic communication then, empathy entails more than just feelingful identification with another person. While in psychoanalytic theory there continue to be differences concerning the definition and application of empathy, psychoanalytic and counseling practitioners recognize empathy and actively employ it in therapist/client relations. As composition theorists and practitioners, we are in a similar situation. Regardless of our theoretical inclinations, empathy is useful for teaching and learning writing if we identify it as a significant part of the substance and procedures of our classes (Brand 1980).

Applications of Empathy

Some aspects of teaching reading and writing already engage the empathic process. We point out to students that empathy is integral to the basic acts of reading and responding. Kohut's definition of empathy as "vicarious introspection" is an apt, if tricky, term consistent with our current understanding of how readers construct meanings from texts. "Vicarious introspection" refers to our adopting an introspective attitude toward our perceptions of another person's feelings, thoughts, and experiences. What is vicarious is not the introspection of our own responses; rather, *vicarious* applies to the situation in which the subject of our introspection is another person's feelings and ideas, which we cannot experience directly from that person's standpoint. Empathy, as "vicarious introspection," fits with descriptions of the reading process, as readers recreate characters and formulate meanings from texts.

Empathy also fits with conceptions of the writing process, evident from the 1980s when theorist-practitioners like James Moffett, Ann Berthoff, and Toby Fulwiler introduced applications of the dialogue process that foster empathy. Although called by different names, these methods range from the strictly personal activities of individual monologues and internal dialogues with ourselves or others, to the classroom settings of pairs and groups involved in individual, cooperative, and adversarial public activities.

Dialogue from Personal Journal to Peer Group

Empathy is fostered on the personal level by assignments in "dialectical" or "double-entry" journals.[2] In a format derived from Berthoff, the left column of a page is labeled "note taking" and the right column is labeled "note making" (1981, 44–45). First, students record quotations and citations from a text in the left column and, next, their own responses (analyses, feelings, personal associations, inferences, questions) in the right column. As a third step, students might reflect on their responses and even on the assumptions and thought processes that led to them. These responses and introspections serve as the raw materials for initiating empathic understanding in discussions and written assignments that follow.

Empathic understanding is fostered on a more public level when students share their journal entries in pairs, small groups, and large groups. They often expand their ideas and feelings about classmates as persons as well as about characters in stories. If pairs or groups are then asked to reach consensus on an issue, individuals may modify their positions as a result of these new perceptions.

This willingness to change our minds, according to Carl Rogers, is fundamental to empathic understanding and mutually satisfactory solutions to problems or conflicts. But it is most difficult to do (as I acknowledge throughout my discussion). The risk of being changed, Rogers said, "is one of the most frightening prospects most of us can face" (1961, 333; see Teich 1987).

Teaching for empathy is best accomplished by modeling all the activities from journals to consensus building. When students do not fear that their personal responses will be ridiculed or misjudged, exploratory and honest journals and discussion emerge and trust is built. To provide guidance before students begin their dialectical jour-

[2]See Berthoff in Fulwiler (1987, 11-18) and Andrasick (1990, 45-58).

nals, I show and discuss excerpts from journals that record feelings, thoughts, and personal associations.

Open-ended questions or sentence starters are valuable for distinguishing the exploratory aspects of "note making" from the textual references of "note taking."

1. What is going on here? I don't understand . . . .
2. Does this character remind me of someone whom I know, or have read about?
3. What kind of person would hold such ideas?
4. Why do I feel this way about . . . ?
5. How or why did I arrive at my idea or feeling?
6. What's coming next? Can I predict where this story or argument is going?
7. Why did the author do this or say it this way?
8. This is important because. . . .

When students finish their journals, Madden (1986) suggests that they meet in pairs for active listening and questioning strategies; they rotate partners two or three times. After about fifteen minutes of discussion in pairs, groups of two or three are allotted ten to fifteen minutes to summarize individual positions and attempt consensus. The remaining class time might include presenting and discussing the small-group summaries and achieving a further synthesis of views.

To model the dialogue process after describing it, Madden holds practice dialogues in front of the whole group, either with volunteer student pairs or with the instructor as one of a pair. During this process two levels of questioning are distinguished. At the lower levels of abstraction, questions are posed about the substance and structure of a work, which originate from specific textual references in the "note taking" column. Madden also prompts dialogue at higher levels of abstraction asking questions about entries in the "note making" column:

1. What do you think is the text's central meaning or purpose?
2. What features help support this meaning?
3. What aspects of your own values and experiences do you find reflected or challenged in this work?

If questions like these are also suggested to students when they write in their dialogue journals, they can direct their responses (recorded or not) to the next session of live peer dialogue.

Active Listening

In the 1940s and 1950s Carl Rogers and colleagues developed in their counseling practices what they came to call "active listening" techniques. To Rogers "active listening" represented the communication skills that facilitated empathic understanding:

> Real communication occurs . . . when we listen with understanding . . . to see the expressed idea and attitude from the other person's point of view, to sense how it feels to him, to achieve his frame of reference in regard to the thing he is talking about. . . . Mutual communication tends to be pointed toward solving a problem rather than toward attacking a person or group. It leads to a situation in which I see how the problem appears to you, as well as to me, and you see how it appears to me, as well as to you. (1951/1961, 331–32, 336)

He summarized the "active listening" process:

> Each person can speak for himself only *after* he has first restated the ideas and feelings of the previous speaker accurately, and to that speaker's satisfaction. It . . . would be necessary for you to really achieve the other speaker's frame of reference—to understand his thoughts and feelings so well that you could summarize them for him. (1951/1961, 332)

Although Rogers presented this restatement "rule" for "mutual communication" in oral dialogue, composition theorists and practitioners have adapted it to writing instruction for argumentation, negotiation, and problem solving.

In the classroom the rational and ethical dimensions of active listening provide well-established and dogma-free ways to develop empathic understanding. Dialogues structured to practice active listening lead students to focus on issues, not attack opponents. The goal, according to Rogers, is "to increase the amount of listening *with,* and decrease the amount of evaluation *about* others" (1951/1961, 335).

Active listening is also integral to cooperative learning. The pioneering work of educational psychologist David W. Johnson and his colleagues is an example. What Rogers called active listening, Johnson and Johnson (1991, 153) called paraphrasing:

1. Restate the sender's expressed ideas and feelings in your own words rather than mimicking or parroting her exact words. [Rogerian active listening]
2. Preface paraphrased remarks with: "You think . . . ," "Your position is . . . ," "It seems to you that . . . ," "You feel that . . . ," and so on.

3. Avoid any indication of approval or disapproval. [Rogerian acceptance]

4. Make your nonverbal messages congruent with your verbal paraphrasing; look attentive, interested, and open to the sender's ideas and feelings, and show that you are concentrating upon what the sender is trying to communicate. [Rogerian congruence]

5. Put yourself in the sender's shoes, and try to understand what she is feeling and what the message means. [Rogerian empathy]

Johnson and Johnson (1991, 152) also stressed the importance of "owning" the message by using personal pronouns like "I" and "my," rather than disguising "who" thinks and feels with such expressions as "most people" or "our group." Because the goal of active listening is an agreement that speakers and listeners are understood, listeners may need to negotiate with speakers until agreement emerges on the meanings and feelings communicated in the message. If listeners realize that mere paraphrasing does not reflect genuine understanding, additional dialogue must get beyond the paraphrased words to negotiate adequate clarification (154).

The following questions suggested by Madden (1986) help students restate meaning:

1. The listener asks for further clarification: "I don't quite understand. Would you please explain that more? Could you give an example?"

2. The speaker being questioned ends a statement by asking: "Is that clear? Should I explain it further?"

3. The listener prefaces restatement of the speaker's views with: "I'll restate your position now. Would you please correct me if I get something wrong?"

The steps in seeking consensus in a pair or group may not take much time if considerable agreement has already emerged. However, depending on the issues, building consensus may not always be possible. Limited discussion time may not permit adequate exploration of complex problems or multi-layered texts. For highly-charged issues in which emotions and beliefs produce volatile differences, consensus may prove impossible. In such situations dialogue can be redirected toward establishing the basis of the different or conflicting views. The following questions may help:

1. Is the disagreement based on structural elements of the text and their interpretation?

2. Is there ambiguity that supports different points of view?

3. Is the disagreement based on personal beliefs, values, or ideologies?

If students identify and explore a range of explanations for disagreements, they may be able to propose a broader consensus, or acknowledge differences and be satisfied with "agreeing to disagree." In my advanced composition classes I have been pleasantly surprised by the use of unconventional expository or argumentative modes. Through personal experiences, extended dialogues between speakers (actual or fictional), and dramatic vignettes, students discussed conflicted issues like abortion, affirmative action, censorship, and gay and lesbian rights. When employing active listening and empathy, students may explore a broad repertoire of genres for writing about controversial issues.

But students may also be susceptible to peer group pressure—to the easy conclusions of relativism or absolutism. To avoid being perceived as hostile and disruptive or to defer to a dominant individual, some students surrender their honest views or are pressured into consensus. They fall back on either the "democratic" solution, in which all people's opinions are considered equally valid, or the "authoritarian" one, in which there must be only one correct answer. Students may discuss this predicament directly. But the best guarantees for genuine problem solving are active listening, empathic understanding, and risk taking.

Reaching consensus, however, is not simply a matter of giving in to the other side. Critics of Rogerian communication allege that the Rogerian approach leads to weak or passive positions and unrealistic compromises for the sake of consensus. While it is certainly true that each of us has some issues that are non-negotiable and some values we will not change, in other situations we can accept the need to cooperate for mutual goals. Students can practice compromise in competitive and adversarial situations created in the classroom context.

Cooperative Controversies

What psychologists Johnson and Johnson (1991) called "creative controversy" and Bredehoft (1991) called "cooperative controversy" resemble the debate format, except that the adversarial elements are subordinated to consensus building. While the primary goal of these psychologists is teaching inquiry and critical thinking skills, the means to these ends clearly involve active listening and empathy. In Johnson and Johnson's approach the goal is a collaboratively written or oral report based on the best thinking of all group members and a thorough consideration of different sides of a controversy. Students start in groups of four, with one pair assigned the "pro" position and the other pair the "con" position. Students then:

1. Prepare the best case for their assigned position.
2. Advocate this position to the opposing pair in their group.
3. Refute the opposing pair's position and thinking, while rebutting attacks on their own.
4. Reverse positions by presenting the other side as sincerely and forcefully as they can.
5. Reach consensus by agreeing on a conclusion, making a decision, or proposing a plan of action that synthesizes the best ideas and reasoning of both sides.

Bredehoft discussed adapting Johnson and Johnson's strategies in the college classroom. He made two notable changes, however. First, he changed the name to "cooperative controversies," a label I prefer for its positive connotation. Second, his goal for written products is separate student papers rather than a group report. This allows individual assessment of each student's written work. He found that cooperative controversies enabled students to consider other points of view rather than their own predisposed opinions. In addition students might draft a reflective or meta-cognitive journal entry about what went on as they worked through the assignment, especially how they felt during the cooperation phase.

Cooperative or "creative" controversy is closely connected to the role playing and role reversal of "creative dramatics," which have proved effective for teaching empathy. For example, Bill Bigelow and Linda Christensen prepared a series of topics and activities for the Portland, Oregon, schools based on historical events. In one assignment students read about the Montgomery bus boycott and then wrote and played roles of either blacks or whites aboard the bus when Rosa Parks refused to give up her seat. After gaining knowledge about a historical situation, students might be asked not only to script their roles, but also to reflect on the extent of their empathic understanding.

For their first cooperative controversy or role play, students seem to grasp the process better if assigned short works of literature or less controversial social issues that involve less personal risk. Students engaging in cooperative controversy should experience the real-life dynamics of disagreeing with positions without personally attacking the people who hold them. Johnson and Johnson stressed being critical of ideas not of persons, just as Rogers rejected adversarial and personal criticism when using active listening to restate, clarify, and reflect another person's ideas and feelings. Being respectful of the other side, we tell students, is the courtesy we give in order to receive it.[3]

Teaching for and about empathy, however, does not guarantee the spread of goodwill and reciprocity. Both Rogers and Kohut recognized that empathy is value-neutral. Like adversarial rhetorics, it can be exploited to the disadvantage of others, as in brainwashing or a sales pitch (Teich 1992, 56, 268). The more extreme objection to the rhetoric of empathy and collaboration would demand: "How could you exhibit empathic understanding or unconditional positive regard for the likes of Hitler?" Yet the empathic approach remains a personally and socially beneficial option. The challenge for instructors and students alike is to examine their assumptions, opinions, and values in the act of entering emotionally and intellectually into other people's worlds.

[3]Thanks to the teachers in my 1992 Oregon Writing Project-II workshop for suggestions and refinements in implementing the "cooperative controversy" approach.

14

Defining Our Emotional Life
The Valuative System—
A Continuum Theory

Alice Glarden Brand

Let's for the sake of argument agree that the mind is one hundred percent constituted by the intellect and emotion (an egregious over-simplification) which are in continuous interplay. Now put these components on a sliding scale, similar to the cold-to-hot air knob on a car heater. Sometimes the cognitive-emotion ratio is cool, tilt-ed toward cerebration. Other times the ratio is reversed; the tilt is warm or hot, weighted toward feeling. Sometimes things are about fifty-fifty. Like real numbers, the "amounts" of intellect and emo-tion at any given moment have the capacity to be infinitely subdi-vided into finer and finer gradations. But they always add up to one hundred.

Positions along this continuum stretch from highly visible bio-physical and emotional activity with infinitesimal social and cognitive content to the other polar extreme of imperceptible physical change and emotional display but high cognitive and social content. The first or hot end of the continuum is saturated with emotion expressed, for example, through such unequivocal and irrepressible behaviors as an infant crying. At this end the lowest common emotional denominator is represented by pleasure/pain. At this end emotions virtually desert-ed by thought could create a monster—infant or adult. At the cold end of the continuum, mental content is heavily processed and seemingly barren of emotion and could create a monster of another kind. Except for motivation,[1] other members of the Valuative System—arousal, emotion, mood, preference, attitude, belief, and value—may be plotted in between according to their contribution of cognition and emotion. This is what may be called the Valuative System, my term for describing the full range of emotionally based mental experience.[2] My intention is not to establish definitive meanings of the terms so much as to arrive at working concepts that go beyond the formulations of Kristie Fleckenstein, David Krathwohl, George Mandler, and Susan McLeod.

It may seem odd for a collection advocating the integrated mind to contain two essays that separate emotion and cognition. While such a separation has heuristic utility, it also has inherent problems. One difficulty is that occupants of the "domain beyond" can easily become isolated. On the other side, because the divisions between higher-order mental interactions are imprecise, the occupants of the "domain beyond" can also penetrate neighbors more easily. The whole point of the continuum is to help organize our thinking about affectively based mental activity while simultaneously to help us understand its members as seamlessly connected, almost chemically blended. There is also the danger that in plotting the terms on a sliding scale, they appear overly simple when their distinctions and interactions are profoundly intricate. These simple relationships are really not simple.

Faced with a generosity of material and limited space, I concentrate on the concepts of arousal, emotion, values, and motivation but only touch on mood, preference, attitudes, and beliefs. The discussion is divided between two essays: The first addresses arousal and emotion; the second, values and motivation.

With the exception of innate arousal and baseline motivation, the residents of the Valuative System share two features: First, they do not just appear whole as themselves. The members of the Valuative System are made up of cognitive, emotional, social, and behavioral components. And, second, they follow from these components; they are derived.

The *cognitive* component refers to our *knowledge* about particular evaluations. To say that we evaluate is to say that we *understand* the correct way to behave, a feeling, a taste we cultivate, or an end-state we strive for. The cognitive component represents our concepts about

[1]Motivation, an overlapping but somewhat different order of internal functioning, is excluded from this list for the time being.

[2]The term, Valuative System, should be distinguished from a value system (see page 169). Few terms linked to the evaluation system—passions, instincts, motivation, drives, moods, needs, sentiments, emotions, attitudes, beliefs, judgments, appraisals, and preferences—have been spared ambiguity or redundancy.Hence, the reason for these essays.

a value judgment—what we know about it.[3] The further along the continuum, the greater the cognitive tilt in the affective-cognitive blend, the more accessible the evaluation is to our consciousness, and the more willing cognitivists are to address it.

Regarding *emotion*, to the extent that the members of the Valuative System are conscious, rational, and verbal (i.e., cognitive), they are technically outside of the scope of this book—if we take its title at face value. To the extent that the Valuative System has *hedonic* or *positive* and *negative* capabilities, the Valuative System falls inexorably within it. As I stated, evaluating is the cognitive counterpart of emotion. But because the affective bases of emotion and evaluation are one and the same, where I talk about evaluation, emotion should also be understood.

While the *social* component is not addressed in these essays, this component recognizes the norms, rules, and cultural skills that shape and perpetuate the Valuative System. As we move along our developmental paths, the biology governing our internal experiences becomes progressively "relaxed" (Averill 1990, 399). Replacing it are socialization processes that serve as standards of public decorum and vehicles for establishing and maintaining particular emotional and intellectual patterns. These social constructions also account for cross-cultural variations.

Last, the *behavioral* element indicates what we *do* as a result of our evaluations. It is often observable like hives but, like a pulse rate, not necessarily so. The behavioral element embraces unnumbered manifestations of bodily activity: physiological, somatic, and physical as well as socially grounded display and expressive behaviors. A valuative experience can barely take place without heightened perception, biophysical changes, and impulses to act in certain ways. Members of the Valuative System are postulated to account for sensibilities as specific as irritation or as mild as appreciation. But they all start with attending and arousal.

Arousal: The Bottom-Up View

Although paying attention to stimuli is undoubtedly the beginning point of all human activity,[4] without physiological arousal we could not think or feel anything—much less write about it. Physiology is

[3]This also depends on two other variables: our familiarity or past experience with the phenomenon and our expectations for it.

[4]The infinite regress: And what sets up attending? Why do we attend to some things but not to others? On what basis does selective attention operate? Paying attention is largely a matter of choice though we may be unaware of that choice (LeDoux 1989, 271; Neisser 1967; see also Edelman 1992 and Luria 1973).

located in territory where writing specialists are understandably reluctant to tread. It is of some consolation to know that few terms have
such neat, agreed-upon meaning as arousal does. It concerns us here
to the degree that neurophysiological, biochemical/hormonal, somatic, and/or motor expressive energy—in a word, our body—serves as a
starting point for all mental and physical response.

The mid-twentieth century ushered in two schools of thought on
arousal: early drive and instinct perspectives evolved into neurophysiological arousal and activation theories. And the cognitive system became the hypothetical construct postulated to explain them
(Appley 1983, 280). In the neurophysiological view cortical arousal
is basic. It is nonspecific excitation that has survival functions.
Alone, arousal is inadequate for distinguishing ordinary neural messages from emotional ones. When cortical arousal motivates, sus-
tains, or terminates activity according to a hedonic principle or a
positive or negative feeling, it becomes affective (Brand 1989a).
Cutting across all organisms phylogenetically and ontogenetically,
affective arousal is as primitive as the withdrawal of a protazoa when
stimulated and as subtle as human hope. For the simplest forms of
life arousal means approach and avoidance responses. Not only is
our brain larger than that of lower animals, but its biology is infinitely more complex than is necessary for sheer approach or avoidance
(Langer 1967, 1972).

It is true that our advanced brain regulates positive and negative
emotional intensity—including excitation and the top-down blunting
of emotions (Luria 1973). But it is also true that our early or "proto-
brain" is far from useless (Pugh 1977). According to psychologist
Tucker, without our *rudimentary* brain, housed in the oldest part of
forebrain, "we could not achieve the attentional control required for
tenacious reasoning, or for an expansive imagination. Without the
controls of our '*old* cortex,' we could not access memories to provide
the experiential context for current emotions" (163–64). We could
not express our feelings.

And this is the point. Emotional arousal affects our intellectual
processes (like priming our memories) even without recruiting intellectual thought (Clark 1982, 281; LeDoux 1989). Which may
explain why we often react to things emotionally first. And why
once we learn something, it is hard to let it go. As Langer pointed
out, emotions are not just subjective products of the mind; they
actually produce it.

There are several cognitive perspectives on arousal. Some
researchers envision the feeling component of evaluation as having
only a neurophysiological phase within the wider mental experience (Izard 1982). Others question the contribution of our biology

or separate the cognitive from the neural (Weiner 1982). Still others contend that arousal is integral to valuing (Berlyne 1960; Mandler 1990).

It is here that one of the more popular cognitive paradigms for processing evaluations is postulated. Psychologist Mandler[5] claims that affective experience and behavior are the interactive result of autonomic arousal and cognitive interpretation. Drawing first on human physiology, he identifies two functions of autonomic arousal. One function is to restore and maintain homeostasis and physiological readiness. The other signals the mental organization for attention, alertness, and scanning of the environment. This last requires analysis and interpretation of the environment by the sensory and cognitive apparatus. This means that emotional arousal is the result of 1) sensory-external or 2) perceptual-internal events. In other words:

cortical arousal equals sensory input + interpretation

or

biology + memory

(Wyer and Srull 1989, 370)

The autonomic nervous system is the signal system that not only regulates emotional intensity or arousal but also enters into evaluating the experience.

Cognitivists use the term evaluation or valuation in a special way. For them, a valuation is a simple valenced judgment. This mean a positive or negative stance with a label assigned to it—like bad or good. A simple valuation ignores arousal (Simon 1982). No emotion is necessary. It is an intellectual yes-no, on-off judgment. Only when this valuation is combined with arousal does it become emotional (Mandler 1982). Two things then occur. First, we analyze its meaning which produces an emotional quality like irritation, resentment, or anger. Second and biologically based, we respond viscerally.[6] This provides its intensity and peculiar emotional "feel."

Cognitivists seem to agree that likings or preferences are experienced with little or no arousal. Arousal is produced, however, when incongruity arises. Incongruity in judgments results from experiences that are the novel, complex, curious, or discrepant, regardless of whether they are pleasant or unpleasant. The way we determine our "evaluation" is by the degree of our arousal and the

[5]Current neuroscience finds that patterns of cerebral arousal characterizing different emotional states are far more complicated than Mandler's work suggests (Heller in Stein, et al. 1990; LeDoux 1991).

[6]According to LeDoux (1991) the visceral brain equals the emotional brain.

"meaning analysis" or thought that we attach to it (Berlyne 1971; Mandler 1982).

Arousal also has its optimum and distorting values that may be depicted as curvilinear. Originating almost a century ago, the Yerkes-Dodson theory depicts arousal as a composite of both positive and negative influences. Intermediate levels of emotional arousal are considered optimum and yield high performance. Low levels of arousal, inadequate to produce or influence performance, generate boredom. Highest levels of arousal overwhelm and paralyze performance in the opposite direction.[7]

A parallel can also be drawn between emotional arousal and Gendlin's felt sense. Sometimes something simply "feels" right. Or something simply doesn't? Intersecting with Gendlin's (1991) three elements of meaning—feeling, language, and situation—are two levels of felt experience. The first and primary level is our internal bodily experience of literally "feeling" our emotions. Something stirs. Something visceral calls attention to itself. But it is not emotion per se. It is preverbal and preconceptual (and I might add where therapeutic progress is best made). To understand meaning experienced at this felt level we focus on its sensory and kinesthetic components, as in meditation. At the second level of experiencing we bring the felt sense into conscious awareness, conceptualizing and labeling it, usually at the same time. A typical emotion has a name[8]; a felt sense does not. The actual "feel" of a protoemotion is therefore different from a report of it. Arousal thus provides a key to understanding simple binary emotions as well as the intricate and subtle emotions resulting from intellectual processing.

Affect, Emotion, Feelings

While I wouldn't go so far as William James in proposing that emotion is little more than the feeling of a bodily state, taken together, the constructs of affect, emotion, or feeling are situated next to bodily arousal at the "hot" theoretical pole. They are the cornerstone of the Valuative System insofar as they are simultaneously themselves and the seminal component of all other members of the system.

To start, the language of these constructs is bewildering. Some psychologists like Simon claim that *affect* is a household word when it is quite the opposite. *Affect* is the high-brow term for emotion. It stands for emotion in its most scientific sense. Affect is also used as a

---

[7]There may also be a rebound effect; when thought becomes too active, some individuals become catatonic.

[8]However, an unnamed emotion may be as real and felt as keenly as a named one.

superordinate or umbrella construct, under which are included concepts embued with emotion such as moods, interests, sentiments, passions, and so on. On the other hand, the term *feeling* is vernacular. It is the word everyone understands, a blue-collar word, so-to-speak. Last, *emotion* is the term used by the educated but that most people also understand.

Acceptable use of the term *emotion* reflects its elusive quality. Emotion may mean excessive arousal at one time, motivation at another, or a specific feeling at still another. The term feeling may refer to complex as well as simple emotions but generally not to the physical act of touching. Nor is *I feel* used here to mean *I think* or *I believe*. Also independent of emotion are primary needs like hunger or thirst that may share the physiological and subjective aspects of feelings but originate organically.

Given those caveats, emotions may be distinguished on the basis of intensity, duration, and valence. The sensation of intensity is the biophysical experience contributed by our nervous system. Duration has to do with the length of time that any emotion lasts, including its weakening or strengthening. Valence, consisting of a positive or negative feeling *and* often an additional quality, is its unique and consummate attribute. So that if these three properties constitute emotion and some measure of emotion constitutes all members of the Valuative System, then it follows that some degree of emotional intensity, duration, and valence comprise the members of the Valuative System. In fact, the subjective reality of that inner experience constitutes its central feature, and it is commonly called feeling or emotion.

One method of categorizing emotion is by trait emotion and state emotion. Originating with Gordon Allport's psychology of personality, trait emotions are affective characteristics of long-standing. They predispose us to particular state emotions but do not have a locus in time. The construct of personality, the relatively permanent organization of our behavior and responses, explains differences between us. In the sense that trait emotions are regularities of emotional response, they are associated with temperament and may be likened to personality characteristics. State emotions are characteristic of our affective life at a given moment. They refer to temporary departures from the trait emotions. Unlike the trait emotions, state emotions occur within specific points in time and have identifiable beginnings, middles, and ends. They tend to run through short characteristic courses and may vary widely in intensity (Brand 1989a).

What I have left out is the cognitive component of emotion. Mainstream psychology recognizes two types of emotion: theoretically pure emotions and the cognized emotions—the ones we think

through. The theoretically pure emotions are considered the non-
propositional parts of evaluations. By this is meant emotions that are
innate, biologically predetermined, nonrational, and occur with little
or no learning. Emotions like surprise, fear, and anger are believed to
be inborn and universal, developing ontogenetically and phylogenetically earlier than cognitions (Bain 1894; Darwin 1894). These "*un-
cognized* universal psychobiological experiences*" (Kleinman 1980,
173) evolve into "secondary" emotions which are mediated by cognition (i.e., meaning analysis) and appraisal—as well as by social and
cultural specifics.

You may remember the cognitive position from the discussion
on arousal: simple affective reactions involve straightforward positive
or negative elements. When emotional response is limited to a binary
positive or negative, it may be possible to make a case for the inclu-
sion of emotion in a cognitive system. Cognitive structures can
accommodate bipolar descriptions with exquisite clarity.

But when bad and good no longer reflect the subtleties of our
feelings, we move to specific emotions about which we need to think.
That is when our feelings become cognitive. Our emotional state is
then defined after we analyze and appraise the situation. By that time
our emotions are also conceptualized and labeled. We give them
names: happy, guilty, frustrated. While states of consciousness may at
bottom be reduced to positive or negative, they are in fact enormous-
ly varied, as the abundance of terms used for them reflects: joy, anger,
elation, fear, sorrow, curiosity, and so on. Each of these nouns refers
to a slightly different condition, even though, according to psychologist Bartlett, "no working vocabulary . . . comes anywhere near [to]
matching the delicate distinctions of affective response of which [we]
are capable" (1932, 223).

Indeed, emotion is a different order of information. When explanations of it are offered by psychologists these days, it is not surprising that they involve *representations*. But the fact is that mainstream
cognitive theory cannot apply directly to phenomena that it was not
developed to explain. How does one *represent* the duration of sorrow,
the intensity of joy, the frequency of anxiety, the kind of anticipation,
the centrality of belief, the stability of attitude? How does one depict
the temporal sequencing of emotion? Does one make the line on the
flow chart thicker or longer? Does one make the box heavier? Darker?
And what do we do with emotion expressed through metaphor?
Gesture? Try diagramming guilt!

Schemas are capable of being modified but incapable of reflecting
minute shades of meaning or the dynamics of frequency, duration,
intensity—despite noteworthy attempts (Bower and Cohen 1982;
Mandler 1982; Wyer and Srull 1989).

Also questionable is the account of emotions as interruptions in otherwise lawful and stable intellectual events. As I stated in the discussion on arousal, cognitivists claim that emotions are invoked by discrepancies and the meaning attached to them. Furthermore, *major* incongruities result in negative emotions. These explanations seem naive first because it is altogether possible for *major* incongruities to result in positive emotions. Second, it is possible for us to recruit *equal* intellectual effort to modify positive as well as negative emotions. Third, assigning terms like interruption and incongruity to emotions suggests a pathology when it is plain that negative emotions can actually be positive and healthy and positive emotions can be negative and unhealthy. Put plainly, the language itself is troublesome. In a more balanced perspective, emotions, regardless of valence, should be considered as signaling a redirection of attention and as organizing new behaviors. This is precisely why we need a theory of composing that accounts for emotion in extracognitive ways.

It seems that at one extreme cognitive evaluations are believed to be produced without corresponding emotion (Simon 1982). At the other more popular extreme, emotions are viewed as just another—albeit discrepant—form of cognition (Leventhal 1982). In the latter view there is no privileged access to affective information (Mandler 1990). Nor is any postulated—especially for pleasant feelings. Instead, emotions are handled like other higher-order semantic operations, in a path analysis or typical flowchart fashion. Feelings are stored as integral parts of schemas or scattered around them, or efficiently summarized or wholly represented by them (Bower 1981; Fiske and Linville 1980). Psychologist Bower particularly hypothesizes an Associative Network Theory of memory and emotion. Propositions are recorded in memory by establishing nodes that describe and gather various events or concepts within them. Activation travels from concept to concept or event to event through associative links, like nerve cell activity with its synapse and dendrites. When considered cognitive, the emotional aspects of an experience also attach to or become nodes. And, when activated, the emotions undergo the same associative process.

In contradistinction social and neuroscientists lobby for the speed of emotion, the parallel development of emotion and cognition, and their partial autonomy (LeDoux 1989; Zajonc 1980). Psychologist Zajonc maintains that "feeling accompanies all cognitions" (1980, 154) and can become functionally independent from the original experience in terms of day-to-day activation. Emotions linked to a stimulus may survive after we no longer recall the experience itself. We may remember liking a book but not remember why. Moreover, certain parts of the brain mature earlier than others which may explain why we have no autobiographical memory when we are first born (LeDoux 1989, 281). There may also be technical grounds for separating the two:

> If there are circumstances at all where affect and cognition are conceptually separate systems, it is useful to treat them as such, so as not to preempt answers to the question of how they interact. We can always collapse them into one system if the benefits of the distinction do not outweigh the benefits of parsimony. But if we start with affect and cognition as one system we will never move beyond it. (Zajonc, et al. 1982, 214)

In the end emotion appears to be at one and the same time a most elemental as well as supple and quintessential constituent of all members of the Valuative System. As basic emotions become established, they become a function of social learning. Ways of regulating emotion are culturally reinforced, so that the social ultimately educates the emotional. Social phenomena not only shape personality but become increasingly correlated to the rest of the Valuative system.

Mood

We've all heard the expressions: "Oh, never mind him. He's just moody." Or: "Our children are cranky." Others have sunny dispositions. Mood is a more diffuse, global, and less intense form of affect than its corresponding emotional state. Unlike emotion it is unrelated to a particular cause, consequence, or object. It is: "I feel just plain grouchy today" as opposed to "I am irritated by the book review." Moods may be shortlived insofar as we snap out of them, or more enduring. Habitual moods may be likened to trait emotions, predispositions to respond that resist change regardless of context.

Moods are differentiated from other evaluative processes to the extent that we are generally unaware of the factors giving rise to them. In cognitive terms mood is applied to emotion that is not acute or interruptive. In other words, mood is located within ongoing thought without noticeably disturbing it (Simon 1982). At the same time so influential is mood that it can enhance or debilitate perception as well as memory. In a watershed study of induced mood states, Bower demonstrated that emotional congruence between past experience and an induced mood produced greater recall of that experience — including its details: Positive personal experiences were more likely recalled in happy moods. Negative personal experiences and negative words were more likely recalled in depressed moods. Its biophysical explanation is that recall of a event with, say, a negative emotional tone is more probable from a current negative mood because the arousal linked to both time periods is similar (Clark 1982, 281).

Preference

Situated in the approximate vicinity on the continuum as mood because of its moderate nature, a preference is defined as a mild wish for or like of something. There is a difference however. Unlike moods, preferences are particular. They are linked to objects or ideas. To the extent that their properties are described (recognized and verbalized), preferences are cognitive.

From the cognitive point of view preferences become affective when combined with arousal. While preferences tend not to be heavily emotional, social psychologists believe that strong emotional elements are prevalent when preferences are acquired in childhood. Unlike the cognitive position that claims that before you can prefer something you must *know* what it is, they claim that, like emotions, preferences can precede that knowledge. However, also like emotions, even when preferences originally arise out of intellectual thought and mental structures are consolidated before a preference is developed, the original intellectual justification for it may be forgotten or dissociated from its emotional component. The source of the preference goes underground, so to speak. But the stimulus is still capable of invoking its emotional element as well as a particular response (Zajonc and Markus 1982). Furthermore, preferences can become the affective springboard for the formation of attitudes, beliefs, and values. To which I devote the next essay.

15

Defining Our Emotional Life
The Cool End
(Plus Motivation)

Alice Glarden Brand

Attitudes

Following mood and preference there is a decided shift in the makeup
of the members of the Valuative System. This location marks a notice-
able decrease in emotional intensity, an increase in the stability of
emotions, and an increase in concentration of cognitive content.
Although attitudes, beliefs, and values may initially be learned from
actual encounters with objects and situations, their emotional component also tends to be global. We thus feel generally positive or negative about things, but not specifically frustrated or guilty as we might
with standard emotions. Attitudes, beliefs, and values are broader and
more ideational than emotions are. This means that they embody more
knowledge about the phenomena in question. Attitudes become more
conscious, more capable of representation, and more accessible to
analysis.

At this point the scale also tips toward the social, for these forms
of evaluation are especially validated consensually. With its heyday
decades ago when attitude was regarded as the sine qua non subject
of social psychology, the science of attitude (see Brand 1991 for a
fuller history) still remains communally constituted. Divested of its
cognitive properties, attitude, for all intents and purposes, would be
social emotion.

Composite definitions establish attitudes as "a relatively enduring
organization of beliefs around an object or situation predisposing

individuals to respond in some preferential manner" (Rokeach 1972, 112; see also Allport 1935). This definition couples both active and static properties. Dynamic definitions underscore a mental or neural state of readiness or a preparedness to act. Static definitions underscore a stability but also introduce another member of the Valuative System: belief. This definition in fact attributes to attitudes "bundles of interlocking beliefs" about objects or situations that may be true or false (descriptive or existential) or desirable or undesirable (prescriptive or proscriptive) (Rokeach 1972, 159).

Among their properties, attitudes may be subdivided by their degree of centrality, organization, specificity, and breadth. Centrality means that attitudes are rank ordered by personal significance. Organization has to do with temporal matters — past, present, or future, and the scope of the period. Specificity refers to the extent that attitudes are differentiated and the ability to predict one attitude from another. Breadth refers to the entire range of ideas that attitudes encompass (Rokeach 1972).

Beliefs

We express an attitude about essay tests. But we believe in the power of the written word. So central are attitudes that beliefs have also been defined in terms of them (Rokeach 1972). Organized like attitudes on an axis from greatest to least importance, beliefs continue to reflect a tendency toward or away from real objects or things. One difference between attitudes and beliefs is that beliefs are held more and more in terms of classes of objects rather than in single objects themselves. While beliefs do not necessarily result from direct contact with these objects, they are accompanied by ideas about their *worth*.

We normally do not believe "against" something. Rather, beliefs take something in our experience as correct or good. They are propositions about the world held as true. To make a judgment about something is also to express a belief about it. Although beliefs are commonly associated with lofty and spiritual phenomena, faith is commonly assigned that meaning, leaving belief with the intellectual state or process of giving something credence. When not used to replace *I think*, say, that we should use pencil not pen, a computer not typewriter, belief like faith operates on the grounds of authority, evidence, or facts beyond observation or material reality. Because beliefs generally cannot be confirmed or denied, psychologists do not seem to find them interesting.

Based on acceptability, Milton Rokeach's classification specifies a first subset of beliefs as axiomatic and not controversial ("People write with a tool"). The second is private and can be impervious to persuasion ("Everybody writes better than me"). In a third subset beliefs may be substantiated by authorities and/or by knowledge derived from them (Peter Elbow advocates free writing for discovering ideas). Last, inconsequential beliefs are a matter of preference or taste ("I like writing poems more than fiction"). A more useful taxonomy of beliefs (Rokeach 1973) roots them in emotion and subdivides them into: Descriptive or Existential, wherein a belief is capable of being true or false (e.g., "Writing is learned"); Evaluative, wherein something is judged as good or bad (e.g., "Freewriting is effective"); and Prescriptive or Proscriptive, wherein some means- or end-activity is judged to be desirable or undesirable (e.g., "Direct instruction in writing is more useful than strict writing-intensive classes").

More stable than attitudes, beliefs are composed of an affective component that recedes in prominence and display except when challenged or changed. Because of the conceptual intimacy between attitude and belief, when the affective component of an attitude is altered, a reorganization of the corresponding beliefs also occurs (and vice versa).

Beliefs form systems around what I call spheres of experience: hedonic, aesthetic, religious, economic, ethical, logical, political, and so on. Our spheres of experience have represented within them some organized psychological but not necessarily logical hierarchy. So that beliefs are vulnerable to the usual distortions of our subjectivity. Writing lore abounds with misconstruals about the process: Think before you write. A simple sentence reflects a simple mind. Sticks and stones will break my bones but names will never harm me. But never argue with anyone who buys ink by the gallon.

While in a top-down view beliefs are treated as ingredients of attitudes and values as "versions" of beliefs within a belief system (Rokeach 1972), the continuum here posits the reverse or bottom-up approach. Ontogenetically and conceptually, attitudes interlock to form a belief, and beliefs are the building blocks of values, to which I now turn.

Values and Value Systems

The relationship of values to attitudes and beliefs is considerable. Like attitudes and beliefs, values are generally considered learned and expressed in choices. Like attitudes and beliefs, values accrue slowly, situation by situation. Like them both, values form systems which are ranked by social or personal priority. However, unlike attitudes and beliefs, values are becoming viewed as set partly by evolutionary selection (in the form of emotion- or value-laden brain structures) (Edelman 1992; Pugh 1977). Unlike attitudes and beliefs, values are only indirectly responsive to objects or things or classes of them.

Social scientists define values as prescriptive and proscriptive beliefs that reach *beyond* specific objects or situations. They transcend judgments about the immediate world to ideal modes of conduct or end-states of existence (Rokeach 1973). And values embody standards. To the extent that we have as many values as beliefs, some psychologists confer a one-to-one equivalence between them, making them interchangeable (Csikszentmihalyi and Larson 1984; Mandler 1982).

An etymologically obvious member of the Valuative System, values occupy a point closest to the cool or cognitive end of the continuum. Once more or less exclusive to philosophy and religion, values have become interesting to the sciences. Although, as I have noted, the prevailing cognitive position on "valuations" raises questions, cognitive psychology nonetheless neatly bases values in:

1. innate emotional and adaptive or biological tendencies like approach and withdrawal;
2. social or cultural learning; and
3. schemas or representations.

Concerned with structural evaluation, schemas or representations bridge values and a cognitive meaning analysis (see page 159). This is how the cognitive process of valuing works: Descriptive meaning refers to pure information ("The story is five hundred words long"). Affective meaning is evaluative and refers to judgments that cannot be reduced to objective information ("The story is joyful"). These form the basis of a cognitive values system. In other words, an evaluation consists of 1) identifying the internal features of an object; and 2) judging their value or appreciating the relationships among the features (Mandler 1982). This evaluative judgment then "selects" the appropriate emotion (Mandler 1990, 25).

Values arise out of a match between event and a schema. When a meaning analysis squares with an existing schema, this congruity produces a positive evaluation, one *independent* of arousal, interruption, or discrepancy. These value judgments typically have low emotional intensity; are "cold," familiar, and accepted; and reflect Piagetian assimilation (Mandler 1990, 24-29). When no prior cognitive structure exists or when phenomena and structure conflict, disruption occurs. Arousal is produced, and individuals engage in more meaning analysis, in other words, more thought. In this instance the evaluation is "hot" or affective and reifies Piagetian accommodation. According to the cognitive valuing process, affectively tinged judgments are usually negative while their positive counterparts may or may not be.

Contemporary psychology is to be praised for even a timid incursion into the arena of values. But it seems to ignore its own literature on the relationship between values and means and ends as enunciated by Tolman—one of their own (see page 174). A more likely rationale for regarding values so highly developed intellectually may be found in part in our ability to anticipate, to predict. Csikszentmihalyi and Reed Larson maintain that our biology and habits shape our proclivities from behind "by channelling and structuring psychic energy in terms of past experience" (1984, 17; see also Luria 1973). At this level, we recruit parts of our more primitive selves adaptively. In contrast, values shape our interests in terms of what is to come. Values anticipate. Humans "have the exceptional ability to do things not only because it is their nature to do so ..." [our biology] or "because they benefit from the action at the present time (as habits would suggest), but because they want to achieve some future valued state" (17–18).

In a lucid and compelling account of valuing, physicist George Pugh emphasizes our biology in a different way. He describes the biology of human choice in order to theorize about the real and the ideal. Briefly, in Pugh's system, descriptive values explain the way people *actually behave* and the criteria they use to make decisions about such values. Predictive values *project* the types of decisions they *will* make by understanding how situations guide them. And prescriptive values help people decide what criteria *should* be used and what decisions *should* be made (1977, 327).

Of course when it comes to *shoulds* there is no better source of support for establishing values as an intellectual phenomenon than in theories of moral development. After early cognitivist Edward Tolman and Rokeach subdivided the value system into means and ends: 1) those upholding ideal behavior and ways of living; and 2) those upholding ideal end-states of existence (1979). Laurence Kohlberg, Jean Piaget, David Winter, and William Perry concern themselves with moral stages and idealized conduct across the life span. These development stages are equivalent to instrumental values or means for arriving at future states. Gordon Allport, P. E. Vernon, and Gardner Lindzey as well as Abraham Maslow, on the other hand, focused on end-states. Here values are reified as personal or social goals.

Values therefore concern central beliefs across the broad sweep of life and become standards for future behavior, judgments, and goals. Values may thus be envisioned as the conception of the desirable, the preferred, for ourselves or for humanitarian or altruistic purposes. The highest values such as truth and beauty are virtually independent of practicality and are clearly the makings of ethical maturity and choice.

For all intents and purposes, theories of emotion equal theories of values. While at one level this is true, there is a danger inherent in these approaches to which Kohlberg, Perry, and Winter have fallen victim (Brand 1987). And it besets the work of David Krathwohl and his colleagues. According to Krathwohl, if by affective maturity is meant "conduct," moral character, and conscience (7), by the time we mature affectively "behavior becomes completely internalized and routine," and emotion is no longer part of most responses (30). Krathwohl's arch example of the highest level of value is that students recognize the "good" in books or music (22). But even at lower levels Krathwohl's taxonomy has, for all intents and purposes, been neutered. He commits a cultural fallacy. Recognizing affect as exclusively a high abstraction and disconnected from our day-to-day emotional life is to attribute Olympian impartiality to our students and throw the baby out with the bath water.

Motivation

If we believe that the wish is father to the thought, motivation—the essence of the wish—has the distinction of being one of the two most powerful variables in learning (the other being ability). The complex theoretical term has been troubled by a lack of conceptual clarity since the appearance of the trivium of reason, feeling, and will—the earliest term for motivation.[1] Since that time the prescientific notion of will has been variously called volition, conation, desire, exigencies, or motivation. And it has been confused with humors, affections, passions, sentiments, emotions, instincts, drives, intentions, and purposes. It is no wonder that the word has been on a conceptual roller coaster. Consider these contradictory attributes:

Motivation is predetermined.	Motivation is volitional.
Motivation is conscious.	Motivation is unconscious.
Motivation initiates learning.	Motivation needs reduction for learning to occur.
Individuals may be generally motivated.	Motivational sources are contextual.
Motives are prior to the "wish."	Motives are a product of the "wish."
Motivation is biological/ organic.	Motivation is ideational/situational.
Motivation is compensatory.	Motivation is goal-based.
Emotion motivates and sustains activity.	Motivation subsumes emotion.

[1] Of the three faculties of the mind—intellect, emotion, and will—Piaget blurred the boundaries between emotion and motivation by collapsing emotion and will. He saw them as constituting intellectual energy but separate from structural cognition (Csikszentmihalyi and Larson 1984, 46).

The most straightforward definition refers to motivation as mental initiative. Sounding not surprisingly like arousal, motivation in this definition assumes a baseline physiological state that is valence free. It simply signals a change in our impulse to act. Because the connection between motivation and emotion is time-honored and shares its etymological roots, a distinction must be made between what is sheer impulse and what is affective.

A more comprehensive definition refers to motivation as a hypothetical construct intended to explain the initiation, direction, persistence, and integration of behavior (Appley 1983; Murray 1964; Weiner 1986). The distinction between sheer impulse and affective impulse is embodied in the word *direction*. Insofar as direction implies something as desired or not desired, we are of course dealing in emotion. Insofar as direction reflects a wish to avoid something or a willingness to take something on and take steps to acquire it, motivation is the psychological wellspring of behavior and inferred from it.

Emotion and motivation therefore overlap in several ways. Both emotion and motivation embody impulses to act. The *motivational component of emotion* resides in its behavioral properties (with arousal as its physiological counterpart). By the same token, *motivation becomes emotional* whenever valence is implicated, whenever arousal occurs along with some sense of the positive or negative. The two also overlap to the extent that motivation is broadly based, concerned with whole classes of responses (personal, social, political, intellectual, and so on). But emotion is capable of greater elaboration and differentiation. Emotion may thus be viewed as motivation particularized. And like other affectively embued constructs motivation is to be viewed not in maximum but in optimal terms, curvilinear like the Yerkes-Dodson theory (see page 160). Last, like other members of the Valuative System, motivation is "a complex of things, some biological, some situational, some cognitive, some emotional . . ." (Norman 1981, 290). Whatever the configuration, motivation is more than preparatory. It keeps us invested with psychological energy— conscious or not conscious—until we get what we want or abandon it or accept a substitute.

Two trends are apparent in modern studies of motivation: the first converts drive and instinct theory to arousal and adaptation theories; the second shifts the intervening variables for explaining motivation from mechanistic to exacting mental processes within the cognitive paradigm (Appley 1983, 280).

The first trend put an adaptive and physiological spin on motivation. Silvan Tomkins and Carroll Izard subdivided human mental activity into three systems of which emotion was defined as the primary motivational system. Positing a neurochemical source for affects, they contended that affective processes were derived directly from it. Affective-cognitive relationships evolve into unnumbered structures that constitute the motivational experiences marking human consciousness and behavior. Moreover, the special motivational qualities of emotion insured human survival and adaptation (Plutchik 1980).

The construct of adaptation level has also been postulated to explain the strength and direction of motivation (Helson 1964). Adaptation levels per se are neutral internal states *before* a stimulus presents itself. An adaptive act involves a motivating stimulus, a sensory situation, and a response that alters the situation in such a way as to satisfy the motivating conditions. Motivation is cued by the distance of a stimulus from the prevailing adaptation level. The more a stimulus departs from that level, the more intense its motivating power (Helson 1977). The direction of that departure explains the direction of motivation, once again implicating a positive or negative, or, in other words, an affective model of motivation. Adaptation levels governing motivation can obviously be changed by experience. For one, adaptation levels are altered socially. For another, repetition strengthens adaptation and weakens motivation. That is, repetition can desensitize (Luria 1973, 276) if not evoke opposite reactions.

The second path to a cognitive psychology of motivation was cleared initially by Tolman in the thirties.[2] Motivation thrived in Tolman's purposive psychology to the extent that it served means-ends relationships. Despite his highly technical theory, Tolman gave motivation some of its essential nomenclature: means-objects, means-situations, secondary goals, end-goals, and goal-objects. His legacy produced these fundamental ideas:

1. A limited number of relatively general and stable motives develop in childhood.
2. These include the primary motives of approach or avoidance, which are: to achieve or succeed; to avoid failure; to seek affiliation or social approval, power, and other motives responsive to a reward system or incentives.
3. Expectations of the consequences of various actions arise from the interaction of personality, socialization, and learning (Atkinson 1977).

Indeed, today psychology focuses on motivation as the source of goal-oriented activity or performance. Unlike earlier psychoanalytic and drive or need reduction theories in which motivation was compensatory and biological, the chief tenet of current theory remains: the

---

[2]Although Lewin's (1944) level of aspiration and Maslow's (1954) hierarchy of motivation also helped place motivation in mainstream psychology.

greater the likelihood of attaining a goal, and the greater its value, the more intense the positive motivation. In shorthand,

$$\text{motivation} = \text{what we expect} \times \text{its value}$$

(Weiner 1974)

And with that we come full circle to the cognitive theory of "valuation."

Adding another layer of cognitive mediation, Bernard Weiner (1986) postulates the intervening variable of causal attribution to explain motivation (and distinct emotions). Essentially, how we assign the responsibility for arriving at or failing to reach specific goals is based on internal or external locus, stability, and controllability (51). Goals, of course, depend on the presence and strength of certain values. Pugh calls a preceding value the sensation of value that we experience *before* engaging in the activity it is intended to motivate. The sensation of value following a motivated activity is a *consequence* which Pugh calls a trailing value. Plainly, values serve as both determinants and effects of motivation.

The members of the Valuative System—arousal to values—all participate in motivation by helping specify: 1) the life goals and intermediary values that establish and reinforce motives; 2) the source of the goals or values; and 3) the behavior to satisfy those motivations (Atkinson and Raynor 1974; Rokeach 1979).

Because we as educators are directly concerned with mastery of skills and knowledge, we are concerned with learning them. Achievement motivation restricts goals to those involving learning and performance.[3] Put simply, achievement motivation answers the questions as to "*which* activity will occur, *when* and for how long?" And, most important, "*how* well is the activity executed?" (Atkinson and Raynor 1974, 391).

Extrinsic and intrinsic motivation are forms of achievement motivation. Extrinsic motivation is our inclination to do things for outside rewards, recognition, or goals. In such situations the reward is external to a situation. In fact, sometimes the reward is better than the task; "the activity [may be] performed *in order to* get the reward" (Murray 1964, 74). Intrinsic motivation is our impulse to do something for its own sake or for our own pleasure. An intrinsic orientation means that we identify with the goal of an activity. We experience positive feelings, spontaneous involvement in whatever is going on, and a sense of control over it. Major intrinsic motivations are: manipulatory (sensory and activity), social (affection, approval, affiliation),

---

[3]Theories of causal attribution for successful or failed achievement may also be applied here (Weiner 1986).

interest-oriented (curiosity), and intellectual (mastery or satisfaction). Even when intermediary tasks are perceived as extrinsic steps toward an intrinsic goal, the intrinsic quality of the motivation is not necessarily invalidated.

Whereas many factors influence intrinsic motivation, whether or not we achieve (perform) is first and foremost mediated by our temperamental traits. As I described earlier, traits are *enduring* dispositions of any internal processes—motivational, emotional, perceptual, or cognitive. When definitions about our internal lives refer to an "enduring" organization of anything, they suggest a relationship to personality whose genetic bases may be inferred through the intervening variable of traits (Allport 1961; Brand 1991). Personality shapes the motivations we initially bring to situations, and, as such, is a source of achievement motivation. Personality is derived from our predisposing traits. Our traits, in turn, are a function of our biological predilections. These built-in tendencies guide the motivation for constructing our intellectual lives in the first place. Once that process gets going, these tendencies continue to be at least partly responsible for arousing motivation under certain stimulus conditions. At the same time, they provide the context for interpreting the infinite layers of new data received from experience. And this is learning. So powerful is motivation that it determines which things we notice and selects which activities we repeat (Hilgard 1975). Over the long haul "[m]otivation can make the difference between learning or not, decent performance or not, what one attends to, what acts one does" (Norman 1981, 290). The interaction between our effort (I try) and our ability (I can) (Weiner 1986, 46) is central to a psychology of writing because the psychology lies in that very interaction.

The Valuing Mind

What we discover about evaluating is that it is at one and the same time a sophisticated condition exclusive to humans as well as a "leftover of a primitive alerting system" (Norman 1981, 282) exclusive to no one organism. At the upper reaches of the valuing mind, arousal, emotion, cognition, and milieu become increasingly embedded in each other, horizontally across experience as well as developmentally. At this level the mind serves as a control system. Our feelings in consciousness may be cognized—symbolized, suppressed, contemplated, cultivated. But just because emotion is intellectualized does not mean it is cognitive. Words help bring emotions within cognitive control—allowing me, for example, to do what I am doing now—discuss the complexities of feelings. However, if we applied to our personal lives the sole concept of objective rationality we would miss a major point I am making. In Carl Rogers's words, some of the deepest learning does not seem "to fit well into verbal symbols" (1961, 203). A seminal property of emotion is its verbal ineptitude. As such emotions are a primary fact of human experience; they are a natural and trustworthy heuristic.

But do they develop before or after other parts of our mind? In traditional psychology the role of emotions is passive, a reaction to cognized experience. Emotions are then end-products of mental processes arising from direct experiences, memories of them, or memories of emotions linked to them.

However, just as the mind continues to exceed its own intellectual frontiers, in its most elemental role we are reminded of the fundamentality of emotions as a starting point for virtually all human experience. From the evolutionary perspective, our rudimentary, emotion-driven values stimulate basic attention and arousal. At the other end of the intellectual spectrum, emotions play a central role in higher-order thinking: constructing knowledge, making decisions, and adapting behavior (Luria 1973). Recent research confirms the impact of emotion on free associations, judgments, and predictions often more powerfully than the reverse (Amabile 1983; Tucker, et al. 1990; Wyer and Srull 1989).

The paths between emotion and the intellect are indeed bi-directional. "[N]eurological control structures have dual activations, one from below—from the emotions—one from above—the intellect" (Norman 1981, 282). In the bottom-up model the causal arrow runs from arousal to emotion to intellectual valuing, as my continuum suggests. Emotions shape values through attitudes and beliefs, which emotion—and by extension the whole Valuative System—then reflects. In pyramidal fashion this means that thousands of attitudes toward specific things exist within belief systems and serve several dozen intermediary values, which are connected to even fewer terminal values, ones that you can count on the fingers of both your hands. The important idea here is that valuing is a developmental and socially constituted process—bottom-up, from childhood into adulthood, from biology to rationality (a biology of a vastly different sort).

Then top-down. Only then (but actually all along in layer and loop fashion [Edelman 1992]) is the Valuative System invoked by social and cultural values and comes to express them (Allport 1935; Edelman 1992). Only then do we ascribe values to experience. Only then do values occupy a position more central than emotions, bring them into line, and regulate emotional response. Only then does cognitive content evoke emotion and activity. All the while our biology acts as a filter for sensory information, letting some data in and keeping other data out.

I wish to remind readers that I am not advocating biological deter-
minism. In the sum of human events our potential seems without
limit. I simply want to emphasize the biophysiology that has gone
unappreciated in composition studies—its simplicity and intricacy,
its wonder and mystery. Our Valuative System is composed of primary values that are innate and impregnable, and an elaborate and
evolving system of secondary values that develop out of them and are
carved by experience. Without an understanding of such systems,
current theories can provide only so much explanation of our complex
and functionally integrated mental life.

With the language that has empowered our mental life, there has
had to occur a parallel progression in our capacity to value. The most
important human values are emotional, not intellectual. Our Valuative
System provides a window into our motivations and direction for our
behavior. Our decisions are driven by it, turning potential values into
actualized values—for among the differences between us and the
paramecium is our ability to choose. But we do a lot more than merely move toward what is important and away from what is inconsequential or harmful. The fact that information alone rarely changes
values suggests the power of the emotional substratum. Heartbeat and
pulse, emotion gives experience its stick-to-the-ribs quality. We see
the world from the inside. To the extent that emotions reflect such
reality, they are emblematic of the only conscience we have.

Part Six

The Open Door

The final section of this book, The Open Door, is a sampler of new directions. Taken together, this section represents both the diversity and the promise of teaching and learning beyond the cognitive domain.

"Where do you find your stories?" asks Donald M. Murray, as he writes to find his answer. Murray makes clear that story is central in the lives of writers. Story has a personal history, written in the bloodlines of our forebears. Moreover, story is characterized by paradox and mystery: always present is a darkness we can't comprehend. Our story, our life, is like a small fire at the edge of that darkness. The lines of Don Murray's story reach back into childhood where he finds the origins of his life experience.

Our profession has long neglected the power of writing as a source of healing. Reports of the salutary benefits of writing, however, come from many sources—twelve-step programs, student personal writing, psychologists and their patients, and counselors. The more individuals attest to the efficacy of writing, the more we must listen. Sandra Burkett describes the anatomy of the healing process within the school environment. She traces the therapeutic progress of an adult student who found writing a means to overcome addiction and to regain health.

The idea of healing is extended in Gabriele Rico's "The Heart of the Matter: Language, Feeling, Stories, Healing." Rico tells of her childhood in Germany during World War II, the death of her mother in a bombing raid, and the resulting pain that has continued through her life. Writing is "a whole-making activity," Rico suggests, a process that involves the mythic dimensions of each of our stories.

"The relationship between teacher and student is so much like love it disconcerts," says Richard J. Murphy, Jr. In the writing classroom, especially in small groups, relationships unfold and grow. The idea of the class as community suggests intimacy, connectedness. When instructors read a student paper, are they not reading a life? Murphy shows how feelings, both positive and negative, influence the quality of learning. Instructors need to understand the dynamics of these powerful forces, to be aware of both their dangers and possibilities.

This section hints at the wealth of topics lying in the area outside traditional cognitive concepts and assumptions, though our present level of understanding does not permit us to see its exact shape or contents. In describing the domain beyond the cognitive, the first metaphor that comes to mind is a vast outer space. Ironically, new discoveries will not be "outer" but "inner," found in the genius and inspiration of writers and teachers.

16

Where Do You Find Your Stories?

Donald M. Murray

The question always surprises me. I imagine everyone swims in an ocean of narrative. How else can anyone experience—and understand—the world except through stories? The stories I tell my readers are but a millionth of those I tell myself. Each day overflows with narrative and every night I dream.

When does a fish know it is a fish? I was a writer before I had language. We all are.

Literacy precedes reading, precedes language; literacy is, first of all, the silent-to-others narratives you tell yourself in your head to make order of your world. The story that Mother will return from the other room is made up, tested by reality, and retold before its teller has developed the spoken language to share this wondrous story of abandonment and return.

We all carry stories into this world. My stories were passed down in the blood from flint users who came to the land that would be known as Scotland, inherited from the makers of fire, the ax carriers, herders, sowers, beaker people and cairn builders and on through to Pict, Scot, Celt; their stories all in me at birth, stories of loyalty and betrayal, love and hate, gain and loss, defense and attack, survival and belief. When I first heard the bagpipe tell a story I was not hearing it for the first time.

I was a writer long before I could read, before I could write, before I could speak. I do not make up stories by writing them; the stories are there, grown on their own inevitable telling. I write a few of them down so they can escape and make room for the new stories that are telling themselves.

I was a writer when my finger traced the brown roads in the faded oriental rug on the living room floor of the house I can hardly remember, and even now I can explore the boxed red squares in which there were secret places I later called forts.

Visiting my year-old-grandson, I see him, with one tiny finger, trace the roads on his Oriental rug, different than mine and the same. His stories come from Russia, Germany, Scotland and he knows, now, before we can understand the stories he tells, the terrible, glorious history of the Jews.

Playing on the Oriental rug of my own childhood, I read the mysterious signals sent by strange fingered hand shadows I would later discover matched maple leaf and oak outside the window. When those shadows left, I told myself about the people who lived in the cities Jack Frost etched on the window pane. On bright days I told myself the stories sent by reflected light, bright spots, circular and oblong, that bounced along ceiling and wall.

I was born to a house with a family that lived in the wall. I cannot remember the last name of the tiny family—small as lead soldiers— that lived in the walls, but one boy was named Donald. He had brothers and sisters and was not an only child. Our rooms were small, but the world within the wall was large; it held oceans, mountains, valleys, cities, ships, Indian tribes, Crusader castles.

Only once did I run away from home, making it only to the next block, returning to the family in the wall, knowing I could escape any room in that house of grown-ups—grandmother, mother, uncle, father —tall people who were given to silences and looking away.

Once, I grew careless and talked to the wall family out loud but the giant people with whom I lived only laughed. They were never worried about the family in the wall, never knew they were my favorite family. They did not know how much time I spent within the wall, how little with them; that when they praised me for being a good little boy—"seen but not heard"—they didn't realize that I was not only silent but also gone.

At first stories were my escape, later they would be my vocation. For now, it was enough to pass into the wall, watch what was happening to what they thought was the real Donald. There was violence in our house, discreet Baptist violence kept from the neighbors—our curtains were always drawn to the proper height—and even, it seemed, from ourselves. Everyone ignored an unfortunate sudden rage, a crying out that was quickly choked back down, the slammed door, the night walk alone.

The rod was not spared. My pants were yanked to my ankles and the slick brown leather shaving strap, pronounced strawp, snaked down or the hair brush, its backside dipped in water to make it sting,

beat against me, again and again and again. We were all born in sin.
We could only work towards unachievable virtue, doing good works
that were never good enough, trying to be what we were not, in the
hope of salvation: in the hereafter, when the roll was called up yon-
der, we would be there, rising on a smug column of righteousness
while most of those around us would fall screaming into the sea of
flames.

That was a story, the story of salvation, the story of damnation.
The Bible was filled with stories; the evangelist strode the platform
telling stories. Religion was true narrative—Jonah and the whale, the
loaves and the fishes, Jesus and the money changers in the temple, the
crucifixion and the resurrection.

I also learned family history through stories: how we came to the
lands beyond the sea, from island and moor, croft and textile mill;
how the Black Watch fought in the war against Napoleon and how the
ancestor for whom I was named took a ball in the knee and his brother stepped into his place; how each family made a first voyage across
the ocean, then returned, then made a second voyage back.

Grandmother brought with her the Black Watch shawl, trunks of
clothes and dishes and books—my grandfather had been a bookseller,
his father a poet—as well as stories from Scotland, every story with
its own terror, its own moral. Father brought home deacon stories
from church—we had roast minister for Sunday dinner—and his buy-
ing trips to New York City; Mother told the stories of neighbors,
friends, and her brother's wives.

We talked indirectly, through stories, discovering why people
were hired or let go, were unhappy or happy, married or single, with
family or childless, ill and sick to death or both hale and hearty.

My real family created and defined themselves by their stories
and I created myself by living stories with the family in the wall. I can
remember the joy of myselfness I must still admit to, the pleasure of
solitude, the comforting escape into loneliness, the passage into the
wall. I was not abandoned or punished but grateful to be left alone in
rooms or hallways or on that Oriental rug, doors shut against me.
There were no silences but make believe. The rug was a magic carpet,
I had a Newfoundland dog, my rocking horse was real.

I lived a guerrilla life, a life of surveillance and betrayal; hiding
under tables, covered by the tent of hanging tablecloth; watching from
behind a sofa or sitting on a closet floor, the door cracked open; listening from under the draping forsythia bush where grown-up stories
fell out the summer window, or hearing, hidden by the lattice of the
under porch, their rock-rock-rocking chairs and discovered one night
I could understand what was not said; lying in the upstairs hall at the
heating grate I could follow the stories not for children's ears that rose

like invisible smoke from downstairs. I was spy to my life and grew
to like my secretiveness, what I knew they did not know I knew and
could only share with the family in the wall.

When I came to reading—and I cannot remember when I could
not read—it was all familiar. Others were telling stories, the stories I
had told myself. I knew all about narrative; I lived a life of stories.
My world was make believe: they told the stories I had written in my
imagination from what was not said, the narratives that spring up in
silences, the worlds to which I escaped, within the walls. I slid into
books as easily as I passed into the wall. I walked through the pages
and lived within their narratives—and out of their stories, I made
more stories of my own.

I was Daniel in the lion's den; I was my grandmother when she
was attacked by the bull while taking a shortcut to school in Scotland.
I did not hear stories, I entered stories. I was the Little Engine That
Could, Billy Goat Gruff, Pinocchio, Long John Silver, Little John
ever loyal to Robin Hood.

School was an uncomfortable place for a boy who lived in stories.
In class and playground, I remained for years in my story life, staring
out windows, standing at the edge of the playground, walking to
school alone, watching the street games from the sickly child's window, happy, content to participate in imagination.

I was shy, an only child, late and, I imagine, unexpected; a Scots
Protestant in a world of Irish Catholics; a bookish, bespectacled kid in
a neighborhood of rowdies. I ran to hide from strangers, walked the
long way home to avoid the loud boys, brash and confident, bare
knuckled. "Wanta knuckle sandwich, four-eyes?"

I read in the library and head down—a dangerous habit in my
neighborhood—read walking home from the library. I read on the
worn Oriental rug, kneeling in front of the wicker chair that became a
book rest, curled up in the chair, at the kitchen table, on the back
steps, up in the apple tree, on the pot, in bed at night with a flashlight,
all day when I was taken to Cape Cod by Uncle Will and left alone in
the car. I was blessed with a sickly childhood, spent almost all of one
year out of school with a tutor; experienced in visions in delirium
and was granted long days and weeks convalescence when I could
read and daydream—half dozing—and nightdream—half waking. My
life was narrative, secret narrative, and I remember the fear of growing up, of leaving that secret life, feeling that if I went out in the
world, I would leave behind all my stories and the family in the wall.

Sadly, with enormous fear, I left the family in the wall, left the
world invisible to others and dove, head first, into reality. I survived
the sad way we all learn to survive, by becoming what we are not. I
accomplished this, I suspect, by stories, telling myself the narratives

the world expected and then entering their stories. I did not know this. I thought I had put make believe behind. I learned costumes, manners, and appearance. More masks fitted than I could have imagined: the class play mask, the church youth leader mask, the delivery boy mask, the newspaper reporter mask, the right tackle mask, the combat paratrooper mask.

But I had not left the imagined world. I found these masks were as effective as the table cloth that hid me as I listened to grown-up talk. Wearing a mask I was never seen. I could live my secret life with the families—now there were many—that lived in the wall. My masks were many and none revealed the voices in my head, the cave drawings on the inside of my skull, the stories in which I was both writer and character.

I learned to deny Jesus and not turn the other cheek, to use knuckle and knee, eventually to speak to rooms full of the devout at church, to go to work, to deliver and even sell, to play football, to bump into people who terrified me, and to shoot back when Germans shot at me. I became whoever I had to be to graduate, to advance, to administer, to make my way in the world which was, of course, never my way but theirs.

I learned to dissemble, to smile, to laugh, to agree, to communicate what I was expected to communicate, to cultivate a shell of personality that allowed me to pass as one of the boys. I was hearty, outgoing, a public person who was once even charged with being a "people person" in the 1960s, pleasingly plump, good natured, hale, open.

I survived because of my inheritance from my family in the wall. They had taught me the great worlds within us. They had encouraged my secretiveness, my habit of observation, and, I suppose, my talent for betrayal, comparing what my family and other grown-ups said with what they did. No one saw the fantasies I created going to school and back, in classroom and church, all as much my life as were the stories I read, heard on the radio, or later saw on movie or television screen.

In high school I began to fear this habit of withdrawal. There was great fear in the land—and in my home. I heard my mother confess her worry to her cronies: I was a "bookworm," I was becoming an "introvert." They knew an introvert would not get ahead, would live a lonely life. I worried just the opposite. My interior life was far more interesting than the life of saddle shoes and beer jackets that was going on around me, certainly more interesting than the life of women's hosiery sales and prayer meetings my father led.

I did sense that there would be a price to pay for my escape into myself and there was: I have never had a vacation from observing others and, worst of all, myself, keeping score on all sins of commission—and omission, my own as wells as those of others. The eye that turns on others, turns on the self. I thought that perhaps this habit, this compulsive self-observation, self-examination would end when I grew up and found myself. But myself was the person I was, here, now, and there, now.

When I became a journalist, I found a new word to describe my interview style: empathy. When I talked to victim or criminal, detective or DA, I passed through the wall, found their lives there and entered into them. I could be doctor and patient, alcoholic and social worker, Chairman of the Joint Chiefs of Staff and enlisted man; labor leader and labor exploiter; environmentalist and polluter; politician and statesman; male and female; performer and audience. As a ghost writer I became Vice President Nixon's secretary, Rose Mary Woods; the U. S. Secretary of Labor, the CEO of a national corporation. No problem. They were all in the wall, waiting.

I worried, of course, about such writerly arrogance, my confident stealing of the lives of others. I feared what I made up could never be, what I wrote could never exist in "real" life. But like most writers, I learned that what some readers think could never happen, has happened to the writer—those are often the most autobiographical parts. And when I think I have gone too far, life provides post-draft documentation. My novel opens with a scene that I doubted; then I visited a town where it almost happened. Sometimes I wonder if the family in the wall doesn't even influence the life within the room, causing real people to perform the acts created by imaginary ones.

I have learned to accept the world I first shared with my family in the wall, a life counterpoint to what others call reality. Walking alone through the winter woods of the Ardennes in 1944, my rifle carried before me at the ready, assigned to find the British army turning south to cut off the German advance, I was the boy in Wollaston who had played snowball war or a city teenager at a New Hampshire camp grown comfortable in the woods. This morning, an old man walking to my 6:30 AM breakfast at the Bagelry, my hands still cradle my rifle, my ears hearing the owl, force my eyes to search for Germans. Later, at my desk, I write a story of war, making once again a narrative, drawing on the narratives I have lived, imagined, read, watched, dreamt, heard.

I live by narrative: the life of love and betrayal, fear and courage, said and unsaid, done and undone. Imagination extorts its price. I almost drowned three times but I had died by drowning hundreds of times before I learned to swim. I was captured and tortured, wounded, killed a thousand times in a war from which I returned without a physical scratch. As right tackle I scored one accidental touchdown on the field, ten thousand on my way to school, in class, at night in bed. In life you can only lose your virginity once, but I lost it a million times.

Sometimes I think the ability to live a life of stories is a curse: the sound at night is an animal more terrifying than any I have ever seen, every lump a tumor, the smell of smoke a conflagration, the wife or daughter late a victim of accident.

But I have no choice and each story is, I suppose, a preparation. When I was suddenly paralyzed and took my first ambulance ride, I surprised the attendant by saying it was just as I had described it in a novel years before. The life of make believe allows no escape, I am compelled to tell myself the story of my daughter's dying as it is happening—and the story of the father of a dying daughter. That real story was far worse than I imagined going down the corridor to her bedroom, night after night. The world tilts with vertigo: there is guilt in living in the wall and in the hospital waiting room—and therapy.

During my almost fatal heart attack, as six nurses and technicians bustle above I told myself the quiet story of at last meeting my daughter once more: Lee stands in her blue jumper waiting at the end of the brightly lit tunnel. I do not pass through the tunnel this time but she was there and there are tears in my eyes writing this and, guiltily, enough detachment to write it.

I have wondered at my strange life of narrative I grew to understand, living with the family in the wall, and think I stand apart from those around me, but when I write of what is most private, most personal, most unusual and unexpected in my life, readers write to tell me that I have articulated their stories. I discover my readers have been neighbors, waiting in the walls of my office to have their stories told.

But our stories are not our own. They were passed down and I will pass them down. None of them belongs to me; not the stories I have experienced here, in this world; not those I have experienced in the wall with my make-believe family; not the narratives that have been woven from what was lived here and there, overheard, read, observed, dreamed, made up, drawn up from that memory of the times so long before now, times when we first discovered the shelter of a cave, the warmth of fire, and the satisfaction of narrative.

17

The Butterfly Effect
Writing from Chaos to Composure

Sandra Price Burkett

> Through writing we may use composition to achieve composure.
>
> James Moffett, "Writing, Inner Speech, and Meditation"

"I have just escaped from an insane asylum." With those words David introduced himself during the first few minutes of my course. Everything about him confirmed his statement. Pale, eyes darting, hands and body trembling, his speech spasmodic in tone and rhythm, David said he had just left a recovery hospital for alcohol and drug addicts. That semester we—the other students and I—learned about the horror of David's alcohol and drug problems. And we sustained David while he wrote his way into the deep, swam, and surfaced somehow more whole.

Carl Gustav Jung wrote of a process he called individuation— the natural process of growing toward an authentic self which all humans share. Sometimes it happens spontaneously; sometimes we do something intentional to help the process along. Whichever the case, when it happens, we feel a new sense of integration, a new sense of pattern, new inner relationships, sometimes new outer relationships; we feel born anew in a very holy sense. It is the movement toward realizing the potential with which we are born. Just as an iris seed bears all its "instructions" and potential for becoming a beautiful Iris, so too every person has the potential for becoming a fully beautiful Self. Much of that process happens despite what we do in education. But just as an iris is able to reach its potential if it has proper air and water and nutrients, so our students' growth can be empowered by what we do in our classes.

Recently, my friend Bill, a Jungian analyst, observed that analysands who begin to write seriously often have dramatic breakthroughs in the individuation processes. Something about writing fosters individuation. I call the process moving from fragmentation to wholeness; Jim Moffett calls it moving "from chaos to cosmos"; some physicists call it "a science of process rather than state, of becoming rather than being" (Gleick 1987, 5). Ira Progoff calls it writing to evoke the development of the Self. My student David called it going from insanity to sanity. Whatever its name, writing encourages the process of finding order in disorder, integration in fragmentation, meaning in chaos, pattern in spatter, focus in blur. Why does writing have this effect on David, on Bill's analysands, and on other people I've known? What does that mean to us as educators? In 1981, Jim Moffett wrote:

> What really teaches composition—"putting together"—is disorder. Clarity and objectivity become learning challenges only when content and form are not given to the learner but when he must find and forge his own from his inchoate thought. . . . through writing we may use composition to achieve composure. . . . [A human being] is always in the process of converting chaos to cosmos—or perhaps of discovering the order concealed in apparent disorder—and the particular instance of this composition that we call writing partakes of this general ordering. (140–41)

David's Story

David enrolled in a class called Writing for Thinking, an upper division academic course designed to enhance the professional writing competence of future teachers and to prepare them to use writing as a tool for learning. Because almost all the students had traditional writing instruction—teacher assigns topic, specifies length, student writes before next class, student turns in paper, teacher grades, *finis*—I always have considerable work to do to change attitudes toward writing, especially enabling students to discover their preferred composing style.

The class begins with a positioning statement similar to that used by Progoff in the Intensive Journal Workshop: "This has been a time when . . . ." Then we move to cataloging persons, situations, and events in our lives that still hold significance. From these lists and elaborations we discover a focus from which we compose our first piece.

David returned over and over to the events and people he knew during the period of his alcohol and drug abuse. He re-experienced the traumas of the closing months of his addiction. He rambled, allowed anguish to surface, digressed to AA language, indulged in what he called self-flagellation, and thus relived his trauma. After much preparation, freewriting, focused sharing, and drafting, David's first full piece was as fragmented and chaotic as he looked that first night. Each paragraph began a new train of thought and sustained itself typically for one sentence, occasionally for two or three. Despite his journalism degree from a large Southern university and twenty years of experience as a professional journalist, David lurched his first draft over twelve pages—a portion of which follows:

> . . . . I had reached my bottom. After using alcohol and speed almost daily for several years I was severely depressed. I did not realize that my depression was due to drugs.
>
> At work I would go into the bathroom to snort speed and it made me so hyper that I could hear 5–6 conversations at once. I could not concentrate on my work and would have to drink several beers for lunch in order to calm down from the speed but, that made my mind foggy. . . .
>
> One night I was seeking drugs and someone with a pistol started chasing me down the middle of the street and shooting at me while I was zig zagging trying to miss his shots.
>
> One night, after leaving a bar, I was crossing the street and run over by a drunk driver. . . .
>
> One night I was drunk and picked up two sailors hitch hiking back to the base.
>
> One held my arm and the other beat me until the blood was flowing from my face. Then they threw me into the river.
>
> I was dead until I hit the water. It was pitch black and the bulkhead was 10 feet high. Somehow I climbed out and walked to a nearby hospital.
>
> I fell on the post door step, while bleeding profusely, as they said they were closed for the night. . . .
>
> My higher power has always been the God of the 1st Baptist Church and since I fired him I am now a recovering Southern Baptist. . . .

Response to David's Writing

When David brought this to class, his peer group was shocked by the events of his life, conscious of his vulnerability, and wary about their roles. None had faced the raging violence that David had. Conscious of their challenge, I kept the group in the periphery of my vision as I circulated around the room. Later I scolded myself for worrying because David and his response group quickly became close-knit.

In my classes I encourage students to respond first to writers as persons and then to their writing as artifacts. We practice active listening, that is, being with writers in the feeling tone of their story and practicing the empathic listening skills of a counselor: "I hear you saying — —"; "Sounds like you were feeling — —." Moving gently to the writing itself, we then use such statements as "The best thing(s) in the piece are . . . "; "I'd like to know more about — —"; "I'm unclear what you meant here"; "I offer this word or phrase for you to consider in your piece: — —."

We last move to more probing questions. David's group tiptoed through that process. Their compassion and openness to his story seemed to ease David's tension and relax his fears, while the group remained true to their comments:

> You're very articulate about your addition.
>
> What happened to make you realize you needed help?
>
> What did you mean about turning against the Baptist God? How do you back up your feelings?
>
> I'd like to know more about timing — how long did it happen?
>
> Try to fit each event together. Maybe by using the last paragraph about the hospital close to the front and reliving the other events.
>
> I'd like to know more about . . . .
>
> What made you actually become this, more than heredity?
>
> What made you say, hey, I need help?
>
> Why did you buy valium?
>
> When did you do it? What made you?

In my own work with David, I followed the same sequence, approaching him first as a person, then addressing his writing. All the while David focused more deeply on his experiences and began expressing them in a coherent, more public voice. The night David turned in his first draft, I held a mini-lesson on leads. David wrote this new one:

> Climbing out of the black river into a blacker night, I could not see through the blood streaming down my face. My head, throbbing with pain, felt like it would burst as I staggered to the hospital door and fell at the entrance as the nurse said, "We are closed for the night."

As David imposed his order and coherence and image on his writing, he, himself, seemed to gain a sense of order and coherence. The group helped too. David felt himself cared about and thus care-worthy; he saw himself valued and thus valuable; he found pattern in his perception of their questions and suggestions.

David's Final Draft

David concentrated on the theme of powerlessness for a final product. A portion of that draft reveals his growth in focus and order in his writing:

> I had been locked in a mental institution for three days before I heard an addict give her life story. Because of her breathtaking blond beauty, everyone listened with intensity. She told how her addiction to cocaine and alcohol had progressed to the point that rendered her incapable of responsive or meaningful thought or action. The progression of her illness had left her resentful, hostile, self-centered, and reclusive.
>
> She fell to the ground sobbing after she finished her story. I was also crying because I realized at that moment that I also suffered from the disease of addiction. I remembered horrible things from my recent past and they now proved that I was powerless over drugs and that I had been insane.
>
> The first thing that I recalled was climbing out of a black river into a blacker night. I could vaguely see through the blood streaming down my face; and my head, throbbing with pain, felt like it would burst as I staggered to the hospital and fell at the entrance only to hear the nurse say "we are closed for the night.". . .
>
> Drunk, while driving back to the naval base, I picked up two other drunken sailors. Having blacked out, I came to with blood flowing from my face. One assailant held my arms and the other beat me profusely and repeatedly. These criminals then held my arms and feet and slung me into the St. Johns River. They left the scene of the crime thinking me dead and I was until I hit the freezing, dark water and it mercifully revived me. Proof of a miracle is that I climbed up a seven foot vertical bulkhead and lay bleeding and gasping for breath.
>
> As my illness progressed I sought drugs in hellish places. Country music blared from the jukebox, stale, smelly smoke hung in layers throughout the dungeon-like room. Prostitutes, both male and female, and transvestites sauntered and weaved around the bar looking for tricks that would enable them to buy drugs. . . .
>
> Finally, the blackouts and hallucinations began to harass and torment me. Egyptian hieroglyphics danced on my bedroom walls as I hallucinated after three straight days of snorting pure crystal speed and swilling rot-gut vodka. I had scratched my head until it bled hoping to take my mind off my racing heart and hoped that it would

not explode as it thumped wildly through my shirt. With red swollen eyes, matted, greasy hair, and aching joints I staggered downstairs to pour some more precious scotch for breakfast. . . .

Finally, in desperation, I took my pillow and scotch and entered my darkened closet as I had fantasized for months about living there, alone from this despised world—in black solitude. . . . I prayed for death because I was consumed with depression and despair and could no longer get high.

The next morning I drove myself to the mental institution. . . .

Embracing his powerlessness, articulating it, ordering it, making it real for the reader, David somehow gained control over it. David became empowered. The last draft of this personal piece demonstrated the essence of his composure.

David's Research

As David gained a more objective view of his addiction, he began to investigate alcohol and drug awareness programs in order to develop a curriculum:

I thought I knew everything about my topic when I started out. I thought a drug awareness program should be based on the consequences of drug abuse: jails, institutions and death; however, I reached a different conclusion. . . .

David described the type of program that would generate alcohol and drug awareness. He listened attentively to others and reflected on his own experience: Such programs would help students express their anger, joy, sadness, because addicts use alcohol and drugs to cover them up. He further suggested that alcohol and drug awareness programs emphasize self-awareness and self-esteem. He advocated peer counseling because young people would find peers more believable than police or counselors. And he advocated a focus on values clarification, decision making, and problem solving:

Counseling should focus on the problems of adolescents: sex, love, joy, self-doubt, fear, anxiety, pain, loneliness, and belonging. . . .

I learned that a drug awareness program should not stress the consequences: jails, institutions, and death, but that it should focus on the feelings and fears that all adolescents face. These feelings should be recognized and discussed in regularly scheduled counseling groups consisting of respected peers and teachers. Self-esteem and self-awareness should also be fostered in the schools. The idea that school and an education can help him meet his goals of self-fulfillment and give an immediate sense of usefulness and self-esteem should be fostered.

During his research process David no longer saw himself as an individual in paralyzed turmoil; rather he saw a man of insight and authority, capable of teaching young people.

David's Reflections on Writing and Healing

David's material revealed the impact of his experience in the course. Six weeks into the semester, David described how writing made him face issues more than talking about them:

> I spent $14,000 in that recovery program and never did I deal with the real issues involved until I got in this class and wrote about them.

He got in touch with his history in one reflection:

> By writing down information and things I recalled from the past, I remembered more things and even more important things that might or might not be included. . . .
>
> Each draft got more focused, I hope, and I made a conscious effort with my Thesaurus to use strong verbs and strong nouns.
>
> I feel I have grown because the writing of drafts greatly improved my confidence in that I felt I was improving with each draft. Striving for improvement, not perfection.

Then from a later reflection:

> The most important thing I learned about writing for my personal piece was to focus on a particular area—idea. . . .
>
> I am trying to think and focus and feel the rest will be a lot easier, I hope.

Three years after the course, David still talked about the ways his writing healed him:

1. First, he said the writing helped him remember. The writing anointed him with a certain honesty when remembering both feelings and events. He remembered more vivid details of his experiences. Revisiting those experiences re-membered him to his Self, cleansing him, freeing him, helping him feel whole.

2. The writing also helped him to see, to find clarity. He said, "We addicts cannot accept things as they are." He paused. "Trying to make it clearer to another person who's going to read it [a piece of writing] makes it clearer to me."

3. The writing also helped him confront his denials. He explained: "In telling about experience orally, you can still deny. When you write it down, you are forced to remember the real. And we get so emotional we can't tell something, but in writing it down, you can

say it coherently." David described how feelings become concrete when they are written. And when they become palpable,
individuals can no longer deny them. When he wrote his "fearless
and searching moral inventory," an AA process, he could no
longer deny the reality of traumas. He thus faced and embraced
reality.

4. David also discussed writing as a vehicle for dealing with disturbing feelings, particularly anger and grief. He explained that
   addicts tend to overreact emotionally, stew in resentment:
   "Writing down feelings helps prevent ruminating, hastens the end
   of the grieving process. It provides painful catharsis and frees me
   to 'let it go.'"

5. Finally, David talked about how writing brings order to turbu-
   lence. David taught me that addicts "thrive on chaos, mental
   chaos, doing things you would never do: 'splattering' yourself
   on the sidewalks and streets of your life." As David ordered his
   turbulent memories, he wrenched and squirmed in the safety of
   his response group and the quiet blank page, and found order,
   patterns not only for his writing but for himself.

The Butterfly Effect

About the time David was born, mathematician-meteorologist Edward
Lorenz at the Massachusetts Institute for Technology discovered
something that has come to be called the Butterfly Effect. Trying to
predict weather with his creation of toy weather, Lorenz discovered
chaos caused by tiny little fluctuations—a principle that can be stated
something like this: If a butterfly flaps its wings in China, it can cause
a storm in New York a month later. This means that very small per-
turbations in data send equations into wild gyrations, turmoil. When
Lorenz discovered the Butterfly Effect, he thought it was the end of
weather predicting; yet he kept trying to find pattern. Intuitively he
knew that pattern was embedded in that turmoil. He simplified the
equations until he finally got them down to three equations with three
variables. To graph the data, Lorenz plotted them in three-dimensional space, producing a "sequence of points tracing a continuous path, a
record of the system's behavior." What Lorenz found was a new pattern in the chaos:

> . . . the map displayed a kind of infinite complexity. It always
> stayed within certain bounds, never running off the page but never
> repeating itself, either. It traced a strange, distinctive shape, a kind
> of double spiral in three dimensions, like a butterfly with its two
> wings. The shape signaled pure disorder, since no point or pattern

of points ever recurred. Yet it also signaled a new kind of order.
(Gleick 1987, 30)

Chaos was not all there was. Lorenz's faith in his intuition
enabled him to continue his experimentation after he discovered the
Butterfly Effect. Through persistent explorations of his equations,
Lorenz found a complex pattern of relationships within the chaos
which came to be called the Lorenz Attractor. The force that created
the new pattern was there all the time. Lorenz's process of analysis
shed light on it. And so the Lorenz Attractor became a daring phenomenon in the world of science, of the mathematics of science. Out
of chaos had come a new form, a new composure.

The process of writing allowed David to collect his memories of
traumatic events, to focus on select ones, to elaborate, probe, and discover new relationships within them, to see beyond them, to find the
new pattern, the complex butterfly in him. Discovering the new pattern, David saw himself anew. Integrating patterns of powerlessness,
trauma, and change composed him, made him sane, redeemed him.
He called it by name.

18

The Heart of the Matter
Language, Feeling, Stories, Healing

Gabriele Lusser Rico

We can know little about who we are or what we know until
we express it. Expression is not an appendix to knowing but
an integral part of the process by which something becomes
knowing.

Charles M. Johnston, *The Creative Imperative*

In the final stages of writing my recent book, *Pain and Possibility:
Writing Your Way Through Personal Crisis,* I tried to stop its publication. As an academic, I feared that the personal voice, which had
surfaced as a common thread, made me too vulnerable. I was not a
therapist writing as someone trained in untangling the complexities
of human emotional life. I was a professor of literature whose passion is poetry. Yet this book was clearly about . . . well, about feelings. It was about educating the emotions, about learning receptivity
to feeling and their expression through writing, about the compression of the poetic voice. It was about words and how words help us
give form to intangible feelings. After the publication of *Writing the
Natural Way*, I gradually realized an irrepressible urge to share my
own experience with the power of words. Like most English majors,
I had long been in love with words, particularly with the words of
poems. In *Pain and Possibility* I wanted people who would not ordinarily read poetry to realize that poems express the discursively inex-

pressible. I wanted people who do not ordinarily write to discover writing as a tool, enabling them to move from passive suffering to active participation in healing—the word "heal" from the Old English hål clearly showing the connection to a process of whole-making. But I was uncomfortable.

And so it was published after all, this book whose preface recounts a fairy tale I had never forgotten since early childhood. The story's main character is a princess who had been born with a glass heart. At sixteen, excited by the first crocuses in the palace garden below, she leaned far out over a window sill. The pressure on her fragile heart proved too much. There was a tiny sound, like glass breaking, and she fell to the floor. But as things go in fairy tales, the court doctor found her heart not broken, after all, but it did have a long, slender crack in it. The story evolves from there.

Fragments of my personal story begin to appear here, threading their way through a book intended to help others confront crisis through writing:

> What is most vivid in my memory is my seven year-old's amazement that the princess lived to be very old, and even more amazing, that she continued to find deep pleasure in her life. I remember puzzling, "How can she run and play? How can she be happy and not be afraid every minute of every day?"
>
> My mother died in a bombing raid three weeks before the end of World War II. It left our family vulnerable, confused, afraid, and in great pain. I pictured a long, jagged crack across my small heart. I felt fragile as glass; I wondered if glass could ever heal. There was no one to ask. Then I recalled the princess's words: "What survives a crack and doesn't break on the spot will be all the stronger for it."
>
> At seven, I did not believe it. Now I do. Although not a single one of us is exempt from pain—in fact, we are all damaged somehow, somewhere, somewhen—the issue is not whether, but how, we learn to move through our damage. . . .
>
> This book is based on a profoundly simple premise: empowerment of self. As we follow the unpredictable paths our lives take, we need tools to mediate our unease, uncertainty, sadness, imbalance. Empowerment does not lie in trying to escape these unpleasant states, but in learning to transform our suffering. Running away from suffering intensifies it; denying suffering intensifies it; wallowing in suffering intensifies it; blaming our suffering on others intensifies it. Anesthetizing it will work only for so long. And emotional shutdown is ultimately destructive to mind and body. I know. It happened to me.

What happened to me was that I had little clue that I was denying anything or that my body used immense negative energy to fence in traumatic thoughts and events. Psychologist James W. Pennebaker's

book *Opening Up* (1992) reported the effects on the body of expressing trauma in writing. One pre/post writing study showed a dramatic
drop in illness visits to the student health center. Another study docu-
mented a rise in immune response by students who had written about
traumatic events, producing significantly higher levels of T-cells,
known to fight infections and viruses. Many people stumble onto the
insights detailed in this book from simple need, thus demonstrating its
validity without realizing it.

Yet most people do not write by choice, especially when they are
hurting or hiding. They need to be guided to writing as a means of healing, to be invited into the process. Moreover, many do not perceive
themselves as creative beings. Writing as a whole-making activity
reflects the basic human need to story our lives. Most of us must actually learn how to make use of this innate propensity. Eric Hoffer (1967)
once observed about the human species: "All other animals are perfect
technicians, each with its built-in tool kit, each an accomplished specialist. The human is a technically misbegotten creature, half-finished
and ill equipped, but in its mind and soul are all the ingredients of a creator, of an artist" (80-81). Given my interest in facilitating our predilec-
tion for *creating* reality, writing became a way to document it. Writers
such as Toni Morrison know that whole-making is a profoundly creative
process: "Writing is the place where we can be courageous, where we
can think the unthinkable. It's an exploration of the possibilities of self
and being human in the world" (Tucher 1990, 57).

Educating the Emotions: Using the Indirection of Metaphor

Psychiatrist William Gray (1980) insisted that "because feelings form
the underlying structural matrix of thought, awareness of emotional
nuances is the key to remembering, to recognizing patterns, and to
generating new ideas" (14). He argued that our emotions are a key to
all learning. Of the seven intelligences Howard Gardner (1983) identified in his landmark work, our feelings are certainly central to educating two: the *intrapersonal intelligence* and the *interpersonal intelligence*. According to Gardner, the *intra*personal intelligence reflects
an inward movement into the self in order to discriminate between
emotional states and to apply this understanding to one's life. The
*inter*personal intelligence moves outward from the self to embrace
the perspectives of others, enabling us to be responsive to their personalities: their moods, desires, and intentions. Educating these two
intelligences cannot be accomplished directly. In fact, they necessitate
indirection. One of the most difficult things to learn is to be receptive

to our own feelings; the second most difficult is to own them; the
third most difficult is to become expressive of them. Neither receptivity nor expressiveness happens on command. Let me give you an
example of the circuitous route of feeling.

My daughter, Suzanne, at age nine, handed me an Easter card she
had fashioned out of red construction paper. It was large, with a huge
Easter egg on its cover. Pleased, I opened it, assuming I would read a
nine year-old's conventional expression of love. Thus, I was totally
unprepared for the contents of the black, scribbled felt-tip writing on
the red construction paper:

My Easter Card

BAD things about you:
1. You yell to [sic] much.
2. You never listen to my side of things.
3. You let Steph [her older sister] beat me up and don't
   do anything about it.
4. You seem to always pick on me!

BAD things about me:
1. Yell to [sic] much.
2. Swear to [sic] much.
3. Pick on Simone [her younger sister] to [sic] much.

GOOD things about you:
1. <u>You are understanding.</u>
2. You do things for me.
3. You are nice (most of the time).
4. Other less important things

GOOD things about me:
1. I am understanding
2. I am nice most of the time.
3. I'm pretty (ha ha).
   P.S. Let's try not to get into so many fights.

Stunned as I was, I understood this child was struggling to give
form to some uncomfortable—perhaps unsayable—feelings. Here
was a pattern of meaning articulated in list form, first for herself.
Second, through writing, she was attempting to reach me in a way she
had apparently been unable to do in speech. Third, she structured the
polarities of good/bad as if to reconcile them. Fourth, the format she
chose led naturally to what was most important to her: "P.S. Let's try
not to get into so many fights." Yet it came almost as an appendix, an
aside. Now, looking back, I doubt she would have known to articulate
this crucial P.S. had she not worked out the pattern of good/bad polarities that spoke volumes. I took her P.S. much to heart, and it produced results. Writing had been an emotionally expressive vehicle

for Suzanne in a way speech could not be. The process of listing enabled her to get at something she could not say directly: "Let's not get into so many fights."

When we perceive writing as intrinsically valuable to us, we begin to *re*-cognize (to know again and again) the elusive fabric of emotional meaning. Over the years I have come to see the engagement of the feeling dimension before logic as critical to genuine expressiveness. British scientist Michael Polanyi (1966) observed, "We know more than we can tell" (1)—discursively, that is. Educating the emotions necessitates a process of indirection; it depends on metaphoric leaps, on the compression of the poetic before the expansion of the expository, and on an individual's sensitivity to recursive images which carry emotional freight. A story, recalled by Dr. Paul Witty about Einstein, illustrates the power of such indirection:

> Professor Einstein went to a party one night and the hostess said, "Professor Einstein will tell us the meaning of relativity."
>
> "I shall tell you a story instead," he said: "I was going down the street the other day with a blind friend and I remarked that I should like a glass of milk.
>
> "What is milk?" asked my blind friend.
>
> "A white liquid," I answered.
>
> "Liquid I know, but what is white?"
>
> "The color of swan's feathers"
>
> "Feathers I know, but what is a swan?"
>
> "A bird with a crooked neck."
>
> "Neck I know, but what is crooked?"
>
> By that time I had grown impatient and I seized his arm and bent it: "This is crooked."
>
> Then I straightened his arm and said, "This is straight."
>
> "Ah," said my blind friend, "now I know what you mean by milk."
>
> Then Mr. Einstein turned to his hostess and said, "Would you like me to tell you more about relativity?" (Martin 1973, 27)

When we mistrust or misjudge the grammar of the emotions, we lose the ability to distinguish between the feelings we think we *ought* to feel and our actual feelings. Novelist and poet Alice Walker argued that the consequences are serious:

> In blocking off what hurts us, we think we are walling ourselves off from pain. But in the long run, the wall, which prevents growth, hurts us more than the pain which, if we will only bear it, soon passes over us. Washes over us and is gone. Long will we remember pain, but the pain itself, as it was at the point of intensity that made us feel as if we must die of it, eventually vanishes. Our memory of it

becomes only a trace. Walls remain. They grow moss. They are
difficult barriers to cross, to get to others, to get to closed-down
parts of ourselves. (1989, 123)

How do we "bear" our emotions, particularly those that hurt? How
can we recognize and accept them as valid because they belong to us?
Gritting our teeth is not the answer. Since we cannot disown them, we
might as well do something constructive with them. Acknowledged,
our emotions are signposts. Expressed, emotions lead to healing, to
wholeness, to major shifts in our understanding of ourselves and others. Denied, they make us emotionally dull and unresponsive, as incapable of genuine affection as we are of honest anger. Emotionally
deaf and dumb, we begin to think the world is supposed to be this
way. So emotions become blind or blocked. Read the revealing comments of two adolescents:

> I keep my emotions pretty bottled up inside me. Sometimes, I will
> build up to a point where I can't stand it anymore. Then I vent my
> frustration through football. I just love trying to hurt people! What
> will I do when I don't play football anymore? I don't know. Jon,
> Lake Ronkonkoma, N.Y.

> If I don't get all my anger out, I won't be able to sleep. I get, like,
> insomnia. So I'll play soccer. I want to talk to a friend, but I can't do
> it. It just doesn't come out. Damien, Lake Ronkonkoma, N.Y.

No wonder psychiatrist Arthur Janov (1970) warned: "In healing the
widening split between thinking and feeling, we must understand that
only unfelt emotions distort the mind. Emotions have precise purposes. Emotions are only blind when they are blocked" (161).

Creativity, Storying, and Whole-Making

Healing oneself again and again in the course of a lifetime may be the
ultimate creative act. But it is not automatic. We need to develop
resiliency. We learn resiliency, says M. C. Richards (1963), by re-
learning "to trust the invisible gauges we carry within us. We have to
realize that a creative being lives within ourselves, whether we like it
or not, and that we must get out of its way" (40). Psychologists Sybil
and Stephen Wolin (1993) define resiliency as "the capacity to rise
above adversity and forge lasting strengths in the struggle, not the
ability to escape unharmed, not about magic" (6).

If we need to learn by trusting, we re-learn to trust by *do*-ing,
and one of the ways we learn to do is to be released into language, as
Adrienne Rich said so eloquently:

> What does it mean to be released into language? Not simply learning
> the jargon of the expected, but by learning that language can be used

as a means of changing reality. What interests me in teaching is less
the emergence of the occasional genius than the discovery of language by those who did not have it (Jelpi and Jelpi 1993, 249).

We are by nature pattern-makers; we are by nature storytellers.
We have an in-built need to name and tell and record. That is what it
means to be expressive. It is a distinctly human trait. Writers of
fiction, such as Tobias Wolff (1992), know:

> In the arms of language children will discover the family of man.
> They will learn what has gone before, and they will learn what is left
> to be done. In language they will learn to laugh, and to grieve, to be
> consoled in their grief, and to console others. In language, they will
> discover who they are.

Psychobiologist Renee Fuller (1982) has spent much of her professional career arguing that the "story" was Carl Lashley's lost
engram, his name for the basic unit of learning. That is, our brains are
literally programmed to story:

> No one has considered the neurophysiological reasons for stories
> having such a curious fascination for all of us. . . . What is the func-
> tion of this emotional and intellectual preoccupation? Is story cohe-
> sion fundamental to human thinking? Is it our cognitive organizer
> and the reason why all human languages take the same form? . . .
> The way we process information seems to be linked to the human
> need to make life coherent, to make a story out of it. . . . Science was
> to give us some of the most fascinating of all stories. In the 19th cen-
> tury, it told us the story of evolution and the origin of our species. In
> our 20th century, it was relativity and the story of the cosmos. And
> so, what we are most proud of, our logic, our rationality, seems to
> have its origin in story cohesion. (132)

Fuller laid out an elegant argument for story cohesion as the lost
"engram of our species." Lashley was looking for something too small,
she insisted, when he searched for the engram: "Lashley spent years
removing more and more cortical tissue from rats, but he found his rats
had to be almost nonfunctioning before they would forget what they
had learned." Acknowledging what teachers and therapists have long
known about enhancing understanding through stories, like others
(Brand 1980, 1989), Fuller argued that something more happens—and
that something more is the connection between intellect and emotion:

> The storymaking process gives the event a heightened reality. It rais-
> es them into consciousness; they become "real." With the con-
> sciousness of this reality which we ourselves seem to create, we
> come into being. . . . For the story is more than a cognitive unit. It is
> the extension of our emotional selves with an extraordinary capacity
> to elicit every emotion known to our species. . . . This association of

emotion and cognition links the richness of our emotional life to the richness of our intellectual capacity. . . ." (128)

Anthropologist Laurens van der Post (1960) echoed the importance of storying:

> The extreme expression of the Kalahari Bushman's spirit was in his stories. The story was his most sacred possession. . . . These people knew what we do not: that without a story you have not got a nation, or a culture, or a civilization. Without a story of your own to live, you haven't got a life of your own. (18)

Unlocking Expressive Potential: Four Voices

Our own "stories," snippets here and there over time, allow us to perceive patterns of meaning over time. They need not be long; they need not take much time. Brief vignettes, written spontaneously without a deliberate aim, often become the carriers of an incipient fruitfulness—a delicate moment of *re*-cognizing, thus contextualizing, a feeling or a feeling-laden event. The vignette, emerging from within and framed on the page without, illuminates our inner emotional landscape with lightning speed.

The exploratory nature of facing our emotional being through the safety net of words, giving them metaphoric resonance, creating stories from our experiences, letting them surprise us into insight depends on moving into unknown territory, according to Michel Foucault: "The goal of life is to become someone you were not in the beginning. If you knew, when you began writing, what you would say at the end, do you think you would have the courage to write it?" (1978, 33) The following writing samples of four unpublished writers are, each, in its own way, testimony to the imperative for getting to the heart of the matter. My advice to my students, for years now, has been, "Always begin where you are," and that is the risk they have learned to take. Each writer has a distinctive voice; each knows what to do with words at her level of expressiveness; each is a growing human being because of a willingness to be receptive, which in turn invites the expressive. I let each voice speak for itself.

Andrea Sandke

Last year, Andrea, a very young, very shy English Master's degree student and a gifted fledgling poet chronicled the discovery of her own voice and the nuances of her feelings:

> I learned to listen to myself with total acceptance. I didn't have to write perfect poems or papers. I could say what I mean and see

where that took me. . . . The route of the open eye, ear, mouth, and hand, is the most courageous and rewarding. . . .

Patterns are the treasures that wait down in that formidable ocean. The patterns we discover when we let go and allow ourselves to follow the thrust of the spiral are the patterns that point to our meanings. For instance, in my *Writing the Natural Way* notebook, one recurring image is that of hands: open hands, closing hands, warm ones, mine, his. As I wrote on all these different days, I came back to my issues naturally, feeling their shapes, finding their meanings. . . .

The recurring image of the hand offers a picture of myself, my emotions, expectations, the way I view other people in my life. How was I before? "Closed small fingers," "thumb bending inward," "opening only to crouch"—I was frightened, closed away. Why did I close? "Because the hand never comes." The hand is the hand of my mother, who inadvertently sent me a message that I could not be touched. Through my writing, I become aware of an assumption made long ago and acted upon ever since. I verbalize this assumption, and suddenly I can question its validity. . . .

The Andrea who has learned to take care of herself speaks in acceptance: "I take it, yes, I accept." And, notice that I accept "the mystery," the chaos. Instead of constantly imagining horrid failures in these depths, I have a trust in the patterns I have found in chaos. . . .

A year ago, I might have said, "I feel so depressed, I don't know why." Now, I can identify the source of my feeling. I can identify and claim the feeling: "I'm sad because Dion isn't available." This is the voice of someone who has learned to face her world with open eyes. It is the voice of one who recognizes she cannot control everything. Indeed, she does not have to. . . .

If I do teach writing, then my personal experience is where I will begin, to expand outward in many directions, to offer a model for students to follow. I myself have done this: written vignettes, kept a notebook, using clustering, said what I meant when I could have kept silent. These are truths and processes I have learned and taught myself. Why couldn't I teach them to others, whatever waits for me in the future? And here we are, back to the chaos: sometimes still the swirling mass, but more often the deep, new, and yet somehow familiar ocean. Through writing, I am learning how to swim.

Last year Andrea applied for, and was selected as, a teaching assistant, responsible for teaching freshman composition. By August, fearing failure, she wanted to back out. I suggested she attend our three-hour T.A. meeting before she made a decision. Quietly she listened to her peers planning their semester—and chose to go ahead. To my astonishment and hers, her freshman composition classes came alive with language. Her shyness was the risk factor propelling her into experiments with the language, words, and writing of her students. As an instructor, she began where she was, knowing little but challenging herself daily with writing activities she herself would want to engage in. As a learner, she blossomed into a gifted teacher, more a guide and facilitator than an authority. Students knew she put herself "out there." They wrote for her. They wrote with her. They owned their writing. They were becoming willing wordsmiths. Andrea, too, wrote. She wrote with her students. She wrote on her own, and still does, as a way of exploring her wholeness, her who-ness, her what-ness. A recent Word Sculpture, generated by an activity in *Pain and Possibility* explores questions, fears, issues, images, metaphors—in short, patterns ultimately nameable, frameable. Figure 18–1 shows Andrea's Word Sculpture; it resonates with complex feelings. The square box reflects the text around the inside of it, which in turn, reflects the key statement in the center of the frame: "I AM SCARED."

Figure 18–1

ANDREA SANDKE

Heide Geiger

I know Heide Geiger only through her words, the words of the German language, at that. I know only a small piece of her childhood story and even less about her life today. She lives in Stuttgart, Germany. She wrote to me some months ago. This stranger sent four vignettes written in German, along with a letter written in English, whose P.S. read: "Please excuse my not so good English. I learned it all by myself for not going to school any time. I'm paralyzed. But this is another story." I was so moved by the power of her four vignettes, I wanted to share them. Impulsively, I sat down at the computer and translated them into English. I reprint her shortest vignette in both the original and translation:

Dann	Then
Wenn die harten spitzen	When the hard, sharp
Hagelkörner des Zweifels	hailstones of doubt
mich treffen	pelt me,
wenn Verzweiflung mir	when despair drives
in die Knochen fährt	into my bones
wie ein eisiger Schauer	like an icy shower
dann	then
hülle ich mich fester	I wrap myself ever more tightly
in den Mantel des Vertrauens	in the coat of confidence,
All die kleinen Blumen	I take to heart
die je für mich blühten	all those small flowers
nehme ich mir zu Herzen	which ever bloomed for me,
Ich hebe den Kopf	and I lift my head
und gehe weiter	and walk on
Schritt für Schritt	one step at a time
bis mir	until
der Regenbogen leuchtet	a rainbow glistens
	(trans. G. Rico)

More recently, Heide sent me a fourteen-page poem chronicling her early childhood, alluding to the illness that resulted in her paralysis. Thus far I have only translated its beginning and ending lines, giving a taste of her style and her voice and her story. But I do know this about her writing: it is powerful, it is honest, it is clearly whole-making. Much of her freedom lies in the act of writing. For Heide Geiger, confined to a wheelchair, her world is the word, guided by a stream of images calling out to be named. I may know Heide Geiger only from her words on a page, but I already know her:

1.
When my mother delivered me,
closed the door behind her,
actually walked out,
leaving me behind alone
in the high white room,
I did not want to believe
that it could happen.
My screams should have
shattered the glass panes of the door
to bring her back.
. . . .

14.
In the beginning I still cry and scream, because
I am afraid of their hands,
the needles, the cold plaster.
But they say I must be a good girl
if I want to get well,
stop being homesick,
swallow spinach and castor oil.

I swallow the spinach,
I vomit the castor oil.
I am still homesick.
No one talks about getting well again.

I split myself from my body—
because I cannot live in it.

Lakiba Pittman

Lakiba participated in a Writing Seminar. On the last day of the
semester during which each student presented a creative project, she
explained to the class that her primary way of expressing herself creatively had always been to sing, and for this reason she would lead us
in an African chant. In preparing us and talking about her creative
process, she explained, "Something bad happened one day that
silenced my song. I couldn't sing for a long time. As a way of surviv-
ing, I began to doodle (Figure 18–2) and created a whole notebook
full of shapes. That was in 1988. For this project, I found myself
writing vignettes to go with the shapes I made." She passed out copies
of her writing juxtaposed with her face shapes and read aloud:

Figure 18-2

Our Wondrous Ride

Polarities of heart
and mind free the soul
from certainty,
from definition
from stagnation.
Somewhere in the
middle,
between
black and white,
beauty and deformity,
humility and deceit,
conflict and peace,
lies a truth
we can sometimes touch,
sometimes feel,
sometimes know,
and thus we grow.
We create by
moving between
the polarities
flowing us down life's
rivers, across boulders,
slipping and sliding,
sometimes sinking,
sometimes bobbing,
sometimes floating, and if
we're lucky enough to
survive the trip,
we return and
tell the
story
of our wondrous ride.

"Oh, well," she said suddenly, her long fingers flicking the air as if making a snap decision, "I probably won't see any of you again since I'm graduating, so I might as well tell you what happened. In 1988 I was raped by two men; that's when I couldn't sing any more. That's when I began to doodle my faces. About a month ago, at a wedding, I saw those same two men again. I went back to my doodles and wrote a vignette for each of them, and these are my gift to you." She presented each of us with a sheaf of her juxtaposed visual/verbal patterns. She then launched into an African chant, leading the entire class in several refrains.

Machiko Yoshida

I only recently met Machiko in a Writing Seminar which I taught at
The College of Notre Dame near San Francisco. Below is her first in-
class writing, produced after we discussed—at some length—process
and trust and the improvisational nature of the initial stages of the
composing process. A second language learner, Machiko did not volunteer in class. After clustering but before the first three-minute writing I suggested that we can only set out from where we are, namely
here, now, in this place, this space. "Always begin where you are and
trust your natural urge for creating patterns of meaning." Machiko
apparently listened, for she produced this vignette—despite the unfamiliar language—rich with metaphor and simile:

> To start writing makes difference,
>   but awkward.
> Idea is larger than sail,
> wide enough to be ocean.
> To confess makes me fear
>   like being in fire.
> My ideas are branches of tree,
> but sticky wind takes them away.

In a review of a book on creative process that we had read, Machiko
revealed how significant her leap toward risking failure had been:

> . . . some of what he says made me realize my inner feeling toward
> writing. As you could see, English is not my native language. It
> made me foolish before. One day I handed my essay to an English
> teacher. He just looked it over quickly and said, "This is not
> English—it is not organized at all. . . ." I was shocked and disap-
> pointed. I felt like an educationally subnormal student. I could not
> get back to myself for a couple days. This is not only about my writ-
> ing, but also my speaking. My fear of criticism, of shame, and of
> foolishness made me not speak and talk to people. My feeling of fear
> toward writing, speaking, and myself overwhelmed me even in my
> native language. That is, I began to avoid talking to Japanese friends
> and also started to stutter even in my native language. Today still,
> when I have to talk to a stranger, words cannot come out well.
>
> So, for me the significant points of *Free Play* are in his state-
> ment: "There is a time to experiment without fear of consequences, to
> have a play space safe from fear of criticism." I have to withdraw my
> fear in order to be totally involved in writing, speaking, music. I
> should not be afraid of making mistakes as judgments like I used to.
> This book made me realize that mistakes advance one. Without fear of
> mistakes, I will be able to practice more to create myself and to reveal
> myself so I can connect my interior world with the outer world.

After typing each writer's piece, I noticed—almost incidental-
ly—that each one had used an ocean or river metaphor. Water, of
course, elicits all the standard symbolic meanings of limitlessness,
life circulating throughout nature in the form of blood, rain, sap, and
milk. However, Cirlot (1962) pointed out that water images are also
identified with intuitive wisdom—the vital potential of the psyche—
struggling to formulate messages comprehensible to consciousness.
All four writers—each in her unique way—struggle toward wholeness
through writing. As they *in*-volve themselves in the creation of meaning, their growing trust of process and of their own words on the page
e-volve into patterns of feeling that clarify and illuminate. Poet
Maxine Kumin (and lifelong friend of fellow poet Anne Sexton)
observed this about the power of words to illuminate whole-making:
"The person who writes out of an inner need is trying to order his cor-
ner of the universe; very often the meaning of an experience or an
emotion becomes clear only in this way" (1976, 67). And Robert
Frost echoed this primal drive to pattern, form, and the tangible
expression of feeling into wholeness, healing:

> Any psychiatrist will tell you that making a basket, or making a
> horseshoe, or giving anything form gives you a confidence in the
> universe . . . that it has form, see. When you talk about your troubles
> and go to somebody about them, you're just a fool. The best way to
> settle them is to make something that has form, because all you want
> to do is get a sense of form. (Vendler 1991, 115)

Echoing Frost is a writer unknown to most of us, a woman who
wrote an entire book about her voluntary confinement in a mental
hospital in the 1930s, a sad and eloquent but life-affirming book,
chronicling the power of words. Lara Jefferson (1974) wrote words
on a page to stay sane in an insane asylum. She learned that writing
was a way of survival:

> The very fact that a thing—anything—can be fitted into a meaning
> built up of words, small black words that can be written with one
> hand and the stub of a pencil, means it is not big enough to be over-
> whelming. It is the vast, formless things we fear. (25)

The healing gained through writing reflects a potent form of consciousness. Our feeling life is responsive primarily to indirection. We
cannot order our feelings into—or out of—existence. Under such direct
assault, our feelings retreat into the furthest recesses of our minds and
bodies and continue a life of their own, often finding destructive paths
of expression. When we withhold our emotional selves from our selves,
the price is high. Enter writing, giving us permission to acknowledge,
educate, and own our feelings, our stories, our lives:

When I Am Asked

When I am asked
how I began writing poems,
I talk about the indifference of nature.

It was soon after my mother died,
a brilliant June day,
everything blooming.

I sat on a gray stone bench
in a lovingly planted garden,
but the daylilies were as deaf
as the ears of drunken sleepers
and the roses curved inward.
Nothing was black or broken
and not a leaf fell
and the sun blared endless commercials
for summer holidays.

I sat on a gray stone bench
ringed with ingenue faces
of pink and white impatiens
and placed my grief
in the mouth of language,
the only thing that would grieve with me.

Lisel Mueller (1987, 294)

"Writing," I stated in *Pain and Possibility* (1991), "leaves footprints marking our trail—where we have been, are now, and where we are going. . . . Sometimes writing illuminates questions we have no answers for, questions we didn't even know we had" (7). And so it is. The language of the emotions is elusive, fragile, multifaceted. The written word is a way of flowing with the logically undefinable through the powerful indirection of images, metaphor, and story.

19

Symposium

Richard J. Murphy, Jr.

Every few years since 1968 I have received a letter or call from a boy I taught at Moreau High School. Then fifteen, he must be nearly forty by now. In sixth period he watched me pick up a pencil that had rolled off another student's desk and hand it back. "I'd never seen a teacher do that," he told me later, "be kind like that."

It was enough to make him want to reciprocate.

Many afternoons at school thereafter, the two of us sat together in my office or in the classroom or on the stairs at the end of the corridor. He taught me to play chess. In the evenings he visited a chess club in Hayward, watched, played some, and then brought back the tricks he had seen. He overwhelmed me. He was so much stronger a player than I that we never got as far as the endgame, but it was bracing for me and so satisfying for him that he brought his small chess set to school everyday.

I can see him still—black curly hair, short-sleeved shirt—leaning on his thin arm on the stair, looking down intently at the plastic board, waiting, waiting, then swooping up a piece and clapping it down on its new space with a smack.

His letters are handwritten in ball-point ink on loose-leaf notebook paper, the pages crammed with words. Sometimes the envelopes themselves are covered with afterthought. His voice has the same insistence when he calls. He stands at a pay phone (I can hear the road traffic behind him) and races the operator to the three-minute mark, telling me as much as he can in the time he has about himself and the plight of man in the world.

I listen, thank him for calling, say it is good to hear his voice. But his calls and letters are difficult for me.

Part of the reason is that I no longer know him. He is married. He has children (two, I think). He works and lives in a city I have never seen.

Neither does he know me. I was a boy in 1968, a boy in a tie. We talked after school. He invited me to his parents' house; he visited mine. Then I left Moreau to enroll in a doctoral program, and he graduated. He has no more accurate a sense of me now than I have of him. And his words make me think he has less. Passionate disquisitions on the nature of society, long biblical quotations, prophetic statements about the duty of human beings in the modern world—his words orate, as if they were addressed homiletically to someone of like mind, or to no one. They seem completely impersonal. At the same time they are so full of urgent respect for me that they embarrass.

I am his teacher still. He reaches his words out toward me as if I were still one of the most well-read, most thoughtful and inspiring people he has ever known. Sometimes he says as much. More often, for all their prolixity, his letters are reserved. Timid. His voice on the phone apologizes. Unable to speak to me as a person in the present, he wants a relationship that is past. It is a yearning I am unable to satisfy.

The relationship between teacher and student is sometimes so like love it disconcerts. Teaching writing and literature now at Radford University, I imagine I am simply fulfilling an institutional role. Sometimes I notice it is something more. I recoil, withdraw, straighten my tie. The same student stays after class day after day on one pretext or another. I listen, answer his questions, but I do not encourage him. I do not prolong our talk. Walking along Fairfax Street after an unusual Sunday afternoon meeting on campus, I see a young woman sitting beneath a tree near the sidewalk, apparently absorbed in a book. She is a student in one of my classes. Our eyes do not meet, but she appears again and again on the periphery of my days—along the regular path I take to my car, walking in the neighborhood of my house, in my rear view mirror. We do not speak; I do not let on that I notice.

When I was an undergraduate at the University of Santa Clara, a student friend told me that she checked the class schedule of one of her teachers and scouted his daily itinerary. She wanted simply to see him, to cross his path. One day he did the unimaginable. He stopped, spoke to her, congratulated her on winning an academic prize: "I hear they've created a medal for you," he said. And he smiled. Twenty-five years later, she can still see the other students walking by in the afternoon sun on Santa Clara street, just between Kenna and Alumni House. She can see her teacher's black cassock and his white hair and his eyes squinting in the light. She can still

hear his paradoxical voice—soft, yet clipped; gentle, but exact. In
her mind she runs her fingers still over his caressing words.

I admire the handsomeness of his gesture. I wish I could think to
say such lasting, nourishing things. Yet that much influence worries
me. That much power. I want to be professional, ethical. I do not
want to be courted or pursued through my days and years. Our eyes
should not meet, I tell myself, and look away. We have nothing more
to say (I think this while we are still talking), and I begin to devise
ways to end the conversation, to disengage myself from their desire.

But.

I feel the desire myself. One spring afternoon I walk out onto the
front porch of the library and there, running in the distance on Muse
Lawn—I cannot quite believe it—is a naked girl. I shield my eyes
from the sun and look more closely. No, she's not naked, after all.
She has shorts on and a string bikini top, but I could have sworn. . . .
She was running to catch a frisbee thrown from somewhere, but now
she seems to me completely alone, the lawn deserted, she standing
with her feet spread wide and her arms up, lifting her hair like a wild
crown into the warm air. She is a silhouette, an apparition out of
James Joyce, an angel of mortal youth and beauty. I feel her beckon-
ing to me.

I say she was a "girl." Some would say "young woman." I am
uncertain how to refer to her. She is a student in my class. She lies
out on the grass in the midday sun then comes to class poached, a
loose t-shirt and shorts over her thin bathing suit. I concentrate on the
work at hand, keep my eyes from lingering on the purple strings at
her neck and hip. I appreciate her covering herself, try not to imagine
her otherwise.

Her modesty in class is a token. She and her friends, college students all over America these days, men and women, sunbathe nearly
naked outside the windows of faculty offices. Here at Radford on the
lawns of Moffett and Muse, for several weeks each year, the grass is
covered with beach towels and books and bodies. Aristophanes might
write an adaptation of *Lysistrata* to examine the ways in which the
work of school is intertwined with the work of sex, a comedy of sexual harassment. I try not to notice, but I am less candid than the main-
tenance workers on the roof who stop spreading hot tar and stare.

I do not want to notice, but when I read a draft of a story I have
written about Teresa Simpson to a small group of colleagues, one
says, "You sound like you're in love with her."

"Oh . . ." I am unsettled. "Really? But that's not what I meant at
all."

"Sure," he shrugs, smiles at my protest, "but look: the way you
say her father stares at her, savors her hair and neck and shoulders,

follows the line of light and shadow in her body in memory of her mother. . . . See, that's *you* savoring her. And when she's in your office, settling herself in your chair, tucking her bare legs up . . . she is so physically present to you that it's obvious you're attracted to her."

"Oh, my goodness," I say, trying to sound as if I think we are talking about a writing problem, when in fact he is presenting me with a secret I have not even recognized in myself.

Its signs are everywhere. Teresa has the body I fashioned, red hair, sweater, voice, and mannerisms. The same thing happens when I remember the evening Sandra Miyoshi sat late in my office reading to me about her grandmother in Hawaii. I pause at the scene. Brown shoulders, the inky blackness of her long hair—one strand stretching across the page of her paper—the whiteness of the page itself—the whole moment is charged in memory with sexual current. I rush to revise. I try to hide my own desire like an Aristophanic fool with an erection.

It would be just as well to admit it and accept it and inquire into its meaning: I want to love my students; I want to be loved by them.

This is not the same as being liked by them. I do not scorn their liking, as some do, but it is not the same. If I construct courses with fresh variety, bring muffins to class (as my colleague, Nick Pappas, inspired me to do), smile a lot (freshman John McKinney said, "You're always smiling; I like that."), or bop around the room with contagious energy and cheer—if they "like" me for these things, I am glad. But I want more.

I want them to enter into my life. I want to enter into theirs. Reading Wilfred Owen's "Dulce et Decorum Est" in class, I am hoping for a moment when we will fall silent together, amazed beyond saying at the "old lie" about war. Reading *Hamlet*, I wait for a student to say quietly (though I fear for us both in wanting this) that she suspects it is her story, that she thinks her mother actually killed her father. I tell them I am Gabriel Conroy, shoes buffed and dinner speech notes in my pocket, self-conscious, middle-aged, wondering what it would have been like to have ever been young. When we puzzle together over "The Horse-Dealer's Daughter," I admit what I think at least is surely true: we kiss sometimes in order to avoid looking in each other's eyes.

A woman student who came back to college after years of work and a marriage that had dissolved, sitting in a room full of students the age of her grown children, told me she was amazed by the things I said in class.

"They are daring," she said. "Intimate." She was not being critical. She was thanking me. And then, unexpectedly, she reciprocated, in a story about her divorce, about the very moment it happened in her mind. One night after a banquet, back in an elegant hotel room (like Gretta and Gabriel in "The Dead"), she watched her husband's body emerge from his worn tuxedo, and she realized she felt no more loathing, nothing.

Intimate. The word comes from Latin (*intimus*, inmost, deepest). Often used with sexual connotation, its denotative meanings are more general and more profound. The intimate is the deeply private, the deeply personal viewed from the perspective of the self in relation to another person. The intimate is what is ordinarily *not* exposed, *not* shared with another. Yet in its very definition it allows the possibility of exposing to, sharing with, knowing by another. The philosopher Michael Polanyi suggests that a large part of our knowledge itself is intimate. Not only is it what he calls "tacit," beyond expressing to ourselves or others. It is known *by* intimation (Polanyi helps us see that intimacy is active): we know by entering into what we know, by interiorizing it. We dwell in it. We participate in it imaginatively, feelingly. "Our knowledge of life," Polanyi says in *Knowing and Being*, "is a sharing of life—a reliving" (1969, 150–51).

The subjects I teach—the reading of literature, the writing of expository essays—require of students precisely this kind of intimation. What does it mean, slipping on wet trunks after a summer rainstorm, to feel in one's groin the chill of death? What does it mean to remember in one's fingertips, with nameless grief, the labored breathing of a dying seal? One must enter into these moments of experience in order to understand them. I know no other way. One must love.

It seems to me just as true, just as necessary, that in order to understand the work of students in my courses, I must enter into *it* imaginatively, into *them*. When they read their papers to me, when they ask me questions or tell me stories—even when they lose heart or lie or cheat—it seems to me that teaching them is indistinguishable from loving them, whatever the frustration or satisfaction, suffering or joy.

There will be suffering.

A student comes into my office to read a draft of an essay-in-progress. He introduces it by saying he is very dissatisfied with the whole thing. I ask him to read; then we will talk. He does. I pause to think about my reaction. He cannot endure the wait.

"I think it's too wordy," he says. To fill the silence.

I think: what's the point of talking about its wordiness if he's dissatisfied with the whole thing? Why is he dissatisfied?

"Well, let me ask you this," I say. "What did you mean when you said you didn't like what you've got here? Is it what you're writing about that bothers you or how you're handling it or what?"

"Both. All. I just don't feel right about it."

"OK." And then I go on to ask him what he wants to say, what he thinks *will* make him feel more satisfied.

Our exchange lasts maybe two minutes. Suddenly he looks straight at me.

"Can we talk about my paper," he asks, "and not about me?"

I cannot answer immediately. I do not believe it will do him any good to talk about the "wordiness" of this draft. That is a side issue, less than a side issue, a diversion. I feel slapped by his question. I watch his face. Then I say, "Sure."

One semester I asked students to write in their journals about the course, to keep track of their thought and feeling about their work. They knew I would read what they wrote:

> Ya know, I used to really love English. Really love it. I still love reading, but you have made me hate it, and dread it. I'm not taking another English course Next year because I am afraid I might End up in another class like this. You have made me scared to learn, scared to take another course. You have shown me a darker side of English I never saw, Papers after Papers, Articles after Articles, Shit upon Shit. I'm never going to forgive you for this, Ever.

I was amazed by these words, battered by them, left soiled and trembling. I still see the student around campus who wrote them. We talk as if nothing had happened. He seems to have forgotten them. I have not. Some days his is the only face I see. I try not to look.

Every semester students in my courses write evaluations of me and of my work with them—using either the official university system of anonymous written comments or writing me personal letters. After every semester is over, grades computed and recorded with the Registrar, I brace myself and read what they wrote.

> I've been sitting here in my bare room for what seems like an eternity (oblivious of the time and the fact that I have two exams tomorrow) just staring at this blank piece of paper, trying desperately to pull my thoughts and feelings together in some logical order . . . I think you're an excellent professor, Murph. You have a special talent for *teaching* and so much to give. You seem to enjoy what you are doing and you do it well . . . You have taught me so much—much more than British lit. and how to footnote a term paper correctly. You have taught me to look more closely at things (all things) and think seriously about what I see—from this I have learned more about myself. What can I possibly say? Bravo, Murph, and thank you.

I read this letter once, set it down, then read it over again.

We have all had teachers we loved—and love still in the memory of having worked with them. I still have the notebook from Terry

Loughran's ninth-grade history class. When we walked through the steam tunnel together on our way to the workshop to make model catapults, I walked just a step behind; he was my teacher, after all. I can remember his room, his books, his radio playing Vivaldi. I never wrote an evaluation for him, never told him. He does not know.

Seven years ago, I received the following letter. Though I quote only part, I think you will be able to sense something of its full effect.

Dr. Murphy:

> Please understand that I respect you as a professor and admire your vast knowledge of literature. However, I feel that the course I completed this Spring in British literature was, at best, a disappointment.
>
> My first complaint is about your attitude both during lectures and outside of class. As much as you professed to be open-minded in class and willing to listen to other's views and opinions, it became apparent that this wish was not genuine. I had listened to what classmates had to say about various poems, stories, etc., and felt that they often had valid suggestions to make to the group concerning the interpretation of the literature, only to find that if their ideas were not in line with what you were thinking, Dr. Murphy, you were quick to shrug it off or to dismiss it with a laugh which was not appropriate. As you are in a position of authority, I have no objections to your telling students what you believe is true; however, if we are to be responsible for and held accountable for your views and opinions, you should make this clear.
>
> Also, I am not impressed with your idea of a test. I do not feel that literature that has not been discussed in class should be included on an exam covering the contents of a course. Also, I think that you should concentrate on the message that various works deliver, rather than on petty details which have little or no significance to the story.
>
> I was not pleased to be scheduled for a conference at 9:20 p.m. You were obviously tired, as you yawned several times, and it really would have been better to postpone the appointment until a time when you were feeling more rested. Perhaps then you could have viewed my paper with a fresher outlook, rather than dealing with it as if it had fallen off an assembly line. I did not like your telling me that I did not mean to write a particular word in my essay, when indeed, I meant to use precisely that word. You were not the least bit encouraging to me as a writer. As a matter of fact, you were most discouraging. You have no right to tell others what they meant to say or what they did not mean to say. When evaluating an essay, you should not be concerned about whether you think the person has written what you think he feels or not, but should try to concentrate on what the person has actually written.
>
> If this evaluation seems negative, that is because my reaction to the course was entirely negative.
>
> Ms. E. Sanders

My gradebook tells me that Ms. Sanders earned a B in that course. I cannot remember what she wrote her papers about (I marked them with Bs, too). I have no face to go with her name (Ellen? Elizabeth?), no memory of the conference in which I yawned. But I still have her letter.

I feel her fingers at my throat still as I read, her nails in my eyes. I tell myself I do not deserve her contempt, but my self-justifications are pathetic. I keep them—and the anger and sadness—largely to myself.

So do my colleagues.

But sometimes our masks slip.

On the first day of class in September, a fellow teacher says to me, "Have you met the little bastards yet?"

One of my colleagues (students tell me) has a special-order stamp. He sets it out on his desk with mock glee whenever he begins reading a stack of student papers. The red stamp pad. The stamp with its shiny walnut handle. He looks like a mail clerk, pounding those papers as they pass beneath his eyes. A neat rectangle enclosing one word: "bullshit."

Listen to Jacob Neusner, a professor from Brown University. He wrote a graduation speech in 1981, submitted it to the student newspaper, then permitted it to be reprinted in newspapers and magazines across America:

> For four years we [the faculty at Brown] created an altogether forgiving world, in which whatever slight effort you gave was all that was demanded. When you did not keep appointments, we made new ones. When your work came in beyond the deadline, we pretended not to care.
>
> Worse still, when you were boring, we acted as if you were saying something important. When you were garrulous and talked to hear yourself talk, we listened as if it mattered. When you tossed on our desks writing upon which you had not labored, we read it and even responded, as though you had earned a response. When you were dull, we pretended you were smart. When you were predictable, unimaginative, and routine, we listened as if to new and wonderful things. When you demanded free lunch, we served it. And all this why?
>
> Despite your fantasies, it was not even that we wanted to be liked by you. It was that we did not want to be bothered, and the easy way out was pretense: smiles and easy Bs. . . .
>
> That is why, on this commencement day, we have nothing in which to take much pride.
>
> Oh yes, there is one more thing. Try not to act toward your co-workers and bosses as you have acted toward us. I mean, when they do not give you what you want but have not earned, don't abuse

them, insult them, act out with them your parlous relationships with your parents. This too we have tolerated. It was, as I said, not to be liked. Few professors actually care whether or not they are liked by peer-paralyzed adolescents, fools so shallow as to imagine professors care not about education but about popularity. It was, again, to be rid of you. . . . (1981, 652)

My first reaction to this "speech" was astonishment. The current of Neusner's spleen ran so deep I was amazed that he would let it be known. He should stop teaching, I told myself piously, if that is what he thinks about students. But then, in the wide press coverage his words received, I heard the message that he was speaking for more than himself. He was speaking for us all. Teachers in Young Hall taped photocopies to their office doors for the edification of passersby.

I think of Ms. Sanders and the furious student who promised never to forgive me, and I realize that sometimes we are of like mind: we hate each other.

This should not surprise. It is love I am talking about. There are no guarantees. Our desire is deep, sometimes reckless, always insatiable.

In *The Symposium*, Plato's Aristophanes presents a comic myth to explain our desire. Human beings—originally whole, complete circles—were cut in two by the gods. Ever after, they have sought one another, desiring to reunite, to complete, to heal themselves. It is a ludicrous myth. Zeus is a bumbling god. Perfect humans are as odd as cartoons: one head, two faces, four hands and feet, two genitals. But this wild premise allows Aristophanes to describe the human condition with great precision: we cannot explain what we desire of one another. It is a yearning the soul cannot express. According to Aristophanes,

the intense yearning which each of them has toward the other does not appear to be the desire of intercourse, but of something else which the soul desires and can not tell, and of which she has only a dark and doubtful presentiment. (1960, 337)

Polanyi would call that presentiment an intimation. Just as he would say it cannot be expressed, Plato would say (through Aristophanes) that it cannot be fulfilled. We are human. We are divided, incomplete. It is the comic rendition of our fallen state. We are not what we desire to be in memory or dreams. "Human nature was originally one," Aristophanes says, "and we were a whole, and the desire and pursuit of the whole is called love" (337).

The comedy of school is that it is so ill-designed for love. Our reaching into and out of ourselves is scheduled by a computer. We meet one another two or three days a week for a semester. Reading this poem or writing this essay is one requirement in a list of others which teacher and student both check off upon completion.

"OK, people. This is essay #7. Just two more and we're done."

"I still need nine hours to graduate, so I'll be going to summer school."

"Eleven semesters. That's it. Eleven more semesters, and I can retire."

From the point of view of love, the very structure of school is ironic. Teacher and student are strangers. Their paths cross for a moment, by chance. Even as they approach one another, they are drawing apart. And if this were not the system already, we would want it to be so. For all our desire, teachers and students do not want to love each other. Can we talk about my paper, please, and not about me? We look closely at each other, and then we look away.

Sometimes, however, our small bit of work together is so fine that it transfigures the business of school and seems to satisfy the inarticulate yearning of our souls.

A student wrote to me once to tell me what she had learned. In her letter, she did not mention me or the work at all. Instead, she told about a walk she had taken alone one winter dusk into the mountains behind her home. Everything was quiet, deserted, frozen in beauty. Beyond a shed, past a ridge, into the valley of a stream running black, she traveled. Dimly, she recognized the danger in it, in the cold and dark. She knew she was beyond any call for help. Finally, she stopped. Stood still. Listened to the water. Let the night fold her up. When she got back home, neither her mother nor her sister asked where she had been or what she had done. It was good that they didn't, she wrote, because she would have been unable to explain. It was just that up there in the woods alone that night she felt connected to absolutely everything. And she hoped I would understand. I do.

Yet it is still difficult for me to know how to reply to her or to the boy who was my student many years ago at Moreau High School. We knew one another for a short while, talked and worked together, loved one another. Then we grew apart. Neither of us has forgotten. We played chess together after school in the stairwell. He said that I was the kindest teacher he had ever known.

References

Adams, James L. 1986. *Conceptual Blockbusting: A Guide to Better Ideas.* 3rd ed. Reading, MA: Addison-Wesley.

Allender, Jerome. 1991. *Imagery in Teaching and Learning.* New York: Praeger.

Allport Gordon W. 1935. "Attitudes." In *A Handbook of Social Psychology*, edited by Carl A. Murchison, 798–844. Worcester, MA: Clark University.

———. 1961. *Pattern and Growth in Personality.* New York: Holt, Rinehart and Winston. Originally Published 1937.

Allport, Gordon W., P. E. Vernon, and G. Lindzey. 1960. *A Study of Values.* 3rd ed. Boston: Houghton Mifflin.

Amabile, Teresa M. 1983. *The Social Psychology of Creativity.* New York: Springer-Verlag.

Anderson, Merrill P. 1981. "Assessment of Imaginal Processes." In *Cognitive Assessment*, edited by T. Merluzzi, C. Glass, and R. M. Genest, 149–87. New York: Guilford.

Anderson, Walt. 1979. *Open Secrets: A Western Guide to Tibetan Buddhism.* New York: Viking Press.

Andrasick, Kathleen Dudden. 1990. *Opening Texts: Using Writing to Teach Literature.* Portsmouth, NH: Boynton/Cook.

Anson, Chris, ed. 1989. *Writing and Response.* Urbana, IL: National Council of Teachers of English.

Appley, Mortimer H. 1983. "Motivation Theory: Recent Developments." In *International Encyclopedia of Psychiatry, Psychology, Psychoanalysis, and Neurology Progress*, 279–83. New York: Aesculapius.

Aristotle. 1981. *Aristotle's Posterior Analytics.* Translated by Hippocrates G. Apostle. Grinnell, IA: Peripatetic Press.

Arnheim, Rudolf. 1969. *Visual Thinking.* Berkeley: U. of California.

Atkinson, John W. 1977. "Theories of Achievement Motivation." In *International Encyclopedia of Psychiatry, Psychology, Psychoanalysis, and Neurology Progress*, 190–97. New York: Aesculapius.

Atkinson, John W., and Joel O. Raynor, eds. 1974. *Motivation and Achievement.* Washington, DC: V. H. Winston.

Averill, James R. 1990. "Emotions in Relation to Systems of Behavior." In *Psychological and Biological Approaches to Emotion*, edited by Nancy L. Stein, Bennett Leventhal, and Tom Trabasso, 385–404. Hillsdale, NJ: Lawrence Erlbaum.

Aylwin, Susan. 1985. *Structure in Thought and Feeling*. London: Methuen.

Bain, Alexander. 1984. *The Senses and the Intellect*. 4th ed. New York: D. Appleton.

Barfield, Owen. 1928. *Poetic Diction*. Middletown: Wesleyan.

Bartholomae, David. 1980. "The Study of Error." *College Composition and Communication* 31: 253–69.

Bartholomae, David, and Anthony Petrosky. 1986. *Facts, Artifacts, and Counterfacts*. Portsmouth, NH: Boynton/Cook.

Bartlett, Frederic C. 1932. *Remembering: A Study in Experimental and Social Psychology*. Cambridge, England: Cambridge UP.

Basch, Michael Franz. 1983. "Empathic Understanding: A Review of the Concept and Some Theoretical Considerations." *Journal of the American Psychoanalytical Association* 31: 101–26.

Bastick, 1982. Tony. *Intuition: How We Think and Act*. Bath: Wiley.

Beaugrande, Robert de. 1984. *Text Production: Toward a Science of Composition*. Norwood, NJ: Ablex.

Belenky, Mary, et al. 1986. *Women's Ways of Knowing: The Development of Self, Voice, and Mind*. New York: Basic Books.

Benson, Herbert, and Miriam Z. Klipper. 1975. *The Relaxation Response*. New York: William Morrow.

Berkenkotter, Carol. 1983. "Decisions and Revisions: The Planning Strategies of a Publishing Writer." *College Composition and Communication* 34: 157–69.

Berlyne, D. E. 1960. *Conflict, Arousal and Curiosity*. New York: McGraw-Hill.

———. 1971. *Aesthetics and Psychobiology*. New York: Appleton-Century-Crofts.

Berthoff, Ann E. 1984. "Recognition, Representation and Revision." In *Rhetoric and Composition*, edited by Richard L. Graves, 27–37. Portsmouth, NH: Boynton/Cook.

———. 1981. *The Making of Meaning: Metaphors, Models, and Maxims for Writing Teachers*. Portsmouth, NH: Boynton/Cook.

———. "The Intelligent Eye and the Thinking Hand." 1983. In *The Writer's Mind: Writing as a Mode of Thinking*, edited by Janice N. Hays, Phyllis A. Roth, Jon R. Ramsey, and Robert D. Foulke, 191–96. Urbana, IL: National Council of Teachers of English.

Betts, George. 1909. *The Distribution and Functions of Mental Imagery*. New York: Columbia UP.

Bigelow, Bill, and Linda Christensen. n.d. *Writing to Think: Teaching About Social Conflict Through Imaginative Writing*. Portland, OR: Portland Public Schools.

Bly, Carol. 1990. "Growing Up Expressive." In *Eight Modern Essayists*, edited by William Smart. New York: St. Martin's.

Bornstein, Melvin. 1984. "Introductory Remarks." In *Empathy II*, edited by J. Lichtenberg, M. Bornstein, and D. Silver, 107–12. Hillsdale, NJ: Lawrence Erlbaum.

Bower, Gordon, and Paul R. Cohen. 1982. "Emotional Influences in Memory and Thinking: Data and Theory." In *Affect and Cognition: The Seventeenth Annual Carnegie Symposium on Cognition*, edited by Margaret S. Clark and Susan T. Fiske, 291–331. Hillsdale, NJ: Lawrence Erlbaum.

Bower, Gordon. 1981. "Mood and Memory." *American Psychologist* 36 (1981): 129–48.

Bradbury, Ray. 1990. *Zen and the Art of Writing*. New York: Bantam Books.

Brand, Alice G. 1980. *Therapy in Writing*. Lexington, MA: D.C. Heath.

———. 1985. "Hot Cognition: Emotions and Writing Behavior." *Journal of Advanced Composition* 6: 5–15.

———. 1987. "The Why of Cognition." *College Composition and Communication* 38: 436–43.

———. 1989a. *The Psychology of Writing: The Affective Experience*. Westport, CT: Greenwood P.

———. 1989b. "Composing Styles and the Power of Writing." Paper presented at the annual Conference of College Composition and Communication. Seattle, WA, 16–18 March.

———. 1991. "Social Cognition, Affect, and the Psychology of Writing." *Journal of Advanced Composition* 11: 395–407.

Brand, Alice G., and Jack L. Powell. 1986. "Emotions and the Writing Process: A Description of Apprentice Writers." *Journal of Educational Research* 79: 280–85.

Bredehoft, David J. 1991. "Cooperative Controversies in the Classroom." *College Teaching* 39: 122–25.

Britton, James, Tony Burgess, Nancy Martin, Alex McLeod, and Harold Rosen. 1975. *The Development of Writing Abilities (11–18)*. London: MacMillan.

Brown, Cynthia S. 1988. *Like It Was: A Complete Guide to Writing Oral History*. New York: Teachers and Writers Collaborative.

Brown, Marshall. 1992. "Unheard Melodies:The Force of Form." *PMLA* 107: 465–81.

Brown, Robert T. 1989. "Creativity: What are We to Measure?" In *Handbook of Creativity*, edited by John A. Glover, Royce R. Ronning, and Cecil R. Reynolds, 3–32. New York: Plenum.

Brown, Victor, et al. 1978. *Elementary Counselor's Notebook*. Christian Outdoor Education Committee of the United Methodist Church, Western Pennsylvania Conference.

Browning, Christopher R. 1992. *Ordinary Men: Reserve Police Battalion 101 and the Final Solution in Poland*. New York: HarperCollins.

Bruner, Jerome S. 1962. *On Knowing: Essays for the Left Hand*. Cambridge, MA: Belknap P.

Bruner, Jerome S., and Blythe Clinchy. 1966. "Towards a Disciplined Intuition." In *Learning About Learning*, edited by Jerome Bruner, 71–83. Bureau of Research Co-Operative Research Monograph.

Buber, Martin. 1970. *I and Thou*. New York: Scribner's.

Cage, John. 1974. "Lecture on Nothing." In *America A Prophecy*, edited by Jerome Rothenberg and George Quasha, 369–70. New York: Random House.

Campbell, Joseph. 1976. *The Portable Jung*. New York: Penguin.

Cassirer, Ernst. 1946. *Language and Myth*. Translated by S. Langer. New York: Harper.

Cirlot, J. E. 1962. *A Dictionary of Symbols*. New York: Philosophical Library.

Cixous, Helene, and Catherine Clement. 1975/1986. *The Newly Born Woman*. Translated by B. Wing. Minneapolis: University of Minnesota P.

Clark, Margaret S. 1982. "A Role for Arousal in the Link Between Feeling States, Judgments, and Behavior." In *Affect and Cognition: The Seventeenth Annual Carnegie Symposium on Cognition*, edited by Margaret S. Clark and Susan T. Fiske, 263–90. Hillsdale, NJ: Lawrence Erlbaum.

Clement, John. 1989. "Learning Via Model Construction and Criticism: Protocol Evidence on Sources of Creativity in Science." In *Handbook of Creativity*, edited by John A. Glover, Royce R. Ronning, and Cecil R. Reynolds, 341–80. New York: Plenum.

Clinchy, Blythe. 1975. "The Role of Intuition in Learning." *National Education Journal* 62: 48–51.

Collins, A. 1986. *A Sample Dialogue Based on Theory of Inquiry Reading: Technical Report 367*. Urbana, IL: Center for the Study of Reading.

Connors, Robert J., and Andrea A. Lunsford. 1988. "Frequency of Formal Errors in Current College Writing, or Ma and Pa Kettle Do Research." *College Composition and Communication* 39: 395–409.

Corrington, Robert S. June 1989. "Transcendence and the Loss of Semiotic Self." Paper presented at annual convention of the Semiotic Society of America. Indianapolis, IN.

Crowley, Sharon. 1989. *A Teacher's Guide to Deconstruction*. Urbana, IL: National Council of Teachers of English.

Csikszentmihalyi, Mihaly. 1975. "Play and Intrinsic Rewards." *Journal of Humanistic Psychology* 15: 41–63.

———. 1990. *Flow: The Psychology of Optimal Experience*. New York: Harper & Row.

Csikszentmihalyi, Mihaly, and Reed Larson. 1984. *Being Adolescent: Conflict and Growth in the Teen-age Years*. New York: Basic Books.

Daiute, Colette. 1981. "Psycholinguistic Foundations of the Writing Process." *Research in the Teaching of English* 15: 5–22.

Dalke, Anne. n.d. "Silence in Women's Fiction: A Lament for the Acquisition of Language." Bryn Mawr, PA: Unpublished Manuscript.

Darwin, Charles. 1894. *The Expression of the Emotions in Man and Animals.* New York: McGraw-Hill.

Dass, Ram. 1982. *Who Dies? An Investigation of Conscious Living and Conscious Dying*, edited by Stephen Levine, vii–x. New York: Doubleday.

Davis, Millie. March/April 1991. "The Impressions Series: Reading or Witchcraft?" *Council Grams* 54, no. 4: 1.

Derrida, Jacques. 1974. "White Mythology." *New Literary History* 6: 5–74.

———. 1976. *Of Grammatology.* Translated by Gayatri Chakravorty. Baltimore: Johns Hopkins UP.

———. 1978. *Writing and Difference.* Translated by Alan Bass. Chicago: University of Chicago P.

Dillard, Annie. 1982. *Teaching a Stone to Talk.* New York: Harper & Row.

Edelman, Gerald M. 1992. *Bright Air, Brilliant Fire: On the Matter of the Mind.* New York: Basic Books.

Edelson, Marshall. 1975. *Language and Interpretation in Psychoanalysis.* New Haven: Yale UP.

Edwards, Betty. 1979. *Drawing on the Right Side of the Brain.* Los Angeles: J. P. Tarcher.

———. 1986. *Drawing on the Artist Within: A Guide to Innovation, Invention, Imagination and Creativity.* New York: Simon and Schuster.

Elbow, Peter. 1981. *Writing With Power.* New York: Oxford UP.

———. 1985. "The Shifting Relationships Between Speech and Writing." *College Composition and Communication* 36, no. 3: 283–303.

———. 1986. *Embracing Contraries.* New York: Oxford UP.

———. 1992. "Voice in Writing: Three Senses of the Term." Unpublished Manuscript.

Elbow, Peter, and Pat Belanoff. 1989. *A Community of Writers.* New York: McGraw Hill.

Emig, Janet. 1964. "The Uses of the Unconscious in Composing." *College Composition and Communication* 15: 6–11.

Epes, Mary. 1985. "Tracing Errors to Their Source." *Journal of Basic Writing* 4: 4–33.

Eppley, Kenneth, et al. 1989. "Differential Effects of Relaxation Techniques on Trait Anxiety: A Meta-Analysis." *Journal of Clinical Psychology* 45: 957–74.

Feldman, David Henry. 1988. "Creativity: Dreams, Insights, and Transformations." In *The Nature of Creativity*, edited by Robert J. Sternberg, 271–97. New York: Cambridge UP.

Fischer, Kathleen. 1988. *Women at the Well: Feminist Perspectives on Spiritual Direction.* New York: Paulist Press.

Fiske, Susan T., and Patricia W. Linville. 1980. "What Does the Schema Concept Buy Us?" *Personality and Social Psychology Bulletin* 6: 543–57.

Fleckenstein, Kristie S. 1989. *Connections: The Cognitive and Affective Links Between Expressive Writing and Aesthetic Reading*, 2875A. Illinois State University. *UMI* 50-9A, no. 1990: 2875A: 9004083.

———. 1991a. "Defining Affect in Relation to Cognition: A Response to Susan McLeod." *Journal of Advanced Composition* 11: 447–53.

———. 1991b. "Inner Sight: Imagery and Emotion in Writing Engagement." *Teaching English in the Two-Year College* 18: 210–16.

Flower, Linda, and John R. Hayes. 1981. "A Cognitive Process Theory of Writing." *College Composition and Communication* 32: 365–87.

———. 1984. "Images, Plans, and Prose: The Representation of Meaning in Writing." *Written Communication* 1: 120–60.

Flowers, Betty S. October 1981. "Madman, Architect, Carpenter, Judge: Roles and the Writing Process." *Language Arts* 58, no. 7: 834–36.

Forman, Robert K. C. 1990. *The Problem of Pure Consciousness: Mysticism and Philosophy*. New York: Oxford UP.

Foshay, Arthur. 1991. "The Arts and Transcendence: An Autobiographical Note." In *Reflections from the Heart of Educational Inquiry*, edited by G. Willis and W. Schubert, 127–32. Albany, NY: SUNY P.

Foucault, Michel. 1978. "The Incitement to Discourse," in Robert Harley *The History of Sexuality* 1: 17–35. New York: Pantheon.

Freud, Sigmund. 1965. *The Interpretation of Dreams*. Translated by James Strachey. New York: Avon Books.

Frost, Robert. 1991. *Voices and Visions: The Poet in America,* edited by Helen Vendler. New York: Random House.

Fuller, Renee. 1977. *In Search of the IQ Correlation*. New York: Ball-Stick-Bird Publications.

———. 1982. "The Story as the Engram: Is It Fundamental to Thinking?" *The Journal of Mind and Behavior* 3: 127–42.

Fulwiler, Toby, ed. 1987. *The Journal Book*. Portsmouth, NH: Boynton/Cook.

Gardner, Howard 1980. *Artful Scribbles*. New York: Basic Books.

———. 1983. *Frames of Mind: The Theory of Multiple Intelligences*. New York: Basic Books.

———. 1985. *The Mind's New Science: A History of the Cognitive Revolution*. New York: Basic Books.

Gazzaniga, Michael S. 1985. *The Social Brain: Discovering the Networks of the Mind*. New York: Basic Books.

Gebhardt, Richard C. 1982. "Initial Plans and Spontaneous Composition: Toward a Comprehensive Theory of the Writing Process." *College English* 44: 620–27.

Gendlin, Eugene. 1962. *Experiencing and the Creation of Meaning*. Glencoe, IL: Free Press.

———. 1981. *Focusing*. New York: Bantam.

———. 1991. "Thinking Beyond Patterns: Body, Language, and Situations." In *The Presence of Feeling in Thought*, edited by Bernard den Ouden and Marcia Moen, 22–152. New York: Peter Lang.

Gleick, James. 1987. *Chaos: Making a New Science*. New York: Penguin Books.

Godwin, Gail. 1991. *Father Melancholy's Daughter*. New York: Morrow.

Goldberg, Philip. 1983. *The Intuitive Edge: Understanding and Developing Intuition*. Los Angeles: J. P. Tarcher.

Goldberg, Natalie. 1990. *Wild Mind*. New York: Bantam Books.

Goldstein, Joseph. 1976. *The Experience of Insight*. Boston: Shambhala.

Goldstein, Joseph, and Jack Kornfield. 1987. *Seeking the Heart of Wisdom: The Path of Insight Meditation*. Boston: Shambhala.

Golub, Jeff, ed. 1988. *Focus on Collaborative Learning*. Urbana, IL: National Council of Teachers of English.

Graves, Richard L. 1992. "Some Rivers." *Teaching English in the Two-Year College* 19: 279.

Gray, William. 1980. "Understanding Creative Thought Processes: An Early Formulation of Emotional-Cognitive Structure Theory." *Man-Environment Systems* 9.

Graybeal, Jean. 1987. "The Team Journal." In *The Journal Book*, edited by Toby Fulwiler, 306–11. Portsmouth, NH: Boynton/Cook.

Greene, Yvonne, and Byran Heibert. 1988. "A Comparison of Mindfulness, Meditation and Cognitive Self-Observation." *Canadian Journal of Counselling* 22: 25–34.

Grof, Stanislov. 1985. *Beyond the Brain: Birth, Death, and Transcendence in Psychotherapy*. Albany, NY: SUNY P.

Guerin, Wilfred L., Earle G. Labor, Lee Morgan, and John R. Willingham. 1979. *A Handbook of Critical Approaches to Literature*. 2nd ed. New York: HarperCollins.

Haas, Christina, and Linda Flower. 1988. "Rhetorical Reading Strategies and the Construction of Meaning." *College Composition and Communication* 39: 167–83.

Hall, Stephen S. June 1989. "A Molecular Code Links Emotions, Mind and Health." *Smithsonian*, 62–71.

Hart, William. 1987. *The Art of Living*. San Francisco: Harper & Row.

Heker, Liliana. 1991. "The Stolen Party." In *Ourselves Among Others: Cross-Cultural Readings for Writers*, 2nd ed., edited by Carol J. Verberg, 210–15. Boston: St. Martin's.

Helson, Harry. 1964. *Adaptation Level Theory*. New York: Harper & Row.

————. 1977. "Adaptation-Level(AL) Theory or Motivaton." In *International Encyclopedia of Psychiatry, Psychology, Psychoanalysis, and Neurology*, 225–27. New York: Aesculapius.

Hergenhahn, B. R. 1986. *An Introduction to the History of Psychology*. Belmont, CA: Wadsworth.

Hilgard, Ernest, and Gordon H. Bower. 1975. *Theories of Learning*. 4th ed. Englewood Cliffs, NJ: Prentice-Hall.

Hoffer, Eric. 1967. *The Temper of Our Time*. New York: Harper & Row.

Hoffman, Martin. 1984. "Interaction of Affect and Cognition in Empathy." In *Emotions, Cognition, and Behavior*, edited by Carroll E. Izard, Jerome Kagan and Robert B. Zajonc, 103–31. Cambridge: Cambridge UP.

Hoffman, Eva. 1989. *Lost in Translation: A Life in a New Language*. New York: Penguin.

Housman, Alfred Edward. 1933. *The Name and Nature of Poetry*. New York: Macmillan.

Hughes, Elaine F. 1991. *Writing from the Inner Self*. New York: HarperCollins.

Hunt, Morton. 1990. *The Compassionate Beast: What Science is Discovering About the Humane Side of Humankind*. New York: William Morrow.

Hynds, Susan, and Donald Rubin, eds. 1990. *Perspectives on Talk and Learning*. Urbana, IL: National Council of Teachers of English.

Izard, Carroll E. 1982. "Comments on Emotion and Cognition: Can There Be a Working Relationship?" In *Affect and Cognition: The Seventeenth Annual Carnegie Symposium on Cognition*, edited by Margaret S. Clark and Susan T. Fiske, 229–42. Hillsdale, NJ: Lawrence Erlbaum.

Jacobs, Harriet. 1990. "Incidents in the Life of a Slave Girl." In *Ways of Reading: An Anthology for Writers*, edited by David Bartholomae and Anthony Petrosky, 312–53. Boston: St. Martin's.

Janov, Arthur. 1970. *The Primal Scream*. New York: Dell.

Jefferson, Lara. 1974. *These Are My Sisters*. Garden City, NY: Anchor /Doubleday.

Jelpi, Barbara Charles Worth, and Albert Jelpi. 1993. *Adrienne Rich's Poetry and Prose*. New York: Norton.

Jenkinson, Edward. November 1988. "New Age: Target of the Censor." *Newsletter of Intellectual Freedom* 37, no. 6: 189, 220–22.

John-Steiner, Vera. 1985. *Notebooks of the Mind: Explorations of Thinking*. Albuquerque, NM: U of New Mexico P.

Johnson, David W., and Roger T. Johnson. 1991. *Learning Together and Alone: Cooperative, Competitive, and Individualistic Learning*. 3rd ed. Englewood Cliffs, NJ: Prentice Hall.

Johnson, David W., et al. 1984. *Circles of Learning: Cooperation in the Classroom*. Alexandria, VA: Association for Supervision and Curriculum Development.

Johnson, Mark. 1987. *The Body in the Mind.* Chicago: University of Chicago P.

Johnson, Thomas H., ed. 1890/1960. *The Complete Poems of Emily Dickinson.* Boston: Little, Brown.

Johnson, William. 1979. *Silent Music.* New York: Harper & Row.

Johnston, Charles. 1983. *The Creative Imperative.* Berkeley, CA: Celestial Arts Books.

Jones, Le Roi. 1963. *Blues People.* New York: Morrow.

Jung, Carl G. 1933. *Psychological Types.* Translated by H. Goodwin Baynes. New York: Harcourt.

———. 1968. *The Collected Works of C. G. Jung: Vol. 9. Part 1.* In *The Archetypes and the Collective Unconscious,* 2nd ed. Princeton, NJ: Princeton UP.

Kalamaras, George. 1993. *Reclaiming the Tacit Dimension: Symbolic Form in the Rhetoric of Silence.* Albany: State University of New York P.

Kammer, Jeanne. 1979. "The Art of Silence and the Forms of Women's Poetry." In *Shakespeare's Sisters: Feminist Essays on Women Poets,* edited by Sandra M. Gilbert and Susan Gubar, 153–64. Bloomington, IN: Indiana University P.

Kapleau, Philip. 1965. *The Three Pillars of Zen.* Garden City, NY: Anchor Books.

———. 1980. *Zen: Dawn in the West.* Garden City, NY: Anchor Books.

Katagiri, Dainin. 1988. *Returning to Silence.* Boston: Shambhala.

Katsuki, Sekida. 1975. *Zen Training.* New York: Weatherhill.

Katz, Albert N. 1983. "What Does it Mean to be a High Imager?" In *Imagery, Memory, and Cognition,* edited by J. Yuille, 39–64. Hillsdale, NJ: Lawrence Erlbaum.

Kessler, Shelley. 1990. "The Mysteries Program—Educating Adolescents for Today's World." *Holistic Education Review* 3: 10–19.

Kleinman, Arthur. 1980. *Patients and Healers in the Context of Culture: An Exploration of the Borderland Between Anthropology, Medicine, and Psychiatry.* Berkeley: University of California.

Klinger, Eric. 1978. "Modes of Normal Conscious Flow." In *The Stream of Consciousness,* edited by K. Pope and J. Singer, 226–57. New York: Plenum.

Kohlberg, Lawrence. June 1975. "The Cognitive-Developmental Approach to Moral Education." *Phi Delta Kappan,* 670–77.

Kohut, Heinz. 1959/1978. "Introspection, Empathy, and Psychoanalysis." In *The Search for the Self: Selected Writings of Heinz Kohut, 1950–1978,* 205–32. New York: International Universities P.

———. 1973/1978. "The Psychoanalyst in the Community of Scholars." In *The Search for the Self: Selected Writings of Heinz Kohut, 1950–1978,* 685–724. New York: International Universities P.

————. 1977. *The Restoration of the Self.* New York: International Universities P.

Kosslyn, Stephen M. May 1985. "Stalking the Mental Image." *Psychology Today,* 23–25.

Krathwohl, David R., Benjamin S. Bloom, and Bertram B. Masia. 1964. *Taxonomy of Educational Objectives: The Classification of Educational Goals, Handbook 2. Affective Domain.* New York: David McKay.

Kristeva, Julia. 1979/1981. "Women's Time." Translated by A. Jardin and H. Blake. *Signs* 7: 13–35.

Kroll, Barry, and John Schafer. 1978. "Error Analysis and the Teaching of Composition." *College Composition and Communication* 29: 242–48.

Kubie, Lawrence S. 1958. *Neurotic Distortion of the Creative Process.* Lawrence, KS: University of Kansas P.

Kumin, Maxine. 1976. *To Make a Prairie.* Ann Arbor: University of Michigan P.

Lakoff, George. 1978. *Women, Fire and Dangerous Things.* Chicago: University of Chicago P.

Langer, Susanne K. 1957. *Philosophy in a New Key.* 3rd ed. Cambridge: Harvard UP.

————. 1962. *Philosophical Sketches.* Baltimore, MD: Johns Hopkins P.

————. 1967. *Mind: An Essay on Human Feeling. Vol. 1.* Baltimore, MD: Johns Hopkins UP.

————. 1972. *Mind: An Essay on Human Feeling. Vol. 2.* Baltimore, MD: Johns Hopkins UP.

Langley, Pat, and Randolph Jones. 1988. "A Computational Model of Scientific Insight." In *The Nature of Creativity: Contemporary Psychological Perspectives,* edited by Robert J. Sternberg, 177–201. Cambridge: Cambridge UP.

Langston, M. Diane. 1989. "Engagement in Writing: How Experts and Novices Pursue Personal Agendas While Drafting New Texts." Paper presented at the Annual Conference of the College Composition and Communication. Seattle, WA, 16–18 March.

Larson, Reed. 1985. "Emotional Scenarios in the Writing Processes: An Examination of Young Writers' Affective Experience." In *When a Writer Can't Write,* edited by M. Rose, 19–41. New York: Guilford P.

Laurence, Patricia Ondek. 1991. *The Reading of Silence: Virginia Woolf in the English Tradition.* Stanford: Stanford UP.

Lawson, Bruce, Susan Sterr Ryan, and W. Ross Winterowd, eds. 1990. *Encountering Student Texts.* Urbana, IL: National Council of Teachers of English.

LeDoux, Joseph E. 1985. "Brain, Mind, and Language." In *Brain and Mind,* edited by David E. Oakley, 197–216. London: Methuen.

———. 1989. "Cognitive-Emotional Interactions in the Brain." *Cognition and Emotion* 4: 267–89. Hillsdale, NJ: Lawrence Erlbaum.

———. 1991. "Emotion and the Limbic System Concept." *Concepts in Neuroscience* 2, no. 2: 169–99.

Leventhal, Howard. 1982. "The Integration of Emotion and Cognition: A View from the Perceptual-Motor Theory of Emotion." In *Affect and Cognition: The Seventeenth Annual Carnegie Symposium on Cognition*, edited by Margaret S. Clark and Susan T. Fiske, 121–56. Hillsdale, NJ: Lawrence Erlbaum.

Lewin, Kurt, Tamara Dembo, Leon Festinger, and Pauline S. Sears. 1944. "Level of Aspiration." In *Personality and Behavior Disorders. Vol.1*, edited by J. McVicker Hunt, 333–78. New York: Ronald.

Loewald, Hans W. 1988. *Sublimation: Inquiries into Theoretical Psychoanalysis*. New Haven: Yale UP.

Lourdes, Peter. April 1989. "A Catholic Priest on Vipassana." *Vipassana Newsletter* 16, no. 1: 2.

Luria, A. R. 1973. *The Working Brain: An Introduction to Neuropsychology*. Translated by Basil Haigh. New York: Basic Books.

Lyotard, Jean-Francis. 1984. *The Postmodern Condition: A Report on Knowledge*. Translated by Geoff Bennington and Brian Massurai. Minneapolis: University of Minnesota P.

Macrorie, Ken. 1970. *Telling Writing*. Portsmouth, NH: Boynton/Cook.

Madden, Thomas R. 1986. "Teaching Literature as Dialogue." Paper presented at the Northwest Regional Conference National Council of Teachers of English. Portland, OR (April).

Mandel, Barrett J. 1978. "Losing One's Mind." *College Composition and Communication* 29: 362–68.

———. 1980. "The Writer Writing Is Not at Home." *College Composition and Communication* 31: 370–77.

Mandler, George. 1984. *Mind and Body: The Psychology of Emotion and Stress*. New York: W. W. Norton.

———. 1990. "A Constructivist Theory of Emotion." In *Psychological and Biological Approaches to Emotion*, edited by Nancy L. Stein, Bennett Leventhal, and Tom Trabasso, 21–44. Hillsdale, NJ: Lawrence Erlbaum.

———. 1982. "The Structure of Value: Accounting for Taste." In *Affect and Cognition*, edited by Margaret S. Clark and Susan T. Fiske, 3–36. Hillsdale, NJ: Lawrence Erlbaum.

Mandler, Jean. 1984. *Stories, Scripts, Scenes: Aspects of Schema Theory*. Hillsdale, NJ: Lawrence Earlbaum.

Marrs, Texe. 1988. *Dark Secrets of the New Age: Satan's Plan for a One World Religion*, 230. Westchester, IL: Crossways Books.

Martin Jr., Bill. 1973. *Sounds Freedomring*. New York: Holt, Rinehart & Winston.

Marzano, Robert, and et al. 1988. *Dimensions of Thinking: A Framework for Curriculum and Instruction*. Alexandria, VA: Association for Supervision and Curriculum Development.

Marzano, Robert, and Daisy Arredondo. 1986. *Tactics for Thinking— Teacher's Manual*. Alexandria, VA: Association for Supervision and Curriculum Development.

Maslow, Abraham H. 1954. *Motivation and Personality*. New York: Harper and Brothers.

———. 1968. *Toward a Psychology of Being*. 2nd ed. New York: Van Nostrand.

May, Rollo. 1975. *The Courage to Create*. New York: Norton.

Mayeroff, Milton. 1971. *On Caring*. New York: Harper & Row.

McKim, Robert M. 1980. *Experiences in Visual Thinking*. 2nd ed. Monterey, CA: Brooks.

McLeod, Susan. 1987. "Some Thoughts About Feelings: The Affective Domain and the Writing Process." *College Composition and Communication* 38: 426–35.

———. 1991. "The Affective Domain and the Writing Process: Working Definitions." *Journal of Advanced Composition*, 11: 95–105.

McNally, D.W. 1977. *Piaget. Education, and Teaching*. Hassocks, Sussex: Harvester.

McNeill, David. 1992. *Hand and Mind: What Gestures Reveal About Thought*. Chicago: University of Chicago P.

Merton, Thomas. 1958. *Thoughts in Solitude*. New York: Farrar, Straus, & Cudhay.

Miller, Hildy L., and Mary Ellen Ashcroft. In press. *"Strong," "Typical," and "Weak" College Writers: Twenty-Two Case Studies*. Minneapolis, MN: The Center for Interdisciplinary Studies of Writing.

Milner, Marion. 1957. *On Not Being Able to Paint*. New York: International Universities P.

———. 1969. *The Hands of the Living God*. New York: International Universities P.

Mitchell, Stephen, trans. 1988. *Tao Te Ching*. New York: Harper & Row.

Moffett, James. 1981a. *Active Voice*. Portsmouth, NH: Boynton/Cook.

———. 1981b. "Writing, Inner Speech, and Meditation." In *Coming on Center: English Education in Evolution*, 133–81. Portsmouth, NH: Boynton/Cook.

———. 1990. "Some Thoughts on Integrating the Curriculum." Paper presented at the Curriculum Congress. Aspen, CO, 26–29 August.

Moffett, James, and Betty Jane Wagner. 1992. *Student-Centered Language Arts, K–12*. 4th ed. Portsmouth, NH: Boynton/Cook.

Mueller, Lisel. 1989. "When I am Asked." *Waving from Shore*. Baton Rouge, LA: Louisiana State UP.

Mullin, Anne J. 1991. *See What We're Saying: An Interpretive Approach to Teaching Composition.* Doctoral Dissertation. University of Massachusetts-Amherst.

Murdoch, Iris, and J. Krishnamurti. 1984. "J. Krishnamurti and Iris Murdoch." Video. Oji, CA: Krishnamurti Foundation.

Murray, Donald M. 1978. "Write Before Writing." *College Composition and Communication* 29: 375–81.

———. 1982. "The Maker's Eye." In *Language by Teaching: Selected Articles on Writing and Teaching,* 68–71. Portsmouth, NH: Boynton/Cook.

———. 1990. *Write to Learn.* 3rd ed. Fort Worth: Harcourt Brace.

Murray, Edward J. 1964. *Motivation and Emotion.* Englewood Cliffs, NJ: Prentice-Hall.

Myers, Isabel B., and Peter B. Myers. 1990. *Gifts Differing.* Palo Alto, CA: Consulting Psychologists Press.

Nachmanovich, Stephen. 1990. *Free Play: Improvisation in Life and Art.* Los Angeles: J. P. Tarcher.

Naranjo, Claudio. 1989. *How to Be: Meditation in Spirit and Practice.* Los Angeles: J. P. Tarcher.

Neisser, Ulric. 1967. *Cognitive Psychology.* Englewood Cliffs, NJ: Prentice-Hall.

Neuenschwander, John A. 1976. *Oral History as a Teaching Approach.* Washington, D.C.: National Education Association.

Neusner, Jacob. 1981. "Commencement Address" Brown University *Daily Herald. National Review*, (12 June): 650–52.

Nhat Hanh, Tich. 1987. *The Miracle of Mindfulness.* Rev. ed. Trans. by Mobi Ho. Boston: Beacon.

Nin, Anais. 1958/1989. *House of Incest.* Athens, OH: Swallow Press.

Noddings, Nel, and Paul Shore. 1984. *Awakening the Inner Eye—Intuition in Education.* New York: Teachers College Press.

Norman, Donald. 1986. "The Nucleators." In *The Cognitive Revolution in Psychology*, edited by Bernard Baars, 381–85. New York: Guilford.

Norman, Donald A. 1981. "Twelve Issues for Cognitive Science." In *Perspectives on Cognitive Science*, edited by Donald A. Norman, 265–95. Norwood, NJ: Ablex.

Oliner, Samuel P., and Pearl Oliner. 1988. *The Altruistic Personality: Rescuers of Jews in Nazi Europe.* New York: Free Press.

Padget, Ron. January/February 1992. "Books." *Teachers and Writers* 23: 16.

Paivio, Allan. 1989. *Mental Representations: A Dual Coding Approach.* Oxford: Oxford UP.

Palincsar, A. S., and A. L. Brown. 1985. "Reciprocal Teaching: Activities to Promote Reading with Your Mind." In *Reading, Thinking and Concept Development*, edited by T. L. Harris and E. J. Cogen. New York: The College Board.

Palmer, Parker. 1983. *To Know as We Are Known: A Spirituality of Education.* New York: Harper & Row.

Pennebaker, James W. 1992. *Opening Up: The Healing Power of Confiding in Others.* New York: Avon.

Perl, Sondra. 1979. "The Composing Processes of Unskilled College Writers." *Research in the Teaching of English* 13: 317–36.

———. 1980. "Understanding Composing." *College Composition and Communication* 31: 363–69.

Perl, Sondra, and Nancy Wilson. 1986. *Through Teachers' Eyes; Portraits of Writing Teachers at Work.* Portsmouth, NH: Heineman.

Perry, William, Jr. 1970. *Forms of Intellectual and Ethical Development in the College Years.* New York: Holt, Rinehart & Winston.

Petrie, Ann. 1976. "Teaching the Thinking Process in Essay Writing." *Journal of Basic Writing* 1: 60–7.

Petrosky, Anthony. 1982. "From Story to Essay: Reading and Writing." *College Composition and Communication* 33: 19–36.

Piaget, Jean. 1956. *The Moral Judgment of the Child.* Translated by M. Gaubain. New York: Free Press.

———. 1970. *Genetic Epistemology.* Translated by E. Duckworth. New York: Columbia UP.

Picard, Max. 1952. *The World of Silence.* South Bend, IN: Regnery/Gateway.

Plato. 1960. "The Symposium." In *The Republic and Other Works.* Translated by B. Jowett. Garden City, NY: Doubleday.

Plutchik, Robert. 1980. *Emotion: A Psychoevolutionary Synthesis.* New York: Harper & Row.

Polanyi, Michael. 1966. *The Tacit Dimension.* New York: Doubleday.

———. 1969. "The Logic of Tacit Inference." In *Knowing and Being: Essays by Michael Polanyi*, edited by Marjorie Grene, 138–58. Chicago: U of Chicago P.

Progoff, Ira. 1975. *At a Journal Workshop: The Basic Text and Guide for Using the Intensive Journal.* New York: Dialogue House.

Pugh, George. 1977. *Biological Origins of Human Values.* New York: Basic Books.

Reigstad, Thomas J. 1985. "Perspectives on Anxiety and the Basic Writer: Research, Evaluation, Instruction." *Journal of Basic Writing* 4: 68–77.

Restak, Richard M. 1984. *The Brain.* New York: Bantam.

———. *The Infant Mind.* 1986. Garden City, NY: Doubleday.

———. 1988. *The Mind.* New York: Bantam.

———. 1991. *The Brain Has a Mind of Its Own: Insights from a Practicing Neurologist.* New York: Harmony.

Richards, M. C. 1963. *Centering: Poetry, Pottery, and the Person.* Middletown, CT: Wesleyan UP.

Rico, Gabriele Lusser. 1983. *Writing the Natural Way*. Los Angeles: J. P. Tarcher.

———. 1991. *Pain and Possibility: Writing Your Way Through Personal Crisis*. Los Angeles: J. P. Tarcher/Putnam.

Rogers, Carl R. 1961. *On Becoming a Person*. Boston: Houghton Mifflin.

Rokeach, Milton. 1972. *Beliefs, Attitudes, and Values*. San Francisco: Jossey-Bass.

———. 1973. *The Nature of Human Values*. New York: The Free Press.

———. 1979. *Understanding Human Values*. New York: The Free Press.

———. 1980. *A Way of Being*. Boston: Houghton Mifflin.

Romilly, Jacqueline de. 1975. *Magic and Rhetoric in Ancient Greece*. Cambridge: Harvard UP.

Rushdie, Salman. 1990. "Is Nothing Sacred?" *Granta* 31 (Spring): 97–111.

Rycroft, Charles. 1985. *Psychoanalysis and Beyond*. London: Hogarth.

Sadoski, Mark. 1983. "An Exploratory Study of the Relationships Between Reported Imagery and the Comprehension and Recall of a Story." *Reading Research Quarterly* 19: 110–23.

Sadoski, Mark, Ernst Goetz, and Susan Kangiser. 1988. "Imagination in Story Response: Relationships Between Imagery, Affect, and Structural Importance." *Reading Research Quarterly* 23(Summer): 320–36.

Saloman, Gavriel, and Tamar Globerson. 1987. "Skill May Not Be Enough: The Role of Mindfulness in Learning and Transfer." *International Journal of Educational Research* 11: 623–37.

Schafer, Roy. 1976. *A New Language for Psychoanalysis*. New Haven: Yale UP.

Scheurer, Erika. 1993. *Emily Dickinson and Voice*. Doctoral Dissertation. University of Massachusetts-Amherst.

Schwartz, Mimi. 1983. "Two Journeys Through the Writing Process." *College Composition and Communication* 34: 188–200.

Segal, Hanna. 1986. *The Work of Hanna Segal: A Kleinian Approach to Clinical Practice*. London: Free Associations Books.

Seitz, James. 1991. "Roland Barthes, Reading, and Roleplay: Composition's Misguided Rejection of Fragmentary Texts." *College English* 53: 815–25.

Sekida, Katsuki. 1975. *Zen Training: Methods and Philosophy*. New York: Weatherhill.

Shapiro, Deane. 1992. "A Preliminary Study of Long-Term Meditators." *Journal of Transpersonal Psychology* 24: 23–39.

Shaughnessy, Mina. 1977. *Errors and Expectations: A Guide for the Teacher of Basic Writing*. New York: Oxford UP.

Sheehan, Peter, R. Ashton, and K. White. 1983. "Assessment of Mental Imagery." In *Imagery*, edited by A. Sheikh, 189–215. New York: John Wiley.

Sheehan, Peter. 1967. "A Shortened Form of Betts' Questionnaire upon Mental Imagery." *Journal of Clinical Psychology* 23: 386–89.

Sigel, Irving E. 1978. "The Development of Pictorial Comprehension." In *Visual Learning, Thinking and Communication*, edited by Bikkar S. Randhawa and William E. Coffman, 93–111. New York: Academic P.

Simon, Herbert A. 1981. "Cognitive Science: The Newest Science of the Artificial." In *Perspectives on Cognitive Science,* edited by Donald A. Norman, 13–25. Norwood, NJ: Ablex.

————. 1982. "Comments." In *Affect and Cognition: The Seventeenth Annual Carnegie Symposium on Cognition*, edited by Margaret S. Clark and Susan T. Fiske, 333–42. Hillsdale, NJ: Lawrence Erlbaum.

Sontag, Susan. 1969. "The Aesthetics of Silence." In *Styles of Radical Will.* New York: Farrar, Straus, Giroux.

Stafford, William. 1964. "Writing the Australian Crawl." *College Composition and Communication* 15: 12–15.

————. 1977. *Stories that Could be True: New and Collected Poems.* New York: Harper & Row.

Staton, Jana. 1987. "The Power of Responding in Dialogue Journals." In *The Journal Book*, edited by Toby Fulwiler, 47–63. Portsmouth, NH: Boynton/Cook.

Stein, Nancy L., Bennett Leventhal, and Tom Trabasso, eds. 1990. *Psychological and Biological Approaches to Emotion.* Hillsdale, NJ: Lawrence Erlbaum.

Suhor, Charles. 1991. "Surprised by Bird and Bard—Transcendence and Silence in the English Classroom." *English Journal* 8: 21–26.

Suzuki, D. T. 1956. *Zen Buddhism: Selected Writings of D. T. Suzuki.* Edited by William Barrett. New York: Anchor Books.

————. 1964. *An Introduction to Zen Buddhism.* New York : Grove Press.

Suzuki, Shunryu. 1970. *Zen Mind, Beginner's Mind.* New York: Weatherhill.

Szerlip, Barbara. January/February 1993. "Inventing Memories: An Interview with Isabel Allende." *Poets & Writers Magazine* 21, no. 1: 38–55.

Tannen, Deborah, and Muriel Saville-Troike. 1985. *Perspectives on Silence.* Norwood, NJ: Ablex.

Tart, Charles. 1989. *Open Mind, Discriminating Mind.* San Francisco: Harper & Row.

————. 1990. "Adapting Eastern Spiritual Teachings to Western Culture: A Discussion with Shinzen Young." *Journal of Transpersonal Psychology* 22: 149–66.

Teich, Nathaniel, ed. 1987. "Rogerian Problem-Solving and the Rhetoric of Argumentation." *Journal of Advanced Composition* 7: 52–61.

————. 1992. *Rogerian Perspectives: Collaborative Rhetoric for Oral and Written Communication.* Norwood, NJ: Ablex.

Terkel, Studs. 1972. *Working: People Talk About What They Do All Day Long and How They Feel About What They Do*. New York: Pantheon.

Thomas, Trudelle H. 1992. "Connected Teaching: An Exploration of the Classroom Enterprise." *Journal on Excellence in College Teaching* 3: 101–19.

Thompson, Nancy. 1991. "Imaging for Literacy Learning: A Reflective Teaching Inquiry." ERIC ED 332163.

Tolman, Edward C. 1932. *Purposive Behavior in Animals and Men*. New York: Appleton-Century-Crofts.

Tomkins, Silvan S. 1962. *Affect, Imagery, Consciousness: The Positive Affects. Vol. 1*. New York: Springer.

———. 1963. *Affect, Imagery, Consciousness: The Negative Affects. Vol. 2*. New York: Springer.

Tomlinson, Barbara. 1984. "Talking About the Composing Process." *Written Communication* 1: 429–45.

Tompkins, Jane. 1990. "Pedagogy of the Distressed." *College English* 52: 653–60.

Trimbur, John. 1987. "Beyond Cognition: The Voices in Inner Speech." *Rhetoric Review* 5: 211–21.

Trungpa, Chogyam. 1969. *Meditation in Action*. Berkeley, CA: Shambhala.

Tucher, Andie, ed. 1990. *Bill Moyers: A World of Ideas II*. New York: Doubleday.

Tucker, Don M., Kathryn Vannatta, and Johannes Rothlind. 1990. "Arousal and Activation Systems and Primitive Adaptive Controls on Cognitive Priming." In *Psychological and Biological Approaches to Emotion*, edited by Nancy L. Stein, Bennett Leventhal, and Tom Trabasso, 145–67. Hillsdale, NJ: Lawrence Erlbaum.

Twain, Mark. 1903. *Life on the Mississippi*. New York: Harper & Brothers.

van de Wetering, Janwillem. 1973. *The Empty Mirror: Experiences in a Japanese Zen Monastary*. New York: Washington Square Press.

———. 1975. *A Glimpse of Nothingness: Experiences in an American Zen Community*. New York: Washington Square Press.

van der Post, Laurens. 1960. *The Lost World of the Kalahari*. London: Hogarth P.

Vaughan, Frances. 1991. "Spiritual Issues in Psychotherapy." *Journal of Transpersonal Psychology* 23: 105–19.

Vernon, P.E., ed. 1970. *Creativity*. New York: Penguin.

Walker, Alice. 1989. *The Temple of My Familiar*. New York: Harcourt Brace Jovanovich.

Watts, Allan. 1955. *The Way of Liberation in Zen Buddhism*. San Francisco: American Academy of Asian Studies.

Weathers, Winston. 1976. "The Grammars of Style: New Options in Composition." *Freshman English News* (Winter).

Weiner, Bernard. 1974. *Achievement Motivation and Attribution Theory.* Morristown, NJ: General Learning P.

———. 1982. "The Emotional Consequences of Causal Attributions." In *Affect and Cognition: The Seventeenth Annual Carnegie Symposium on Cognition,* edited by Margaret S. Clark and Susan T. Fiske, 185–209. Hillsdale, NJ: Lawrence Erlbaum.

———. 1986. *An Attributional Theory of Motivation and Emotion.* New York: Springer-Verlag.

Weis, Monica R. 1983."Current Brain Research and the Composing Process." In *The Writer's Mind: Writing as a Mode of Thinking,* edited by Janice N. Hayes, et al., 25–33. Urbana, IL: National Council of Teachers of English.

West, Thomas. 1991. *In the Mind's Eye.* Buffalo: Prometheus.

Winter, David G., David C. McClelland, and Abigail J. Stewart. 1981. *A New Case for the Liberal Arts.* San Francisco: Jossey-Bass.

Wolin, Sybil, and Steven Wolin. 1993. *The Resilient Self.* New York: Villard Books.

Woodrow, Peter. 1976. *Clearness: Processes for Supporting Individuals and Groups in Decision-Making.* Baltimore, MD: New Society.

Worley, Demetrice A. 1991. "Visual and Verbal Transactions: The Effect of Visual Imagery Training on the Writing of College Students," Illinois State University. *UMI* 51–9A: 30006A.

Wyer, Robert S., and Thomas K. Srull. 1989. *Memory and Cognition in Its Social Context.* Hillsdale, NJ: Lawrence Erlbaum.

Yerkes, Robert M., and John D. Dodson. 1908. "The Relation of Strength of Stimulus to Rapidity of Habit-Formation." *Journal of Comparative Neurology and Psychology* 18: 459–82.

Zajonc, Robert B. 1980. "Feeling and Thinking: Preferences Need No Inferences." *American Psychologist* 35: 151–75.

Zajonc, Robert B., and Hazel Markus. 1982. "Affective and Cognitive Factors in Preferences." *Journal of Consumer Research* 9: 123–31.

Zajonc, Robert B., Paula Pietromonaco, and John Bargh. 1982. "Independence and Interaction of Affect and Cognition." In *Affect and Cognition: The Seventeenth Annual Carnegie Symposium on Cognition,* edited by Margaret S. Clark and Susan T. Fiske, 211–28. Hillsdale, NJ: Lawrence Erlbaum.

Zillman, Dolf. 1988. "Mood Management: Using Entertainment to Full Advantage." In *Communication, Social Cognition, and Affect,* edited by Lewis Donohew, Howard E. Sypher and E. Tory Higgins, 147–72. Hillsdale, NJ: Lawrence Erlbaum.

Contributors

Susan M. Becker is associate professor of English at Illinois Central College, Peoria, where she teaches courses in American literature, business communication, and freshman composition. She chairs the committee on Writing Across the Curriculum and serves as advisor to the Phi Theta Kappa honorary society. In 1994, she was sponsored by the Illinois Consortium for International Studies as foreign exchange professor in England.

Alice Glarden Brand is professor of English at SUNY Brockport, having previously served as director of composition. Her first book *Therapy in Writing,* was published in 1980 and her second, *The Psychology of Writing: The Affective Experience,* in 1989. Her essays and poetry have appeared in the *Journal of Advanced Composition, Educational and Psychological Measurement, Journal of Humanistic Education and Development, Journal of Psychology, Rhetoric Review, College Composition and Communication, The New England Quarterly,* and *The New York Times.* She has also published two volumes of poetry, *As It Happens* in 1983, and *Studies in Zone* in 1989.

Sandra Price Burkett is professor emerita of Curriculum and Instruction at Mississippi State University and part-time director of the Mississippi Writing/Thinking Institute. Her passions for writing as a spiritual process and for infusing spirituality into education have called her to retire early and explore spirituality at the Graduate Theological Union in Berkeley, California.

Peter Elbow is professor of English at the University of Massachusetts at Amherst. He has taught at M.I.T., Franconia College, Evergeen State College, SUNY–Stony Brook, where for five years he directed the writing program. He is author of *Oppositions in Chaucer, Writing Without Teachers, Writing with Power, Embracing Contraries, What Is English?,* and (with Pat Belanoff) *A Community of Writers.* His essay, "The Shifting Relationships Betwee n Speech and Writing" won the Richard Braddock in 1986. He is currently exploring the relationships between writing, voice, performance, and the body.

Kristie S. Fleckenstein is an independent scholar based in Overland Park, Kansas. Her research interests include the role of affect and imagery in reading and writing processes. She has published in journals such as *College Composition and Communication, Journal of Advanced Composition, English Journal,* and the *Journal of Mental Imagery.*

Donald R. Gallehr teaches writing in the English Department at George Mason University, Fairfax, Virginia, and is completing a text on using secular meditation techniques in advanced non-fiction writing. Don serves as director of the Northern Virginia Writing Project and co-director of the National Writing Project.

Richard L. Graves is professor of English Education at Auburn University, Auburn, Alabama, and director of the Sun Belt Writing Project. His publications include *Rhetoric and Composition: A Sourcebook for Teachers and Writers* (Heinemann-Boynton/Cook) and articles in professional journals such as *English Journal, College Composition and Communication, Language Arts,* and *Phi Delta Kappan.*

Linda Hecker has taught at Landmark College in Putney, Vermont, a school for high potential learning disabled students, since its founding in 1985. A lifelong teacher, she has worked at all levels from pre-school to college, including a stint as a teacher in a maximum security prison. She lives in the woods of Guilford, Vermont, where she doubles as a freelance violinist/violist.

Elizabeth Holman taught composition, reading, and study skills at the College of Lake County in Illinois before completing the doctorate at Illinois State University. She is currently studying the noncognitive process of writing and serving as assistant editor of *Research Review: The Journal of Little Big Horn Associates.*

Karen Klein has pursued a dual career as a teacher of literature and a visual artist. She is associate professor of English at Brandeis University where she also directs the humanities program. At Brandeis she has developed a writing course for students whose thinking patterns are spatial and simultaneous rather than linear and sequential. Her ink drawings and artist's books have been exhibited in juried or invitational solo and group shows.

Hildy Miller is assistant professor of English and associate director of composition at the University of Louisville. Her research interests include the conceptual role of image and metaphor in writing, the cognitive and social implications of feminist theory, and the effect of instructional context and individual perspectives on writing assessment. Her essays in these arenas have appeared in journals such as *Metaphor and Symbolic Activity* and the *Journal of Teaching Writing.*

James Moffett is an author and consultant in education. Though most of his past works focused on language learning, he is now dealing with total education (*Harmonic Learning: Keynoting School Reform,* Heinemann-Boynton/Cook 1992) and is proposing a thoroughly individualized community learning network for all ages, set in a spiritual and metaphysical framework (*The University Schoolhouse: Spiritualizing Society,* Jossey-Bass, 1994).

Anne E. Mullin teaches composition and directs the writing lab at Idaho State University. Her essay "Freewriting: Good for What?" appears in *Nothing Begins with N,* edited by Pat Belanoff, Peter Elbow, and Sheryl Fontaine. Her poems and other essays have been published in *College English, Black Fly Review, Plainswoman, Timberline, The Maine Sunday Telegram,* and *Sunrise Magazine.*

Richard J. Murphy, Jr. teaches composition and literature at Radford University. He is the co-author of *Symbiosis: Writing and an Academic Culture* (Heinemann-Boynton/Cook), and he has published essays on teaching and learning in *College Composition and Communication, College English, English Education,* and *Into the Field.* His collection of autobiographical essays, *The Calculus of Intimacy: A Teaching Life,* is forthcoming from Ohio State University Press.

Donald M. Murray, Professor Emeritus of English at the University of New Hampshire, practices his craft every morning, surprising himself by what he says in the drafts of his poems, novels, textbooks, and *Boston Globe* column. As a journalist he won a number of awards, including the Pulitzer prize for editorial writing on *The Boston Herald* in 1954. Among his publications are several texts on writing: *A Writer Teaches Writing; Learning by Teaching; Writing for Your Readers; Write to Learn; Read to Write; Expecting the Unexpected; Shoptalk, Learning to Write with Writers,* and *The Craft of Revision.*

Sondra Perl is associate professor of English at Lehman College, CUNY. She is co-founder of the New York City Writing Project and served as director for ten years. Her interests include feminism and composition theory, ethnography, the teaching of writing and literature, and teacher training. She has published, with Nancy Wilson, *Through Teachers' Eyes,* which is an ethnographic account of six teachers teaching writing.

Gabriele Lusser Rico is professor of English, Creative Arts, and Humanities at San Jose State University. She currently directs the teaching assistant program, having previously served as director of composition and coordinator of the upper division of Writing Across the Curriculum program. She has authored *Writing the Natural Way* (1983), *Pain and Possibility: Writing Your Way Through Personal Crisis* (1991), and with Hans Guth, *Discovering Literature, Discovering Poetry,* and *Discovering Fiction.* Her interests include higher level thinking skills, the role of the emotions of learning, and the use of the arts to integrate the curriculum.

Charles Suhor is Deputy Executive Director of the National Council of Teachers of English. A former high school teacher and K–12 English supervisor in the New Orleans public schools, he has written widely on curriculum, media, language, and composition. His recent work reflects his interdisciplinary interests, including semiotics, meditation, music, and the teaching of values.

Nathaniel Teich is professor of English at the University of Oregon. He is formerly director of composition and currently director of the Oregon Writing Project. In 1992 he published *Rogerian Perspectives: Collaborative Rhetoric for Oral and Written Communication* with Ablex. His primary interests are the role of empathy and the composing process.

Trudelle H. Thomas is assistant professor of English and director of the University Writing Program at Xavier University in Cincinnati, Ohio. Her essays have been published in *College Composition and Communication,* the *Journal of American Culture,* and the *Journal of Excellence in College*

Teaching. Her academic interests include autobiography, Writing Across the Curriculum, and Virginia Woolf. She is at present working on the use of journals in the writing classroom.

Demetrice A. Worley is an assistant professor of English and director of writing at Bradley University. Her research interests include visual imagery in writing and reading, contemporary African American women writers, and the creation of "self" in creative writing. She is co-editor (with Jesse Perry, Jr.) of *African American Literature: An Anthology of NonFiction, Fiction, Poetry, and Drama* and author of articles of African American literature, the use of multicultural literature in the classroom, and the relationship of writing theory and writing practice. When she is not teaching or writing, she likes to visualize world peace.